HARVARD EAST ASIAN MONOGRAPHS

71

THE CH'ING IMPERIAL HOUSEHOLD DEPARTMENT

A STUDY OF ITS ORGANIZATION
AND PRINCIPAL FUNCTIONS, 1662-1796

THE CH'ING IMPERIAL HOUSEHOLD DEPARTMENT

A STUDY OF ITS ORGANIZATION AND PRINCIPAL FUNCTIONS, 1662-1796

by Preston M. Torbert

Published by
Council on East Asian Studies
Harvard University

Distributed by
Harvard University Press
Cambridge, Massachusetts
and
London, England
1977

This book is produced by the John K. Fairbank Center for East
Asian Research at Harvard University, which administers research
projects designed to further scholarly understanding of China,
Japan, Korea, Vietnam, Inner Asia, and adjacent areas. These
studies have been assisted by grants from the Ford Foundation.

Library of Congress Cataloging in Publication Data

Torbert, Preston M   1943–
    The Ch'ing Imperial Household Department.

    (Harvard East Asian monographs ; 71)
    Bibliography: p.
    Includes index.
    1. Nei wu fu. I. Title II. Series.
JQ1512.Z66   354'.51'000903   77–10722

ISBN 0-674-12761-7

To the Memory of My Father

FOREWORD

This is the first full-length institutional study of the organization and functions of the Imperial Household Department under Ch'ing rule. That department constituted the emperor's "personal bureaucracy." In tracing the complex structure of this organization, Preston Torbert has avoided an exhaustive listing of nominal offices and their prescribed duties; instead, he has described the distinctive "social functions" of the various "social groups" that made up the department's total personnel—the bondservants, the eunuchs, and the palace maids. It was through the loyal services of these groups that the emperor's personal needs were met: food, clothing, housing, travel, personal security, and entertainment. It was from the bountiful supply of palace maids—selected from among the young daughters of bondservants—that some of the prominent imperial consorts emerged. This provided a major route for the upward social mobility of their bondservant parents and other relatives.

The department's multiple financial functions account for the origins of the emperor's personal wealth. Mr. Torbert examines the various lucrative activities of the department that guaranteed a steady flow of funds into the emperor's personal coffer—the ginseng trade, the salt and copper monopolies, the customs levies, and so forth.

Linking his findings to larger issues, Mr. Torbert raises such questions as whether the indentured-servant system in Ch'ing China might have contributed to the growing authoritarian nature of the imperial government and society; and whether peace and prosperity through the eighteenth century contributed to the rising economic influence of the throne, thereby consolidating the position of the autocracy. These questions are significant in furthering our understanding of Ch'ing social and governmental history.

Mr. Torbert's interest in Chinese history began in preparatory school and continued through his undergraduate years at Princeton. Upon receiving his B.A. in 1966, he left for a year's study in Taiwan as a Carnegie Foundation fellow. Subsequently, as a graduate student in history at the University of Chicago, he turned his attention to Chinese institutional history, particularly to the Imperial Household Department. While working on a dissertation about that department, Mr. Torbert also studied at the Harvard Law School in order to gain a better analytical grasp of law and institutions. He has since combined the practice of law with research on Chinese institutions. At present, he resides in Taipei, where he is associated with a local firm.

Silas Wu

ACKNOWLEDGMENTS

While I enjoyed the benefit of assistance from many quarters in the research and preparation of this book, Professor Ping-ti Ho of the University of Chicago deserves particular recognition. Without his continuing inspiration and constant guidance the work could not have been begun, much less completed. I owe him a tremendous debt.

I am also grateful to others at the University of Chicago. Professor Philip A. Kuhn was especially helpful in leading me to source materials and in making constructive criticisms of the manuscript. Professors William McNeill and Edward A. Kracke gave generously of their time and contributed valuable comments. Other friends and associates at the University of Chicago also rendered continuing and significant assistance to me both during the time I was a student there and afterwards. I much value their interest and encouragement.

I am also happy to acknowledge a considerable debt of gratitude to Professors John K. Fairbank, Jonathan Spence, Silas Wu, Thomas Metzger, and L. Carrington Goodrich for their careful reading of the manuscript and their considered comments. Constructive criticism from those who were familiar with the period and institutions that are the focus of this work has added much to it. Professor Jerome A. Cohen played an indispensable role in encouraging my endeavors on several chapters of this work while I was a student at the Harvard Law School. R. Randle Edwards, Joseph Cheng, and Wejen Chang among others at the Law School's East Asian Legal Studies Program have graced this work with their contributions.

Finally, I would like to express my appreciation to the staffs of the various libraries I visited in the course of my research. Principal thanks go to Dr. Tsien Tsuen-hsuin and the accommodating staff at the University of Chicago Far Eastern Library. The East Asian Library at Columbia University, the Harvard-Yenching Library, and the Library of Congress also deserve thanks for their considerable efforts in aiding my research.

CONTENTS

Chapter I

THE BACKGROUND TO
THE IMPERIAL HOUSEHOLD DEPARTMENT

The Ch'ing Imperial Household Department (Nei-wu-fu) was an unusual and perhaps unique organization which handled primarily the emperor's personal affairs, but whose functions and influence extended far beyond the imperial palace. The department's origins and the details of its early existence are obscure. The general framework of Chinese history and the more specific circumstances of the evolving Manchu state, however, provide an understanding of the context in which the department originated and developed. In a broad historical sense, the department was a result of—and partly a reaction against—the experience of previous dynasties in establishing and administering institutions to care for the emperor's private life. In a narrower perspective, the department was formed by the major influences and circumstances of the Manchu conquest in the seventeenth century. With these two perspectives in mind it is helpful to look at analogous institutions from other periods in Chinese history, especially the Ming dynasty.

The Chinese Eunuchs

Throughout Chinese history those who supervised and cared for the emperor's personal affairs generally were eunuchs. The particular physical incapacity of this group of palace employees had two important implications. First, these men were incapable of disturbing the continence of the imperial consort and concubines. This may well have been the original purpose in appointing castrates to handle the affairs of the harem and the reason why almost no Chinese scholars suggested abolishing the palace eunuchs.[1] Second, they suffered from a peculiar social and psychological dependence because of their physical disability. A eunuch's condition immediately made him an outcast in a society which placed a high value on continuation of the family line. As a social pariah,

1

he had no hope of attaining prestige and power except through the good graces of his master. The generally hostile social environment thus made the eunuch almost slavishly dependent on his master for status and dignity. For this reason, the eunuchs, more than any social group, except perhaps slaves, made obedient servants. Typically, an emperor also valued his eunuchs because their debased nature would inhibit them from challenging him as pretenders to the throne. The eunuchs, then, were the ideal servants—they willingly carried out even the most despicable or sacrilegious commands, yet they did not generally constitute a threat to the ruler.[2]

The importance of the eunuchs stemmed from their physical proximity to the emperor as managers of his personal affairs, and from their complete dedication in catering to and fulfilling his desires. The relationship of the eunuchs to the emperor was an unusual one, not merely in their proximity to him, but also in their continuous attendance upon him. The last Ch'ing emperor, Hsuan-t'ung (reigned 1908-1911), declared:

> No account of my childhood would be complete without mentioning the eunuchs. They waited on me when I ate, dressed and slept; they accompanied me on my walks and to my lessons; they told me stories; and had rewards and beatings from me, but they never left my presence. They were my slaves; and they were my earliest teachers.[3]

Constant propinquity and utter faithfulness were qualities that inevitably drew the eunuchs from their proper sphere of private personal concerns into a political role in public matters. In post-Ch'in Chinese history the eunuchs' role in administration took two basic directions. Forceful and clever emperors deputed eunuchs as secret agents to investigate the activities of regular civilian and military officials and to report their discoveries directly to the emperor. The other, more common, trend was for weak emperors to allow the eunuchs gradually to extend their influence from the secret service into the public realm and eventually to usurp essential functions of civil and military administration.

The Role of the Eunuchs before the Ming Period

The earliest use of castrates as household servants may date as far back as Shang times; in any case, they seem to have existed in the Chou period.[4] They assumed a firm position in the imperial system, however, only in the reign of the Han emperor Wu Ti, when several factors created the potential for eunuch abuses of public power late in the Han period. One of the most significant was Wu Ti's raising the number of concubines from twenty to several thousand,[5] because this necessitated a corresponding increase in the number of eunuchs required to care for them. In addition, Wu Ti employed the eunuchs as spies and as transmitters of documents from within the inner palace to the civil officials outside and thus introduced the eunuchs to political activities.[6]

In the later Han era, the eunuchs assumed greater importance. Their increased strength at this time seems principally related to the physical isolation of the rulers. Officials who were not castrates were banned from the inner palace, and positions there became a monopoly of the eunuchs.[7] In addition, the maternal relatives, who controlled government, secluded the emperor within the inner palace so that they could rule more effectively in his name.[8] This policy of isolation, however, was not successful in the short run for the maternal relatives, nor certainly in the long run for the dynasty. Emperors such as Chih-ti (reigned 146 A.D.) found the eunuchs to be their sole ally in the struggle against the maternal relatives.[9]

The T'ang, however, is the dynasty most famous for eunuch abuses. In other periods the eunuchs were able to misuse and even appropriate the power of individual emperors, but in the late T'ang their power exceeded even that of the emperor.[10] This unique situation stemmed from the institutional weaknesses in succession procedures in the T'ang imperial house. In the first half of the dynasty, at least four of the nine ascensions to the throne were determined by armed struggle, and the deciding factor was control of the northern gate to the palace.[11] During the last half of the dynasty the eunuchs were able to gain control of military units and particularly of the palace guard units commanding this gate.

Eunuch interference in the succession seems to have started in 756, when Li Fu-kuo, a eunuch military officer and aide to the heir apparent, encouraged and supported him in assuming the throne prematurely.[12] As the eunuchs expanded their military power in the following years, their intervention in political affairs became more extensive. In 783 the Te-tsung Emperor, after crushing a mutiny by the Regional Military Commander, Yao Ling-yen, decided to employ eunuchs so as to diminish the influence of military officials. He refused to allow military men to command the palace guard and, instead, appointed trustworthy eunuchs to serve in this capacity.[13] As they gained control of the palace guards and other military forces, the eunuchs were able to secure the northern gate and assure themselves of a decisive role in emperor-making. Although they struggled with officials representing powerful families over the succession of several emperors in the early 800s, from the time of the Wen-tsung Emperor (ruled 827-841) the eunuchs alone controlled succession to the throne.[14] The T'ang emperors for the last century of the dynasty were emperors in name only. In fact they were mere puppets manipulated by their eunuch masters.[15]

The Sung period offers an interesting contrast to the disasters of the T'ang. The Sung founder (reigned 960-975) limited the number of palace eunuchs to fifty and promulgated strict laws prohibiting their exercise of public power.[16] The respect which these laws commanded among successive Sung emperors and among the bureaucracy did much to prevent a repetition of the abuses that had marked the Han and T'ang. General cooperation between the emperors and their ministers and the great power of the chief-councilors (*tsai-hsiang*) were also indispensable elements in the enlightened government of this period.[17] In T'ai-tsung's reign (976-997), for instance, when the secretariat (*chung-shu*) insisted that the eunuch Wang Chi-en be rewarded for exterminating over 100,000 bandits by being appointed a Commissioner of the Hsuan-hui court (Hsuan-hui-shih), the emperor refused. "I have read the histories of the previous dynasties and know that the eunuchs must never be allowed to interfere in government matters;" he said, "appointment of Wang Chi-en would be the beginnings of just such eunuch interference."[18] In a contrasting case some years later, the Chen-tsung Emperor (reigned 998-1022) wished to appoint the eunuch Liu Ch'eng-kuei as an Imperial Commissioner (Chieh-tu-shih). The chief councilors protested so vigorously, however, that in the end he desisted.[19]

In the Sung era, it seems, the eunuchs were unable to traverse the accepted limitations on the scope of their activities. They did, however, function as special deputies of the emperor in clandestine investigatory operations. The Northern Sung saw the establishment of two private eunuch spy organs which were directly responsible to the emperor. One was the Bureau of the Imperial City (Huang-ch'eng-ssu), which employed some 2,000 agents to spy on the military, to inspect and guard the national and the emperor's personal treasury, and to accompany all foreign tributary envoys.[20] The other consisted of the Itinerant Inspectors (Tsou-ma ch'eng-shou), the emperor's personal secret agents who investigated the volatile conditions on the northern borders.[21] Although these privy officials may have shown proper obedience at most times, they were still regarded with suspicion. In fact, eunuchs were prohibited from serving in the Bureau of the Imperial City from the Yuan-feng era (1078-1085) onwards,[22] and the office of Itinerate Inspector was abolished early in the Southern Sung period (1127-1279).[23] These decisions suggest that constraining measures were taken when eunuchs in these positions began to show signs of independence and initiative.

The Chin dynasty (1115-1235), established in North China by the Jurchen forebears of the Manchus, presents a strong contrast, as does the Sung, to the earlier and later periods. The eunuchs, who comprised a decisive minority within chamber administration, were never able to gain control of the household and turn it to their own purposes, although individual eunuchs, such as the traitorous Liang Liu, were able to hoodwink gullible rulers. One such emperor was Hai Ling Wang (reigned 1149-1160), who was so impressed by the military feats of the eunuch general Chang Ch'eng-yeh in the Posterior Han (923-935) that he was favorably disposed to appointing eunuchs to substantive posts.[24]

Taking account of the fate of previous dynasties and desiring, perhaps, to preserve certain aspects of their own national heritage, the Jurchen conquerors set up an unusual institution called the Bureau of Attendants (Chin-shih-chü). This office, which employed an intentionally small number of eunuchs, not only managed the emperor's personal affairs, but also had a definite role in government.[25] Appointment to the Bureau of Attendants was restricted to loyal, upright officials of broad experience, because, as Shih-tsung (reigned 1161-1189) said, "I generally do not listen to slander but, if eloquent insinuators were constantly at my side, I'm afraid that I might gradually come to agree with and approve their nefarious schemes."[26] Besides managing the private business of the emperor, the bureau served as a channel of information, handling the memorials to the emperor from public officials. The bureau's officials not only transmitted documents, but also wrote out summaries of the longer memorials before presentation to the emperor.[27] As might be expected, eventually complaints arose of intervention in government affairs by these supposedly menial servitors. The Hsuan-tsung Emperor (reigned 1213-1223), however, dismissed these remonstrances with the comment: "Since the censors are not fulfilling their duties, I have no way of discovering improprieties among the officials other than relying on the Bureau of Attendants."[28] At this time investigatory officials of the bureau were active throughout the country. Special itinerant censors (hsing-lu yü-shih), for example, checked on all types of civil matters in the provinces.[29] More important were the war supervisors (chien-chan), whom the emperor deputized at times of military crisis to assert imperial control over the armies. The result of this policy, however, was to stifle the initiative and upset the plans of the commanding generals and to bring on repeated military defeats and the extinction of the dynasty by the Mongols in 1235.[30]

The Role of Eunuchs in the Ming Period

The eunuch disasters of the Ming dynasty were more prolonged and graver than those of any other dynasty except the T'ang. To a large extent the high degree of eunuch misgovernment in the Ming period was directly linked to the intensified despotism of post-Sung China. In the Ming era, as in earlier dynasties, the eunuchs were first introduced into the political arena by emperors suspicious of challenges to or restraints upon their prerogatives by the bureaucracy. The profound suspicion with which Ming rulers viewed the bureaucracy prompted them to make more extensive use of private servants in an official capacity than any previous emperors. Although this policy was at first effective in strengthening the hand of energetic emperors, it eventually brought on disaster when inferior emperors of the later half of the dynasty abandoned their responsibilities and completely isolated themselves from public officials. At such times the eunuchs were quick to grasp the power which the emperor had abdicated.

These characteristics of Ming government can be traced in part to two policies of the Ming founder (reigned 1368-1398). First, he issued a strict prohibition against interference by eunuchs in government and took special care to assure that the heir to the throne, later Hui-ti (reigned 1399-1402), learned a proper disdain for them. Second, he abolished the secretariat because he suspected the grand councilor of plotting rebellion against him. In its place he established private secretaries to help him handle the burden of some 1,660 documents dealing with 3,391 separate matters that required an imperial decision during any average ten-day period.[31]

The education of Hui-ti was a temporary success, but ultimately a disaster. His rigid policy of restricting the eunuchs to menial janitorial tasks won for him their unanimous antipathy. Thus, they quickly offered their allegiance to the Prince of Yen, later the Ch'eng-tsu Emperor (reigned 1403-1424), when he revolted. In his military campaign against Hui-ti, Prince Yen intentionally favored the eunuchs with appointments as spies and military commanders. After successfully arrogating the throne, he entrusted loyal and able eunuchs, such as Cheng Ho, with special commissions.

Eunuch intervention in government was no mere accident, but a deliberate policy of the Ch'eng-tsu Emperor, who relied on them to scrutinize an officialdom reluctant to accept his usurpation. For this purpose he created a vast eunuch secret police network to ferret out hidden dissenters from his rule among the bureaucrats. The eunuchs and a newly formed palace guard unit closely associated with them, the embroidered uniform guards (*chin-i-wei*), operated as Ch'eng-tsu's personal agents, arresting and detaining those suspected of disloyalty. A eunuch-managed eastern depot (*tung-ch'ang*) torture chamber was established for the interrogation of these suspects. The depot's agents even spied on the embroidered uniform guards to be sure they were performing their duties properly.

In this period, eunuch intervention in government was not limited to spy functions. Some acted as envoys to foreign countries. Their most significant advances, however, were in the military. Ch'eng-tsu, who had won the throne by force, was determined to preclude that possibility for anyone else. To keep informed of the intentions of the military commanders who controlled the large armies essential to border defense and internal security, he appointed trustworthy eunuchs to the military office of "Grand Defender" and deployed them as spies.[32] The eunuchs not only watched over the armies, but also began to command them; their blunders in the campaign in Annam were one reason for Chinese setbacks and eventual withdrawal.[33] In the economic sphere, the eunuchs inspected the tax quotas on merchants and on the mines and were placed in charge of all foreign maritime trade.

The remaining years of the fifteenth century after Ch'eng-tsu's reign saw a continuing rise in the influence of eunuchs over various aspects of Ming government. Eunuch military power was enhanced by greater responsibilities and the creation of eunuch grand commandants. In fiscal policy, the eunuchs took control of the state lands and the emperor's personal estates which had first come into existence in Jen-tsung's reign (1425). The eunuchs also extended their grasp not only over the emperor's private fisc but also to the public treasuries. Further, eunuchs began to act as regents from the end of the Hsuan-tsung's reign (1426-1455), and, later, the eunuch Wang Chen's intimate relationship with the young Ying-tsung Emperor (reigned 1436-1449, 1457-1464) gave him the power to promote officials to the cabinet.[34] When Ying-tsung traveled in the provinces, eunuchs behind in the capital acted *in loco imperatoris*.[35] The incompetence and corruption of two eunuch military leaders, Wang Chen and Kuo Ching, were indispensable elements in the humiliating defeat and capture of the Ying-tsung Emperor at T'u-mu fort in 1449. Seven years later, eunuchs acting on Ying-tsung's orders went so far as to assassinate the Ching-t'ai Emperor (reigned 1450-1456).[36]

Eunuch intervention in military and civilian affairs continued to increase in the last half of the fifteenth and in the first years of the sixteenth century. The secret service organs expanded considerably. The number of spies in the embroidered uniform guard grew from 500 to 60,000 by the time of Shih-tsung (reigned 1522-1566).[37] The notorious eunuch favorite of Wu-tsung (reigned 1506-1521), Liu Chin, even organized a new spy organ, the *nei-hsing-ch'ang*, to keep an eye on both a recently established western depot and the older eastern depot.[38] In addition, eunuchs gained control over the highest judicial deliberation, the *hui-shen*.[39] In the economic realm, eunuchs expanded their control over the commercial tax revenues by creating new tax bureaus and government storehouses (*huang-tien*).[40] Corruption in eunuch management of the national and personal treasuries, in their inspection of mines and the salt monopoly, and in their supervision of the capital's grain supply grew to unprecedented proportions. During this period, the fortunes made by the eunuch administrators of the imperial textile manufactories were so great that appointment to that bureau was popularly called "elevation to immortality" (*teng-hsien*).[41] In military affairs, the largest army in the empire, the reorganized troops guarding the capital, came under the control of the eunuch Directorate of Ceremonial (Ssu-li-chien).[42]

At the end of the dynasty eunuch tyranny reached its zenith. The number of palace eunuchs had grown enormously, rising from 10,000 during the late fifteenth century to 70,000 or 100,000 by the end of the dynasty.[43] The number of unemployed eunuchs outside the palace may have been even greater. As the authority of the palace eunuchs grew and government and the economy

deteriorated, thousands of impoverished young men sought employment in the palace by castrating themselves. In 1621, for example,
when the emperor expressed a desire to recruit 3,000 eunuchs for
service in the palace, 20,000 castrates applied for these positions.[44]
Bands of unemployed eunuchs roamed the environs of the capital
waylaying travelers and intimidating officials.

Those eunuchs who found employment in the palace managed
one-seventh of all cultivated land in the empire through their control of the emperor's personal estates and state lands.[45] And these
lands did not include the large private estates owned by powerful
eunuchs. In government administration and in military affairs the
eunuchs' arbitrary control of the vast secret police network and
the detention centers (including a new *nei-ch'ang* established in
Shen-tsung's reign [1573-1619]) paralyzed the bureaucracy and
military command, thus crippling the dynasty before the combined
onslaught of domestic rebels and foreign conquerors.

If the Ming founder's zealous efforts to prohibit eunuchs from
participating in government and to educate his grandson Hui-ti
ended in disaster, his abolition of the secretariat was certainly a
contributing factor, for it promoted the isolation of Ming emperors
from public officials. Dynamic rulers like the Ming founder and
Ch'eng-tsu made effective use of the new informal system of private secretaries, but weaker monarchs avoided audiences with their
public secretaries and conducted all communications with them
through written messages. It was the eunuchs who transmitted
those messages.

The first emperor to refuse to meet with the cabinet was
Jen-tsung. Although eunuchs had committed abuses before this
time, their misdeeds were relatively rare, because by order of the
Ming founder they were not permitted to learn to read or write.
In 1436, however, a school for eunuchs was established inside the
palace, and from this time on they were able to take advantage of
their position as intermediaries between the emperor and the
cabinet. The dangers inherent in this situation became most apparent from the end of the fifteenth century.[46] From 1469 to 1497
the two emperors, Hsien-tsung and Hsiao-tsung, had no audiences

with the cabinet, and only from 1497 to 1505, the last years of Hsiao-tsung's reign, was there a revival of fairly regular audiences. The following emperor, Wu-tsung, spent much time traveling about the country and was not available for regular consultation with his cabinet ministers. The Shih-tsung Emperor saw his ministers only once between 1524 and 1550. His successor, Mu-tsung (reigned 1567-1572), was not reluctant to deliberate on policy with his ministers, but he ruled for only five years. The next emperor, Shen-tsung (reigned 1573-1619), followed Shih-tsung's example, meeting with his ministers only once in the last twenty-nine years of his reign. It appears, then, that during the last century and a half of the Ming dynasty, only the last eight years of Hsiao-tsung's reign showed a normal pattern of court audiences. Absenteeism was the rule.

Under these circumstances the eunuchs, who already exercised considerable influence over economic and military affairs, were able to usurp the decision-making authority of the emperor. In Ming times, the process of communication between the emperor and his ministers was supposed to function in the following manner. The chief eunuchs would carry the memorials and draft decisions of the cabinet ministers in to the emperor, wait for his decision, then send lower-status eunuchs to transmit the decisions back to the ministers. Eunuchs such as Liu Chin, however, were even able to prevent memorials to the emperor from reaching him. Instead, Liu Chin carried them back to his own residence where he ordered his nephews to copy out imperial rescripts or edicts according to his whim.[47] A century later the artful eunuch Wei Chung-hsien brought substantive memorials to the attention of the Hsi-tsung Emperor (reigned 1621-1627), an avid carpenter, only when he was completely absorbed in his favorite hobby. The emperor, annoyed at any interruption, would invariably tell Wei: "You handle the matter yourself as best you can. Just don't bother me."[48]

Isolated from contacts with ministers and other officials, the emperors came to rely on their faithful eunuchs for both material and moral support. When Li Tzu-ch'eng's forces were about to enter Peking in 1644, the last Ming emperor to rule from Peking, Ch'ung-chen, took refuge on Prospect Hill and called for help. The only person to respond was his loyal eunuch Wang Ch'eng-en.[49]

Manchu Society and Government and the Origins of the Imperial Household Department

The origins of the Ch'ing Imperial Household Department were linked not only to the general developments in Chinese history, but also more directly to circumstances specific to the sixteenth and seventeenth centuries. Key elements of the department's activities are associated with the development of Jurchen (Manchu)[50] society and government in the late Ming period. The following brief sketch of the development of the household organization among the Jurchen and early Ch'ing rulers focuses on a few major factors in Jurchen and Manchu society and government and the origins of the Imperial Household Department: the tribute system and trade with Ming China; the role of Chinese renegades and captives; and the influence of Chinese political organization.

The Tribute System and Trade with Ming China

One indispensable element in the rapid development of Jurchen power and the conquest of China was the influence of Ming China's system of foreign relations. Upon the defeat of its armies by the Mongols in 1234, the Jurchen Chin Dynasty, which had ruled North China from 1125, collapsed. Many Jurchen were slaughtered or enslaved, while others, disguised as Chinese peasants, were absorbed into Chinese society. Only a few Sinified Jurchen escaped death or assimilation by returning to their original homeland in Manchuria where some Jurchen tribes still survived.[51] The Mongol rulers of China adopted a policy of granting official rank to the tribal leaders in Manchuria and allowing them to manage internal affairs as they wished.

Later, the Ming dynasty followed this same policy,[52] but relations with the Jurchen became closer only after the establishment of a garrison (wei-so) system during the reign of the Ch'eng-tsu Emperor.[53] Under this strategy, sometimes called a "loose rein"

(*chi-mi*) policy,[54] the Ming state attempted to exercise general
control over the Jurchen in order to secure the northeastern border.
The primary means of attaining this end was to extend the political
and economic advantages of participation in the tributary system
to a large number of Jurchen tribes in order to promote the frag-
mentation of political and military power in Manchuria. The
Ch'eng-tsu Emperor exhorted the Jurchen tribes to establish
tributary relations with China and to depute envoys to the Ming
capital at regular intervals. He rewarded their tributary missions
with payments and gifts, which soon became a major source of
wealth for the Jurchen. In exchange, the Jurchen sold to the
Chinese officials, or presented to the emperor, mainly horses,
which they procured from the Mongols,[55] and ginseng. By the mid-
fifteenth century, according to one Chinese observer, the Jurchen
depended on tributary trade with China for all their clothing and
utensils.[56] The Jurchen, of course, had a great interest in the commercial aspects of tributary trade and wished to increase the scope
of these valuable commercial contacts. The Ming government,
however, was pressed by fiscal embarrassments and attempted to
reduce the expenses for tributary missions by transferring commercial contacts to horse markets on the borders at K'ai-yuan in
1439 and at Fu-shun in 1464.[57]

In the sixteenth century, as the fiscal difficulties of the Ming
state became more severe, the conflict between Chinese and Jurchen
interests in tributary trade intensified. The Ming state imposed
limits on the number of Jurchen from each garrison who could
bear tribute, but the Jurchen overcame these and other restrictions
by seeking the creation of more garrisons, by bargaining for increases in the number of tributary envoys, by forging the official
patents which granted permission to bear tribute, and by bribing
Chinese border officials.[58] They competed for the patents and, by
the end of the sixteenth century, were even fighting each other to
secure them. The seizure of a large number of these patents by the
leader of the Chien-chou Left Garrison, Nurhachi, played a significant role in his unification of the Jurchen tribes in the early
seventeenth century.[59] These patents were probably Nurhachi's

most effective means of rewarding his adherents and allies for their past loyalty and of assuring their continued support.

In addition to their political influence, official tributary relations had a significant impact on the development of Jurchen society and economy. The trading privileges and the lavish tribute gifts the Jurchen leaders received from the Ming court not only increased their political legitimacy in the eyes of their followers, but also contributed to the development of the Jurchen economy. As the tributary trade and illegal commercial dealings it stimulated expanded, China and Korea provided a market for Jurchen exports of hides, medicines, and precious stones. Internal trade also developed. During the sixteenth century groups of dozens of itinerant merchants bartering a variety of goods circulated among the recently constructed castle towns which had become commercial centers.[60] The foreign demand for ginseng at the end of the sixteenth and the beginning of the seventeenth century provoked the invention of a new method of processing this root.[61] Indeed, the growing traffic in this medicinal herb inspired the quip by a later historian that "the Ch'ing Dynasty rose on ginseng and fell on opium."[62]

Evidence from the early Ch'ing period suggests that this lucrative trade in ginseng was handled by the private slaves of the Jurchen leaders. The extensive rights of the Imperial Household Department over the ginseng trade and the expeditions of 600 men which the Household Department deputed to gather ginseng in the 1640s suggest that this was the continuation of a long-standing policy of sending out household slaves to engage in trade.[63] One incident from 1640, for example, indicates that corrupt officials tried to extort money from merchants who were the emperor's bondservants primarily because they were known to be the most prosperous traders.[64] It seems that the tributary trade was a significant element not only in the general development of Jurchen society and economy, but also in the commercial proclivities of the Jurchen leaders' household slaves and, later, of the Imperial Household Department.

The Role of Chinese Renegades and Captives
The influence of China on the development of the Jurchen

economy was not limited to the officially sanctioned tributary trade or private commerce. As in the Chin dynasty, Chinese renegades and captives were of considerable importance.[65] From the early fifteenth century, when diplomatic and military contacts with the Chinese of southern Manchuria became more frequent, the Jurchen captured Chinese peasants on plunder raids on border settlements and welcomed renegade Chinese soldiers into their camp. The Jurchen, who practiced a mixed economy of hunting, gathering, and agriculture, employed the newcomers in the fields, because Chinese peasants possessed an agricultural technology superior to their own. The actual status of these newcomers in Jurchen society and their precise role in the economy is, however, the subject of some debate.[66] Some historians have characterized these Chinese as field slaves who provided the economic basis for the spectacular growth of Jurchen military and political power in the sixteenth and early seventeenth centuries. This view, however, has recently been questioned. The nature and importance of these captives and renegades probably differed among the various Jurchen tribes and undoubtedly underwent considerable changes during the span of a century or two.[67] It seems likely, however, that the entry of these Chinese peasants into Jurchen society increased agricultural output sufficiently to enable a greater degree of specialization in agricultural and military pursuits.

The contribution of Chinese and Korean captives to the development of technology and handicrafts was also considerable. In the early fifteenth century, the Jurchen obtained iron agricultural implements from both Korea and China. When they discovered how to beat these plowshares into swords in the 1470s and 1480s, however, both China and Korea prohibited the export of iron implements to them.[68] Nevertheless, by the late fifteenth century, Korean and Chinese craftsmen among the Jurchen were engaged in small-scale production of weapons and implements from iron which they obtained illegally from China or Korea. A century later, over one hundred foreign craftsmen were living in Nurhachi's castle town, Hetuala, making iron implements, armor, bows, and arrows.[69] At the same time, under the guidance of foreigners, the Jurchen began to mine ore for their own needs as well as silver and gold for export. In other handicrafts, such as the production of porcelain, cloth-making, and even naval architecture, the Jurchen relied on Chinese and Korean captives to teach them advanced techniques which they employed to great advantage.[70]

In later years, Chinese captives transmitted other more significant military techniques to the Jurchen. In 1626 Nurhachi suffered his first serious military defeat at Ning-yuan, a Ming city well protected by modern European cannon. After his death—which may have been caused by physical injuries he received at Ning-yuan—his son and successor, Abahai, made efforts to copy these modern weapons but met with little success. A decisive turn came in 1633, however, when the Ming generals K'ung Yu-te and Keng Chung-ming surrendered to him.[71] These turncoats not only presented Abahai with a number of workable cannons, but they also set to work producing more of them. The effective deployment of these new weapons allowed the Manchus to continue their conquest of the northeastern border areas and to invade China proper.

Foreign captives, especially Chinese, also played a crucial role in the origins of the household organization of Nurhachi and Abahai. Among the Jurchen, household slaves may have been a continuation of a Chin dynasty practice or perhaps a later development. Although sources indicate that some Jurchen had household slaves in the fourteenth century and that most Jurchen had slaves of some type in the early seventeenth century,[72] the specific type of bondservants that characterized the Imperial Household Department seems to have arisen mainly during the Jurchen conquest of the eastern fringes of the Liao River basin in the 1610s and 1620s. This conquest greatly increased the number of captives. The taking of Fu-shun in 1618, for instance, added 300,000 people to the Jurchen state.[73] These large accretions of population brought about a change in policy. During the first years of conquest (to 1624), the captured Chinese were generally enslaved, and bore obligations to private persons, while later (in 1624-1625) they were often enrolled in the ranks of the semi-dependent agricultural class, *jusen*, who bore obligations to the state.[74]

The genealogical records of the bondservants of the emperor and other banner leaders, although offering a very restricted picture, are helpful in sketching a general outline of the origins of these private slaves. The personnel of the Imperial Household Department were the emperor's bondservants and most were descendants of Chinese captured during the conquest of this area.[75] The genealogical records, as we might expect, indicate that by far the greatest number of Chinese bondservants of the emperor and other banner leaders came from Fu-shun and Shen-yang, which were captured in 1618 and 1621, a period when most Chinese captives were enslaved.

The Chinese captives were the most numerous group that worked in the ruler's household, but other nationalities were also present. The majority of the bondservants before 1618 seem to have been Jurchen, with substantial numbers of Koreans and some Mongols. After the conquest of the Liao River basin in the 1620s, however, Chinese came to constitute a little over half of the total number of the emperor's bondservants before the conquest of China. At this time Manchus constituted about 30 percent of the bondservants, while Mongols and Koreans were about 6 percent and 7 percent respectively. The Manchu bondservants came from among criminals or indigent peasants within Manchu society, while the Koreans and Mongols were probably, like the Chinese, mainly war captives. Of the Manchu bondservants of the emperor, at least 48 percent seem to have been descendants of men who had entered his service before 1636.[76] For Koreans the percentage was at least 80 and for Mongols at least 14. Comparable information for Chinese bondservants is, unfortunately, lacking.

Many of these non-Chinese bondservants came from a small number of places. More than one-third of the Koreans, for instance, came from I-chou. One-half of the Mongols came from either Ch'a-ha-erh or K'o-erh-ch'in. The geographical origins of the Manchus, on the other hand, were relatively dispersed. While over 40 percent of the Manchu bondservants came from the three areas of Ye-ho, Hui-fa, and Ch'ang-po-shan, the others came from eighty-four separate places with no more than 4 percent from any one of them.

A crucial development closely tied to the introduction of Chinese captives into Jurchen society was the growth of the landed estates of the Jurchen princes and high military commanders. An observer in 1596 noticed that Nurhachi and other Manchu leaders possessed landed estates and employed specialized estate stewards, *kuan-chuang-jen*, to manage them.[77] The capture of extensive areas between 1618 and 1622 provided the opportunity for a vast expansion of these lands, but each estate remained a rather small unit. From 1625 it appears that the landed estate became an artificial (as opposed to natural) village including nine to thirteen adult males, seven cows, and 700 mou of land.[78] The Manchu *beile* (banner leaders), in particular, seem to have acquired a considerable number of these estates. In 1634, for instance, the son of the *beile* Daisan owned twenty-three estates with a total of 503 slave cultivators.[79] The position of the slaves was hereditary, as was the position of the stewards, which was assigned to the wealthiest member of a lineage group in the estate.[80] These stewards, whose main function was to assure the collection of the owners' quota of grain from the estates, were able to enjoy a certain measure of prosperity. A Korean account of 1641, for instance, states that they married their daughters to surrendered Ming army officers and entertained Korean royalty in their homes.[81]

Later, lands in Chihli province were added to these estates in the Liao River basin. When the Manchus entered China in 1644, a number of Chinese living near the capital, fearful of the destruction of their fields in the fighting between the Ming forces and the invaders, commended their lands to the Imperial Household Department and received in return the privilege of perpetual tenancy on the land as the emperor's personal slaves. Under this arrangement they contributed a yearly quota of grain or other commodities to the department in lieu of state tax obligations.[82] Since the practice of commending lands was prohibited in 1646, we may assume that large parts of the department's estates in the Liao basin and within China proper were formed before this time.[83] It was these lands, with later additions, that provided the daily provisions for the emperor and his household during the Ch'ing period.

The Influence of Chinese Political Organization

Another indispensable element in the Jurchen rise to power and their successful conquest of China was political organization. Originally, political power of the Jurchen tribes under Nurhachi was divided. At first Nurhachi ruled jointly with his younger brother or with his son over a loose confederation of tribes, each incorporated intact with its leader into this larger group. Tribal leaders, consequently, still enjoyed a large measure of control over their followers. Nurhachi had begun to centralize power in his hands, however, by appointing combined judicial and investigatory officials, *cha-erh-ku-ch'i*, to handle judicial matters.[84]

His greatest contribution, however, was the division of power in 1615 among eight leaders by organizing all of Jurchen society into eight military units. These units, called "banners," consisted of five battalions or *ts'an-ling*, each battalion containing five companies or *tso-ling* of 300 men each. This new organization, perhaps inspired by the Chin dynasty *muke* military organization,[85] was a device for consolidating power in the hands of Nurhachi and his sons and nephews who became the banner leaders or *beile*. These banner leaders exercised general supervision over the banners, which were considered their property, but they commanded directly only select guard units, *bayara*.[86] Banner administration and direct control of the military forces were in the hands of appointed officials, the *ku-shan-o-chen*.[87]

Nurhachi hoped that the diffusion of power among a small group of related banner leaders would ensure good government. Looking back to the internecine warfare among the Jurchen tribe leaders which he had witnessed, he ordered that upon his death his sons and followers should establish an eight-member oligarchy, whose members would all take part in governing under a nominal leader chosen from among them.[88] He felt that such an arrangement would not only eliminate infighting for a single position of authority, but would also result in joint consultation and decision-making which would prevent rash or arbitrary policies.

When Nurhachi died, however, one son, Abahai, gained control of Nurhachi's two banners and began to reduce the power of the other *beile*. The complete subordination of the *beile* to one leader was not accomplished until the reign of the Yung-cheng Emperor (reigned 1723-1735) a century later, but the major steps were taken in Abahai's reign. Nurhachi had been able to use his seniority to impose his authority over his sons, but Abahai needed a bureaucratic structure responsible to himself in order to govern.[89] On the one hand, he revived the power of the *ku-shan-o-chen* and other incipient forms of control over the *beile* current under Nurhachi, while, on the other hand, at the urging of his Chinese advisors, he adopted the political institutions of the Ming autocratic state. He established secretarial organs to copy out his orders, and in 1631 he established six boards, one each for civil appointments, revenue, rites, war, punishments, and public works, which administered the country and were responsible to him. The creation of a censorate in 1636 to investigate officials' conduct was another important move. As he created new bureaucratic institutions he needed qualified personnel to occupy the positions in them. His need for educated persons was so great, in fact, that, starting from 1629, he allowed bondservants to take the examinations to qualify as officials.[90]

These and other similar measures created a public bureaucracy with an existence and a legitimacy more removed from the ruler's personal authority than before. The government of Jurchen society became, in part at least, a public matter administered by a bureaucratic machine rather than by the leader's personal friends or chamber servants. It was in this decade (1630s) that the distinction between the private affairs of the ruler and his public role first appeared. Prior to this period public administration was essentially the private affair of the banner leader. Then, however, separate organs whose sole purpose was to manage the emperor's personal affairs began to take shape. Unfortunately, the exact date of the first establishment of the formal bureaucratic organ to handle the imperial household affairs is not known. One might surmise, however, that the institutionalization of these duties took place in the 1630s.[91]

The Jurchen leaders' household organization, like Jurchen

government structure, amalgamated different elements as the society changed with the passage of time and the acquisition of new territory. Just as the society at large consisted of two organizations, a military-social one derived from Jurchen experience and a bureaucratic one derived from Chinese history, so did the Imperial Household Department. The department, like many other aspects of Ch'ing society and institutions, possessed a duality that reflected its hybrid origins.

This duality manifests itself in the two common views of the Imperial Household Department. One view, emphasizing the banner system, describes the department as consisting of the bondservants of the three upper banners belonging to the emperor, namely the plain yellow, the bordered yellow, and the plain white. This characterization of the department reflects the earlier Jurchen belief that the banner leader or *beile* was the owner of the soldiers and bondservants who made up the banner. In institutional terms, this view emphasizes the fact that the emperor's bondservants were organized into units similar to those of the banner system. The second view of the department sees it as a bureaucratic institution employing and managing certain personnel considered members of the department. This view of the department reflects the institutional development from a quasi-feudal Jurchen period of private power to a more advanced Chinese period which distinguished public from private power. In a broader context it also reflects Chinese history, for the Imperial Household Department, like analogous organs in earlier times, became a comparatively large and complex bureaucratic organization.

The Immediate Background to the Establishment of the Imperial Household Department

The definitive establishment of the Imperial Household Department occurred in 1661. Prior to that date, a similar organ charged with essentially the same duties existed, but little is known of it. The circumstances surrounding the re-establishment of the department indicate that its re-emergence was the result of a debate over who should manage the emperor's personal affairs, the eunuchs or his bondservants.

The appearance of eunuchs among the Jurchen may mark another aspect of Chinese influence on them. Eunuchs served in the palace in Chin times and may have existed among the Jurchen before 1620. The first mention of them, however, is in an order from Nurhachi to the *beile* in 1621 telling them "to castrate your house slaves while they are young . . . otherwise when they mature they will carry on covert relations with the women in the palaces."[92] Slave eunuchs, then, probably existed in the households of the *beile* from that time until the conquest of China.

When the Manchu forces took over the Ming imperial city in Peking in 1644, the composition of the palace eunuchs underwent a significant change. As the Manchu troops approached Peking, the Chinese eunuchs of the last Ming emperor went out to the city gates to welcome the conquerors to the capital. This cordial display of allegiance to the new rulers perhaps ingratiated them with the Manchus, but, in any case, these holdovers from the previous dynasty soon became the dominant force among the palace eunuchs.[93] These developments upset a number of officials, particularly the older ones who had witnessed the eunuch abuses of the previous dynasty, and viewed the eunuchs as a direct threat to proper government by the regular bureaucratic authorities. Their advice to the Regent Dorgon, who ruled during the Shun-chih Emperor's minority from 1644 until his own death in 1650, apparently convinced him to take measures to curtail the eunuchs' influence. The first eight years of the Shun-chih Emperor's reign (1644-1661) witnessed a spate of edicts which prohibited the eunuchs from handling the income from the imperial estates (1644), from participating in court audiences (1645), and from going to the capital to seek employment (1646).[94] Various eunuch posts, such as those connected with revenue and construction works, were abolished. The government also took measures to alleviate the vexatious oversupply of eunuchs. An order of 1646, for example, provided that those who castrated themselves with the intention of becoming palace eunuchs were to be decapitated.[95]

In 1653 the Shun-chih Emperor, after the death of Dorgon, restored the eunuchs to a secure, if somewhat circumscribed, role in his service. He justified this move in an edict alluding to the role of the eunuchs from their supposed origin in the Han dynasty through later periods, such as the T'ang era, in which they had usurped functions intended for Confucian bureaucrats and military officials. Originally, he said, they had performed menial tasks, such as sweeping the buildings of the palace, but as a result of their close, daily contact with the emperor, they were able to overstep the boundaries of their proper duties and interfere in governmental matters. They used their newly acquired power to connive with other officials and reward their numerous followers and clansmen. Previous rulers who, although virtuous and courageous, had fallen unwittingly into their clutches, served as a lesson for him.[96] He insisted, however, that the eunuchs were indispensable. Rather than abolish them, he settled on the creation of thirteen clearly defined eunuch bureaus[97] with a system of joint management by both eunuchs and bondservants. The eunuchs were to be restrained by specific prohibitions, such as restrictions on their leaving the palace grounds without express permission, on their interfering in matters outside their sphere of administration, and on purchasing land and houses under their relatives' names. Civilian officials were to investigate and uncover infractions of these regulations.[98]

Within a month of the emperor's announcement of this new policy, officials, mindful of the eunuch misdeeds of the Ming period, remonstrated with him over the establishment of the eunuch bureaus. A censor, T'u Lai, while admitting the necessity of eunuchs, voiced a concern that they might gain control of the transmission of documents to an emperor secluded within the palace. The emperor reassured him that he had no intention of cutting himself off from his ministers and explained that lately he had not held court audiences only because he had been indisposed.[99] He assured the censor that the managers (*tsung-kuan*) of the Imperial Household Department were senior officials of merit who were so faithful that there could be no reason for anxiety. While conceding that the eunuchs constituted an organization, nevertheless he insisted that power was not in their hands but in those of his close Manchu officials. Such an arrangement, he claimed, differed radically from the institutions of previous dynasties because it allowed the eunuchs no opportunity to take part in political affairs.

While the emperor's arguments may have temporarily mollified his critics, they were not entirely convincing. Indeed, he himself later expressed qualms about a resurgence of eunuch influence. In 1655, for instance, he commanded the Board of Works to erect in the palace an iron tablet with an inscription proscribing eunuch interference in state matters and ordered that the safekeeping of the emperor's seal be divided between eunuch and Manchu officials.[100]

Later events, like earlier history, indicated that anxiety about the eunuchs was not unfounded. One of the most significant developments of the late 1650s was the discovery of a group of civilian officials who were suborning eunuchs in order to promote their official careers.[101] Their contact inside the palace was Wu Liang-fu, the Shun-chih Emperor's closest and most trusted eunuch. The emperor pardoned these high officials and his eunuch companion and thereby encouraged the expansion of eunuch power near the end of his reign. In 1661, for instance, some of the eunuch bureaus were upgraded. One of them, the Bureau of Palace Ceremony, or Ssu-li-chien, even achieved a position equal in authority to that of the most powerful of the six boards, the Board of Civil Appointments.[102]

These developments were, of course, linked to the Shun-chih Emperor's personal attachment to Wu Liang-fu and other eunuchs, but they may also have been inspired in part by a desire to enhance the emperor's position by counterbalancing the influence of the Imperial Household Department with a grant of power to the eunuchs.[103] When the emperor died, later in 1661, however, a Manchu reaction set in. The high officials and the regents (Oboi, Soni, Ebilun, Suksaha) agreed with the late emperor's mother to make public a posthumous declaration of the emperor. In this document Shun-chih purportedly acknowledged that the thirteen bureaus were no different from the Ming system of eunuch management which had caused the fall of the dynasty, and he took the blame for the abuses which stemmed from the creation of the thirteen bureaus.[104]

This extraordinary and mysterious document was followed, not unexpectedly, by further denunciation of the eunuchs and administrative measures against them. The regents, in the name of the young heir, offered an historical justification for abolishing the thirteen bureaus and for subordinating the eunuchs to the household bondservants of the emperor. They asserted that neither Nurhachi nor Abahai had employed eunuchs, since they had realized that the demise of the Ming dynasty was due to the eunuchs. Furthermore, they said that the Shun-chih Emperor had been deceived by the eunuch Wu Liang-fu and a Manchu, T'ung-i, into ignoring the precedents of Nurhachi and Abahai by establishing the thirteen eunuch bureaus. Wu and T'ung-i had exploited the bureaus and their positions, the regents claimed, to usurp power and gain an authority respected not only within the palace but throughout the entire country. In palace affairs they had allegedly wasted large sums on construction of new buildings and had made efforts to control areas outside their competence. The regents, implementing this denunciation with practical measures, abolished the thirteen bureaus and restored the old institutions of Nurhachi's and Abahai's time.

From this time the Imperial Household Department acquired a significant and expanding role in the affairs of the emperor and even, at times, in state affairs. The eunuchs were not abolished, but the personal bondservants of the emperor took over the main tasks which eunuchs had handled in the Ming period and kept the remaining eunuchs under tight control. It was this subordination of the eunuchs to their functional equivalents, the imperial bondservants, which permitted the Ch'ing dynasty to avoid, for the most part, the serious eunuch interference in government that had plagued previous dynasties. For almost two hundred years, Ch'ing government remained comparatively free of excessive eunuch influence. One notable exception was the attempt by a religious sect with eunuch support on the life of the Chia-ch'ing Emperor in 1813. In the late nineteenth century, the eunuchs gained some authority under the empress dowager, but even at that time the institutional check over them by the Imperial Household Department prevented a repetition of the Ming experience.

Chapter II

A GENERAL VIEW
OF THE IMPERIAL HOUSEHOLD DEPARTMENT

After 1661 the Imperial Household Department preserved
aspects of its dual nature which reflected both early Manchu and
later Chinese influences. We have already mentioned the failure of
Chinese sources to distinguish between the personnel—the bondservants of the upper three banners—and the organization—the
bureaucratic apparatus of the Imperial Household Department.
In Chinese both are known as "Nei-wu-fu." In essence, this con-
fusion stems from the coexistence of both the Manchu socio-
military system—the banner system—and the Chinese bureaucratic
administrative apparatus. Naturally, an acquaintance with both
types of organization is necessary for a full understanding of the
workings of the Nei-wu-fu but, because of limitations in source
materials and considerations of historical importance, the main
focus herein is on the Nei-wu-fu as a bureaucratic governmental
institution, rather than as a socio-military organization. The English
translation of "Nei-wu-fu" as "Imperial Household Department"—
implying a bureaucratic institution—reflects this emphasis. Nevertheless, a brief discussion of the Nei-wu-fu banner system is included in Chapter III, which deals with social aspects of the
department.

Organization

The organization of the Nei-wu-fu as a bureaucratic institution, although clearer than its structure as a part of the banner
system, still presents problems. The general outlines of the organization are perhaps most easily discerned. The Imperial Household
Department as a whole can be viewed as a complete bureaucratic
system. The personnel serving in the department were drawn, with
a few notable exceptions, from the ranks of the bondservants of
the upper three, or imperial, banners. The department possessed a

wide variety of sub-departments to manage education, recruitment, and promotion of personnel, in addition to judicial, fiscal, and supervisory functions. The only aspect of the department's administration managed by an official from the regular government bureaucracy was, not unexpectedly, that of the censorate. But even these censorial duties were actually divided between an official from the censorate and the highest officials in the department.[1] Since the department constituted a complete bureaucratic organization, it should come as no surprise that in several features its organization strongly resembled that of the public government bureaucracy.

Size

The Imperial Household Department was an unusually large and complex organization. Indeed the extent of its competence and the variety of its functions are startling. A complete outline of the various subordinate offices and positions within it could fill a weighty tome. One scholar has estimated that, at the end of the nineteenth century, the department, which was similar in size to what it had been a century earlier, controlled fifty-six subordinate departments, many of which had numerous sub-offices themselves.[2] The sub-departments treated below include the Coordinating Office, the Department of the Privy Purse, the Department of Works, the Palace Stud, the Chancery of the Imperial Household and various schools, all of which were either important in ministering to the emperor's needs or in the administration of the department as a whole.

The Imperial Household Department, like most bureaucracies, was not a static mass but a constantly changing organism. The natural tendency for all healthy bureaucracies may be to expand; such was certainly true of the Nei-wu-fu. A count of the number of officials in the department as a whole indicates that it grew significantly from 1661 to 1796. In later years, expansion continued, but at a slower pace than in the first half of the dynasty. In 1662, for instance, the total of officials in the department was 402, not including those such as managers for whom there was no

fixed number.³ By the end of K'ang-hsi's reign in 1722, the number
had more than doubled to 939. The rate of growth during Yung-
cheng's reign was more than triple that of K'ang-hsi's reign, but the
total number of officials reached only 1,285 because Yung-cheng
ruled for only thirteen years. The long reign of the Ch'ien-lung
Emperor saw the maturation of the department through slow expansion. The average yearly increase in personnel in this period
was 5.6 as compared with 8.8 for K'ang-hsi's and 26.6 for Yung-
cheng's reigns. The total number of officials had reached 1,623
by the succession of Ch'ien-lung's son in 1796.

The growth of the Nei-wu-fu in part reflected the expansion
of the original sub-departments established in 1661, but a significant part of its growth also came about from the creation of new
offices under its jurisdiction. One regular accretion to the department, for instance, was an imperial mausoleum for each deceased
emperor and empress. Less predictable, but more vital, were other
additions in K'ang-hsi's reign, such as the Imperial Manufactories
(Chih-tsao-chü) in 1664, the Bureau of the Imperial Gardens and
Hunting Parks (Feng-ch'en-yuan) in 1671, the School on Prospect
Hill (Ching-shan kuan-hsueh) in 1685, and the Eunuch School in
1696.⁴ The reign of the Yung-cheng Emperor, surprisingly, did not
witness a dramatic increase in the number of new subdivisions
added to the Imperial Household Department. In this period the
only significant addition was the incorporation of the Pasturage
Department (Ch'ing-feng-ssu), originally part of the Department
of Ceremonial, but independent from 1684.

The Ch'ien-lung era witnessed the merging of a relatively
large number of offices into the Imperial Household Department,
but they were relatively small and minor ones. Additions in the
early years of his reign included the Ching-ming-yuan estate
(Ching-ming-yuan), the Mongolian School (Meng-ku kuan-hsueh),
the Imperial Boats Office (Yü-ch'uan-ch'u), the Moslem and Burmese School (Hui-mien kuan-hsueh), and the Imperial Construction
Office (Tsung-li kung-ch'eng-ch'u). The last years of his reign
witnessed the inclusion of the Imperial Dispensary (Yü-yao-fang),
the Pao-ti Monastery, the School for Moslem Students (Hui-tzu

hsueh), and the Office of Buddhist and Taoist Priests (Seng-tao
ssu). This expansion did not fundamentally change the character
of the Nei-wu-fu, but simply added sub-departments roughly similar
in function to those already under its supervision.

The largest offices in the Nei-wu-fu were the Department of
the Privy Purse, the Department of Works (Ying-tsao-ssu), the
Palace Stud (Shang-ssu-yuan), the Imperial Armory (Wu-pei-yuan),
and the Chancery of the Imperial Household (Nei-kuan-ling ch'u).
Each of these sub-departments, except for the Chancery, possessed
over 50 officials in the Shun-chih period (1644-1662) and, when
the Nei-wu-fu was revitalized in 1661, these offices became its
largest components. Over the following century and a half, they
continued to expand: the Department of the Privy Purse became—
and remained—the largest, encompassing more than 183 officials
by the end of the Ch'ien-lung era. The greatest expansion was in
the Chancery of the Imperial Household, which contained only 20
officials in 1662, but had grown to over 160 by 1796. The slowest
growth was shown by the Palace Stud, which increased only from
59 officials in 1661 to 109 by the end of the eighteenth century.
Together these sub-departments represented 72 percent of all
Nei-wu-fu officials in 1662 and 44 percent in 1796. Thus, the
Nei-wu-fu had diversified considerably, but a small number of sub-
departments still held a large proportion of its officials.

Location

The physical location of the numerous and diverse subdivisions
is a troublesome question. The headquarters, or Coordinating
Office, can be clearly located on the western side of the Forbidden
City inside the Hsi-hua Gate and to the west of the Hall of Perfect
Harmony.[5] Ironically, this location, if not the very building, was
occupied in the Ming dynasty by the Directorate of Ceremonial,
the most powerful eunuch bureau.[6] In descriptions of the palace,
the buildings in this area are described as the "nei-wu-fu," but
aside from the Coordinating Office it is difficult to know which
sub-departments of the Nei-wu-fu were also located here.[7] One
description implies that the Department of the Privy Purse and the
Department of Ceremonial were also situated in this area.[8]

Diagram of the Imperial Palace

North

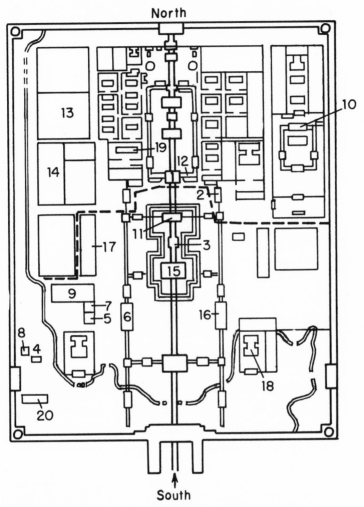

South

1. Ch'ien-ch'ing-men
2. Ching-yun-men
3. Chung-ho-tien
4. Hsien-an-kung kuan-hsueh
5. Hui-mien kuan-hsueh
6. Hung-i-ko
7. Kuo-fang
8. Meng-ku kuan-hsueh
9. Nei-wu-fu
10. Ning-shou-kung
11. Pao-ho-tien
12. Shang-shu-fang
13. Shou-an-kung
14. Shou-k'ang-kung
15. T'ai-ho-tien
16. T'i-jen-ko
17. Tsao-pan-ch'u
18. Wen-hua-tien
19. Yang-hsin-tien
20. Yü-shu-ch'u

− − − dividing line between "inner" and "outer" palace

Source: Adopted from T'an Wen,
Pei-ching chang-ku (Hong Kong, 1974), p. 10.

This location, in the Ch'ing dynasty, placed the Nei-wu-fu in the so-called "outer palace" (*wai-ch'ao*), rather than in the "inner palace" (*nei-t'ing*). This implies perhaps a functional distinction between one location (outer palace) where the administrative headquarters of the Nei-wu-fu was located and another location (inner palace) where the Nei-wu-fu managers met with the emperor to discuss and formulate policies. Other sub-departments of the Nei-wu-fu located in the outer palace section of the Forbidden City were the Workshops of the Imperial Household, which were contiguous to this Coordinating Office, the Fruit Office (Kuo-fang), and the Moslem and Burmese School. Just to the south of this complex of buildings and also located in the outer palace were the Mongolian School, the School at the Palace of Universal Peace (Hsien-an-kung kuan-hsueh), and the Printing Office and Bookbindery at the Throne Hall. Still farther to the south in the outer palace were various storehouses of the Nei-wu-fu and the Imperial Library (Yü-shu-ch'u). On the eastern side of the Forbidden City, also in the outer palace, were located the Palace Stud and the Imperial Buttery (Yü-ch'a-shan-fang). Just outside the Forbidden City to the north was the School on Prospect Hill. Other sub-departments, such as the parks and gardens, were located in other parts of Peking or nearby. Some sub-departments were even located far from the capital. The offices of the three imperial manufactories (*chih-tsao*), for instance, were located in Nanking, Soochow, and Hangchow, all in the lower Yangtze region. Thus, the geographical scope of the Nei-wu-fu's offices was not limited to the Forbidden City or even to the capital.

Principal Sub-Departments
    The seven principal sub-departments of the Imperial Household Department illustrate well the concept of the department as an almost self-contained bureaucratic entity. One author has implied that the department, which contained functional equivalents of the organs of government, was in itself a miniature model, or at least a likeness, of the central government.[9] The department managers, in this view, were analogous to the Cabinet, while the

Department of the Privy Purse, the Department of Works, and the Coordinating Office were equivalent to the Boards of Revenue, Works, and Civil Appointments. In popular parlance the Department of the Privy Purse was, in fact, dubbed "the Inner Board of Revenue" (Nei-hu-pu). Other sub-departments fulfilled the functions of the Boards of War, Rites, and Punishments. While this analogy is a useful analytical tool, a closer examination of the functions of these various sub-departments reveals a slightly different but more accurate picture of the Nei-wu-fu's principal components.

The Coordinating Office appears first in 1661 with the creation of an undetermined number of Nei-wu-fu managers and sixteen clerks.[10] The managers were not only the heads of the Coordinating Office, but also the most powerful officials in the Nei-wu-fu, for they had authority over all other officials and sub-officials in the department. Their broad powers carried wide-ranging responsibilities. Their duties included such diverse tasks as deputing Nei-wu-fu officials to accompany the emperor when he went on tour, sending out an official each year to bring back incense from Taishan, submitting a monthly report on the number of commissions carried out by the Nei-wu-fu, inspecting the condition of the palace maids, requesting the replacement of the assistant superintendent of customs at the Ch'ung-wen Gate in Peking, deputing a high Nei-wu-fu official to recite the classics in the Hung-jen Monastery, collecting communications from the various Nei-wu-fu sub-departments, and checking the expenditures of all Nei-wu-fu offices.[11] The number of managers was indeterminate and varied from two to as many as nine, but in general remained between four and six.[12]

Below the managers, the most important official was the department director. The K'ang-hsi Emperor appointed the first department director to the Coordinating Office in 1703 because it was overburdened with work and possessed no official between the lofty Nei-wu-fu managers and the lowly secretaries. Afterwards this post was temporarily left vacant, but the expansion of the Nei-wu-fu in Yung-cheng's reign led to the permanent establishment of this post in 1735. The department director was fully concerned only with the administration of the Nei-wu-fu. Unlike a Nei-wu-fu manager, who had social obligations imposed on him by his high status and who often traveled outside the capital to investigate or manage parks or gardens, the department director was constantly and directly in touch with the concrete details of bureaucratic management. He inspected the communications and reports from the subordinate departments and the work of the Coordinating Office, as well as bearing general responsibility for the prompt dispatch of business. In the absence of the Nei-wu-fu managers he temporarily assumed their authority. The importance of the department director is evidenced by the fact that the Coordinating Office is given no independent designation in the statutes relating to the Nei-wu-fu, but is simply styled "the various officials under the office's department director."[13] The Coordinating Office, it seems, was seen as the department director's particular, but not exclusive, bailiwick.

The Department of the Privy Purse was a direct descendant of the Privy Purse (Yü-yung-chien), one of the thirteen eunuch bureaus established in 1654. Control of this organ was transferred to the Nei-wu-fu in 1661, but the name was changed to Kuang-ch'u-ssu (Department of the Privy Purse) only in 1681.[14] This Department had originally three department directors, whose status was below that of the Coordinating Office's department director. As the Privy Purse grew, however, the number of department directors was expanded to a total of six by the end of Yung-chen's reign. Under the supervision of these directors were numerous other officials—assistant department directors (yuan-wai-lang), secretaries (chu-shih), clerks (pi-t'ieh-shih), controllers (ssu-k'u), and inspectors (k'u-shih). The Privy Purse consisted of a total of six storehouses. Four of them, the Bullion Vaults (Yin-k'u), the Fur Store (P'i-k'u), the Silk Store (Tuan-k'u), and the Imperial Wardrobe (I-k'u), dated from 1661. The Porcelain Store (Tz'u-k'u) and the Tea Store (Ch'a-k'u) were established only in 1689.

The Department of the Privy Purse was charged with handling the imperial finances. Records, called yellow registers (huang-ts'e), of the amounts of gold, silver, pewter, copper, pearls, furs, silks,

and ginseng in the imperial coffers had to be presented each year
to the department director of the Coordinating Office.[15] Records
also had to be kept of the goods received from or disbursed to
foreign tributary missions, the expenditures for presents to princes
and nobles when the emperor went on tour, the expenses for
bearers and other services entailed in an imperial tour, and many
others. In addition, the Department of the Privy Purse communicated with other sub-departments of the Nei-wu-fu and even offices
outside it, such as the Board of Revenue, and exchanged or transferred funds with them on occasion.[16]

The Department of Works also evolved directly from one of
the thirteen eunuch bureaus. In 1661 it became part of the Nei-wu-
fu and its name was changed to the Inner Board of Works (Nei-
kung-pu).[17] Only in 1681 did it receive the designation Department of Works (Ying-tsao-ssu). The department at first had three
department directors, but after 1699 only two. Below these
directors was a large, but fairly stable, number of assistant department directors, clerks, storehouse overseers (k'u-chang), and storehouse keepers (k'u-shou). A number of storehouses in the Department of Works, such as those for lumber (mu-k'u), iron (t'ieh-k'u),
charcoal (t'an-k'u), firewood (ch'ai-k'u), and others, contained the
materials necessary for this department's work. The main responsibility of the Department of Works was for repair work within the
Forbidden City. Any project that involved the expenditure of
more than two hundred taels was handled by the Nei-wu-fu's
Imperial Construction Office (Tsung-li kung-ch'eng ch'u) or by
the Board of Works.[18] The Department of Works, therefore,
managed small-scale repairs, while larger tasks were left to these
other two organs.

The Palace Stud was another remnant of the era of eunuch
supremacy at the end of the Shun-chih Emperor's reign. In 1661
its name was changed to A-tun ya-men, the Pastoral Office, from
the Manchu term adun meaning "herd."[19] In 1677 the name was
modified to Shang-ssu-yuan, the Palace Stud. The highest official
in this organ was a Nei-wu-fu manager, a position first occupied in
1661. Below him there was a department director established in

1665, and another department director established in 1694 to coordinate the two divisions of the Palace Stud created in that year. Under these high officials was a large group of assistant department directors, secretaries, clerks, supervisors of droves (*a-tun shih-wei*), inspectors of droves (*mu-chang*), Mongol veterinarians (*Meng-ku i-sheng*), and others. Starting in 1694 the duties of the Palace Stud were divided between a First Department (Tso-ssu) and a Second Department (Yu-ssu), the former managing the herds located in the capital and outside as well as rewards and punishments, and the latter handling fodder and salaries for officials.[20] The size of this department indicates the importance of horseback riding to the Manchus, who, although not nomads like the Mongols, glorified the equestrian skills associated with hunting and war.

The Chancery of the Imperial Household was an unusual subdivision which strongly reflected Manchu influence. Indeed, the Chinese term for the Chancery, "Nei-kuan-ling ch'u," is simply a translation of the Manchu term for "inner organs," implying that the Chancery, which was linked to the banner system, was the forerunner of the Nei-wu-fu and later absorbed by it.[21] Originally, there were four overseers (*nei-kuan-ling*), but in the early years of the dynasty their number increased, reaching twenty by 1654 and thirty by 1695. Each of the upper three banners contributed ten overseers to this total of thirty. The overseers were thus recruited through the banner organization. In addition, until the middle of the eighteenth century no superior official in the Chancery was charged with managing the administration of Chancery affairs. The overseers themselves seem to have handled these matters. In 1750, however, a department director and assistant department director were finally appointed, symbolizing the subordination of these overseers to a civilian bureaucratic hierarchy.

Although the institutional organization of the Chancery became more orderly over time, its functional role displayed no similar tendency. The principal responsibilities of this organ seem to be related to miscellaneous services for the court. Indeed, "chancery" seems a noble term for a sub-department that was mainly concerned with menial janitorial and other services. It reported,

for example, the amount of expenditures for vehicles and for fresh
vegetables by the court; it suggested which times were propitious
for cutting the grass by the Throne Halls; it selected the *su-la* or
"disbanded servitors"[22] for odd jobs; and it reported on the conditions in the Nei-wu-fu estate lands in Chihli Province and in Manchuria.[23] As we shall see below, the overseers were also responsible
for supervising the activities of the eunuchs.

The Nei-wu-fu schools served as a means of educating the
sons of the bondservants from the upper three banners for service
in the Nei-wu-fu.[24] Six different Nei-wu-fu schools existed prior
to 1796,[25] including a Eunuch School.[26] Preparation for entrance
into official positions in the Imperial Household Department
through these schools differed from that for entrance into the
regular government bureaucracy. Recruitment into the Nei-wu-fu
did not depend on a combination of private academies and local
schools in coordination with the three-tier examination system.

The first and largest Nei-wu-fu school was the School on
Prospect Hill. In 1685 the K'ang-hsi Emperor ordered the establishment of a school for children of the Nei-wu-fu bondservants because,
as he said, "there is no one in the Nei-wu-fu who can both write
and use a bow and arrow."[27] In accordance with K'ang-hsi's demand that the new school be set up in a place where he could frequently observe the students and insure that they would exhibit
proper diligence in their studies, a site just north of the Forbidden
City was chosen. Three hundred and sixty pupils were selected to
study Chinese and Manchu under the guidance of twenty-seven
teachers recruited from among the elderly and reliable Nei-wu-fu
adjutants (*chih-shih*) or disbanded servitors (*hsien-san*). Indigent
students who entered this school received stipends. In the eighteenth century, examinations were held every three years and the
students divided into four groups according to performance. Those
in the first group were given positions as clerks; those in the second,
posts as storehouse inspectors or storehouse keepers; those in the
third were allowed to continue their studies; those in the fourth
group were expelled. The Ch'ien-lung Emperor, who showed great
interest in preserving certain native Manchu customs, ordered that

the Nei-wu-fu send one or two officials to judge the exhibitions of archery on horseback which he considered an essential part of these predominantly literary examinations.[28]

The founding of the School at the Palace of Universal Peace in 1728 was another effort to cultivate education among the imperial bondservants. This school had nine teachers and ninety students. At first, students were exclusively imperial bondservants, but from 1758 ordinary bannermen were admitted.[29] The professors were chosen by the Board of Civil Appointments from among the *chin-shih* or *chü-jen*. The students took exams every three or five years, and those who did well could expect to receive positions such as storehouse inspectors. This school had more scholastic pretensions than the School on Prospect Hill. The Ch'ien-lung Emperor, for example, rebuked the Nei-wu-fu officials who requested that students in the school be given official posts before they reached thirty years of age, saying that the purpose of the school was "nurturing men of talent and not the appointment of clerks."[30]

The three remaining Nei-wu-fu schools were all established by the Ch'ien-lung Emperor for non-Chinese minority groups within the Nei-wu-fu or for the study of the foreign languages by Nei-wu-fu students. The first was the Mongolian school established in 1747 inside the School at the Palace of Universal Peace in order to promote the study of Mongolian by the Mongol bondservants in the upper three banners. Twenty-four students were taught Mongol classics by Mongol instructors who possessed the *chü-jen* or *sheng-yuan* degree in translating. The curriculum was supervised by two officials from the Court of Colonial Affairs (Li-fan-yuan). The second school, the Moslem and Burmese School, was created in 1756 to teach Arabic and, later, Burmese to Nei-wu-fu bondservants. The ten students were probably Moslems, particularly after 1760 when Moslem artists and craftsmen were enrolled in the ranks of the Nei-wu-fu bondservants.[31] The teachers were recruited from among Moslems resident in the capital. Exams were given every five years, and successful students could take up posts as clerks or storehouse inspectors. The other Nei-wu-fu school, the School for

Moslem Students, was probably an institution for educating the almost 200 Chin-ch'uan Moslems who had been captured in battle and enrolled in the Nei-wu-fu in 1776.[32] This school came under the supervision of the Nei-wu-fu managers in 1790.[33]

Major Functions

The translation of the term "Nei-wu-fu" as "The Imperial Household Department" conveys the general purposes of the organization—to manage the emperor's private affairs. This included the obvious tasks of providing for the emperor's food, clothing, and shelter as well as other responsibilities such as handling his ceremonial duties and his entertainments.[34] These functions in themselves may, at first glance, appear to be somewhat pedestrian, but in fact their execution was endowed with a grandeur and elegance that made them not only impressive but also culturally significant.[35] The food, clothing, and shelter given to the emperor were the best available in China at the time and represent the highest achievements of the Chinese in these fields. Nor was the range of activities under the department's roof limited to these bare essentials of life. The Nei-wu-fu's Printing Office and Bookbindery at the Throne Hall (Wu-ying-tien), to name only one example, published the finest editions of scholarly works. The reprinting of these editions in recent years indicates the wide esteem they still enjoy. The compilation of the mammoth Imperial Manuscript (Ssu-k'u-ch'üan-shu) Library in 36,000 volumes was another scholarly enterprise of the department which transcended the purpose of serving the emperor's personal amusement.

Although the Nei-wu-fu's task of caring for the emperor's daily needs was an essential one, three of its other functions are more interesting and significant topics for investigation. One of these is the role of the Nei-wu-fu in controlling the eunuchs and preventing a repetition of eunuch usurpation of power like the one in Ming times. Other significant functions of the Nei-wu-fu were its social role in Ch'ing government and society and its financial functions. These latter two topics are treated at length in Chapters III and IV.

Strict control of the eunuchs began with the conquest of China, if not before. The Ch'ing dynasty's earliest regulations dealt with reducing the oversupply of eunuchs remaining from the Ming. In 1646, for example, persons who had castrated themselves without official sanction were sentenced to decapitation.[36] In later years, officials became subject to punishment if commoners under their jurisdiction became eunuchs.[37] In the late seventeenth and early eighteenth centuries, as death depleted the ranks of the aging Ming eunuchs and as the palace administration expanded, prohibitions on castration demonstrated a concern for the welfare of Manchu and Chinese young men. The purpose of these prohibitions became to insure that boys were not forcibly or deceitfully castrated and that Manchu bondservants or Manchus themselves did not become eunuchs.[38] By 1724 a regulation required a thorough investigation into the background of all new eunuch applicants in order to prevent Manchu bannermen from entering palace service as eunuchs.[39]

The emphasis on control favored the recruitment of young eunuchs to fill the openings created by the deaths of the older ones. An order of 1723, for instance, limited recruitment to those under seventeen years of age in an effort to discourage older, and therefore less manageable, castrates from applying for positions.[40] A certain suspicion of older eunuchs is manifest in a decision of 1740 which allowed castrated boys of under sixteen to volunteer for service, but required those over fifteen to present a written bond (*wen-chieh*) from local government officials in addition to the usual proof of a guarantor.[41] Some older eunuchs managed to secure employment in the palace, but they were regarded with disfavor. In 1756, for instance, a manager of the Imperial Household Department, in fixing punishments for eunuchs involved in robberies and arson, decided to dismiss a certain Chang T'ai-p'ing. The reason he gave was that "even though our investigation reveals that he did not take part in the crimes, still he has a base character and furthermore he was castrated in middle age."[42]

Aside from these preliminary restrictions on eligibility for service in the palace, there were other institutional checks upon the eunuchs. The two major devices for controlling the large number of menial eunuchs were direct supervision by head eunuchs and indirect supervision by officials of the Nei-wu-fu. The procedures for inspection of new eunuchs are one example of the way in which these two types of control interacted to assure subordination. In 1661, when new regulations were promulgated on eunuch recruitment, generally two types of eunuchs were recruited: those who entered through the Board of Rites of the government bureaucracy, and those who directly offered their loyalty and services (*t'ou-ch'ung*) to the new Manchu rulers. Two sub-departments of the Nei-wu-fu, the Accounts Department (Hui-chi-ssu)[43] and the Department of Ceremonial (Chang-i-ssu), sent out two officials (*ssu-kuan*)[44] to inspect both types of applicants and assure that they were in fact eunuchs.[45] After inspection they handed over the novices to an assistant chief eunuch (*tsung-kuan t'ai-chien*) for assignment to a post. After assuming a position, the eunuch received his salary from an overseer (*nei-kuan-ling*), a Nei-wu-fu banner official.

In later years this process of recruitment, while changing in some details, remained essentially the same. In the first half of the eighteenth century, for instance, eunuchs from certain backgrounds, such as those from the banners (*ch'i-hsia t'ai-chien*), were prohibited from serving in the *chin-shih-ch'u*, the emperor's personal entourage.[46] Later, in the second half of the eighteenth century, an effort was made to improve administration by curtailing the superfluous registration of eunuchs under the Nei-wu-fu managers.[47]

How effective these various measures were in fostering an objective and efficient system of recruitment for eunuchs which would ensure a supply of able, young eunuchs of good character is open to question. Fragmentary evidence suggests that cases of eunuch misconduct were increasing through the Ch'ien-lung era, but this may be merely a result of the apparently increasing number of eunuchs.[48] One indication that administration of recruitment was not fully effective is an order of 1785 by the Ch'ien-lung Emperor that the Nei-wu-fu managers take a more active role in the inspection of eunuchs in order to prevent recurrences of extortion and malfeasance by the officials and clerks from the Department of Ceremonial who inspected the eunuchs.[49]

The organization of the eunuchs once they entered the service of the emperor is not altogether clear. It is obvious that in 1661 they suffered a great blow in power and prestige with the abolition of the thirteen eunuch bureaus and the re-establishment of the Nei-wu-fu. Afterwards, under the general supervision of the Nei-wu-fu, a definite, but informal, hierarchy of authority prevailed among them. In 1726, however, the Yung-cheng Emperor re-established a formal hierarchy by restoring to the various eunuch leaders the official ranks of which they had been deprived in 1661.[50] At the top was the Chief Eunuch (Kung-tien chien-tu ling-shih t'ai-chien, also called Ch'ien-ch'ing-kung tsung-kuan), who was responsible for the conduct of all the eunuchs, first to the Nei-wu-fu managers, and second to the emperor himself. Although certain sub-departments of the Nei-wu-fu, such as the Department of Ceremonial and of Works, bore the responsibility for deciding eunuch promotions in certain cases before 1726, from this year on the Chief Eunuch was entrusted with general authority for reviewing almost all demotions and promotions for eunuchs.[51] The Chief Eunuch himself was probably chosen by the Nei-wu-fu managers from among the assistant chief eunuchs (*tsung-kuan t'ai-chien*).

The assistant chief eunuchs aided their superiors in supervising eunuchs throughout the palace. They played a role in deciding the promotion of their inferiors to positions such as heads of eunuch sub-departments (*shou-ling t'ai-chien*). An edict of 1712, for instance, criticized them for selecting lazy and pretentious eunuchs to these posts.[52] The eunuchs who headed the sub-departments were responsible for the actions of others who served in a specific sub-department. In the Department of Ceremonial, for instance, two eunuchs oversaw the deportment of forty others.[53] In that case, the eunuchs were held in check not only by their own hier-archy, over which the Nei-wu-fu had overall control, but were also under the scrutiny of the Nei-wu-fu officials of higher rank who worked by their side in the department. The heads of eunuch sub-departments were selected from among the assistant heads of eunuch sub-departments (*fu-shou-ling t'ai-chien*), who, in turn, were chosen from the ranks of the unranked eunuchs (*t'ai-chien*).

It appears that, at least in theory, the eunuchs had a clearly defined hierarchy which provided chances for advancement. In practice, however, promotion through the ranks of eunuch officials was probably not as simple, nor were the criteria for promotion as objective, as might appear at first glance. In certain cases, such as for heads of eunuch sub-departments in the Hall of Perfect Harmony (T'ai-ho-tien), in the three Throne Halls (Chung-ho-tien, Pao-ho-tien, and Wen-hua-tien), and in the carpentry, tile, and scroll workshops, the Nei-wu-fu's Department of Works exercised the privilege of selecting eunuchs for promotion until 1726. Nor was the power of selection limited to the Nei-wu-fu, for the Board of Civil Appointments also played a role—at times nominal, at times substantial—in the promotion of eunuchs.[54] The Board of Rites, too, reserved authority for filling certain eunuch posts under the supervision of the Nei-wu-fu's Department of Ceremony even after 1726.[55]

The promotion patterns of the eunuchs remain obscure. Information from 1754 suggests that newly hired eunuchs were sent to serve in the Summer Palace (Yuan-ming-yuan) gardens outside the capital as grounds keepers.[56] Those who performed well in these lowly posts for an extended period were then promoted to employment in the palace. The precise criteria for these promotions and those for promotion of eunuchs inside the palace are not described, but undoubtedly included diligence and loyalty. A case from 1748, however, provides an example of an informal procedure which may have been common in many eunuch promotions. In that case the formal procedures had been supplanted by unwritten ones in which the eunuchs already employed in the office illegally acted as guarantors in recommending and securing approval for the promotion of certain applicants.[57]

In one area in particular, eunuchs were never allowed any significant self-management. This was in financial matters, where control over them was especially severe. The funds available to eunuchs both as salaries and as administrative expenses were meager and closely scrutinized. The salaries of the eunuch officials are unknown, but the unranked eunuchs received a stipend of merely two taels per month.[58] In 1689 the K'ang-hsi Emperor chastized the eunuchs for their tattered clothing and beggarly appearance and later remedied the situation by arranging for loans to needy eunuchs. These loans were supposedly only for unexpected trips or funeral expenses, but were actually used for ordinary living expenses such as clothing.[59] They were dispensed from the coffers of the Tzu-ming-chung-ch'u, the Self-Chiming Clock Office, or the Nei-wu-fu's Department of the Privy Purse, and were supervised by Nei-wu-fu officials.

Later, the Yung-cheng Emperor likewise demonstrated a concern for the eunuchs' low salaries. In 1729 he ordered the Nei-wu-fu managers to discuss with the assistant chief eunuchs how to implement their suggestion of establishing a pawn shop in the Summer Palace gardens or in the palace as a means of earning interest on the 200,000 taels of Nei-wu-fu funds he had given them to invest.[60]

As mentioned above, the eunuchs' salaries, like these supplementary grants, were distributed by the Nei-wu-fu. Until 1723 the salaries were disbursed by the overseers (*nei-kuan-ling*), but afterwards this authority was transferred to higher officials. From this time Nei-wu-fu banner officials, the *ts'an-ling*, prepared the eunuch payroll for presentation to the Nei-wu-fu's Accounts Department which then notified the Nei-wu-fu Coordinating Office.[61] The salaries were then released by a directive from the Coordinating Office to the Board of Revenue. This new procedure for disbursing salaries seems to have been a deliberate effort to curtail abuses in the eunuch payroll by dividing the process of disbursement into several steps. Officials from a different office handled each step, but those from the Nei-wu-fu played the leading role.

Eunuch authority for spending funds on administrative expenses or on other items was also limited by procedures inspired by memories of the squandering of tax revenues by eunuchs in the late Ming period. Thus, the Nei-wu-fu supervised the dispensing of monies to the eunuchs. From 1661, when the thirteen eunuch offices were abolished and the Nei-wu-fu re-established, all administrative expenses (*kung-fei*) for the eunuchs were reported by the assistant chief eunuchs to the Nei-wu-fu, which then ordered the Board of Revenue to release the funds.[62] Further precautions were introduced in 1677, when the K'ang-hsi Emperor ordered the eunuchs to report the use of monies from the coffers in the Yang-hsin Hall to two separate Nei-wu-fu sub-departments.[63] These measures prevented the eunuchs from by-passing the Nei-wu-fu by appealing directly to the emperor for funds, and made it easy to determine the responsibility for any misuse of funds.

In the eighteenth century these restrictions on the disbursement of funds may have directed the eunuchs' attention towards other, covert means of attaining money. Incidents, such as one in 1731, in which the eunuchs, in order to earn money, sold the choice meat provided for imperial sacrifices, seem to have become more frequent.[64] Funds mysteriously disappeared from the vaults of the Yang-hsin Hall, and Ch'ien-lung promulgated stricter regulations on the issuing of vouchers permitting the removal of articles from the palace. This measure was prompted by an incident in 1746 in which a sub-official was caught at the Ching-yun Gate smuggling state-owned silk supposedly "belonging to the eunuch Wang Jui of the Shou-k'ang Palace."[65] In later years the Ch'ien-lung Emperor ordered a yearly inventory of all the articles on display in various palaces so as to uncover and discourage pilferage.[66]

Towards the end of the century, when the eunuchs tried to reassert authority to oversee the upkeep of the palaces, the emperor strongly rebuked them. In 1776, for instance, the eunuchs were soundly berated for ordering, on their own initiative and without the permission of the Nei-wu-fu managers, that workmen from the Nei-wu-fu's Workshops of the Imperial Household (Tsao-pan-ch'u) do repair work on the Yang-hsin Hall.[67] Eunuchs in the first half of the Ch'ing period, then, were unable to overcome significantly the Nei-wu-fu's control of administrative expenditures and turned to thievery to acquire what was otherwise unobtainable.

In theory, responsibility for investigating the eunuchs'

behavior and punishing them for misdeeds rested ultimately with the Nei-wu-fu. In practice, however, it turned out that the assistant chief eunuchs and the heads of eunuch sub-departments often bore immediate responsibility for keeping the eunuchs in line. The early Ch'ing emperors often communicated directly with the assistant chief eunuchs on details concerning eunuch administration, sometimes encouraging them to be diligent in the execution of their duties, but more often threatening them with punishments for misbehavior.[68] Several examples illustrate this point. The K'ang-hsi Emperor in 1682 ordered the assistant chief eunuchs to deliberate on the appropriate punishment for a certain Wang Chin and other eunuchs who had taken their seats at a feast before the princes and ministers had seated themselves.[69] The assistant chief eunuch Ku Wen-hsing, a close companion of the emperor,[70] recommended a punishment of fifty lashes, but the emperor, after reviewing this suggestion, raised the number to eighty. In 1728 the unequal administration of justice caught the eye of the Yung-cheng Emperor, who criticized the assistant chief eunuchs for allowing their subordinates to mete out mild punishments to friends and severe ones to foes.[71] He insisted that the assistant chief eunuchs personally investigate any case involving substantial punishment to insure a fair sentence. Several decades later the Ch'ien-lung Emperor ordered that the assistant chief eunuchs punish the eunuch Wang Ch'ang-kuei of the Chancery of Memorials to the Emperor (Tsou-shih-ch'u) for tampering with the seals on a box containing memorials (tsou-hsia) sent by provincial governors.[72]

In general, the Nei-wu-fu managers seem to have taken an active role in investigating and punishing eunuchs only in substantial cases which the emperor was not willing to entrust to the eunuchs themselves. A case from 1748 illustrates this point. A eunuch in the Imperial Gerfalcon Aviary (Ying-fang) was accused of insubordination by a general commandant of the gendarmerie, who suggested to the emperor that he be delivered to the Nei-wu-fu managers for punishment. Ch'ien-lung denied this request with the terse comment: "There is no need to hand him over to the Nei-wu-fu; simply give him to the assistant chief eunuchs."[73]

Representative cases where the Nei-wu-fu managers did play a role
were those concerning robbery and arson, failure to forward communications to the emperor by eunuchs in the Chancery of Memorials to the Emperor, failure to allow firemen to enter the Shou-
an Palace to extinguish a fire, and possession of a dangerous weapon
by a eunuch from the Palace Drama Office (Kung-hsi-fang).[74]

Perhaps the most serious cases of eunuch misconduct were
handled by the Nei-wu-fu's Judicial Department (Shen-hsing-ssu).
This office generally deliberated on substantial misbehavior by
Nei-wu-fu officials and sub-officials, but it also seems to have had
jurisdiction over the criminal, as opposed to administrative, misdeeds of the eunuchs. Crimes for which the punishment exceeded
one hundred blows were referred from the Judicial Department to
the Board of Punishments, and it seems that homicides were probably referred to the Three High Courts of Judicature (San-fa-ssu).[75]
In the mid-eighteenth century, for instance, cases involving thefts
and assaults by eunuchs were entrusted to the Judicial Department.[76]
The establishment in the 1720s of a Police Bureau (Fan-i-ch'u) and
a jail subordinate to the Judicial Department underlines its criminal,
rather than administrative, orientation.[77] Previously the Nei-wu-fu's
banner institutions, such as the overseers, had carried out police
duties, but by the early eighteenth century the need for a new
specialized organ to apprehend suspects and criminals became
apparent. In 1726, for instance, the newly created Police Bureau
was ordered to ferret out and arrest eunuchs who, after release
from service, did not return home, but remained without permission in the capital.[78]

The Nei-wu-fu's supervision of the eunuchs, as this order of
1726 suggests, did not necessarily end when they retired from
service in the palace. Originally, the K'ang-hsi Emperor had ordered
the Board of Rites to care for retired eunuchs who were unable to
return to their homes and remained in the capital, but this measure
was not sufficient. The Yung-cheng Emperor declared that even
dogs and horses received better treatment in their old age than the
palace eunuchs and demanded that the Nei-wu-fu managers provide them with free housing and use the income from government

(probably Nei-wu-fu) real estate to support them.[79] At the same time, all retired eunuchs living in the capital had to acquire a certificate from the Nei-wu-fu indicating that they had good reason to remain in Peking.[80]

Finally, the Nei-wu-fu not only supervised the eunuchs and punished them; it also deprived some of them of their positions. In 1771, for instance, the eunuch positions in the Wen-hua Throne Hall were abolished, and eleven years later eunuchs in the three Throne Halls were replaced with Nei-wu-fu personnel.[81]

No sketch of the institutions and policies which held the eunuchs in a subservient position would be complete without a brief mention of the attitudes of the emperors who formed the institutions and decided the policies. While the emperors shared many convictions, the Nei-wu-fu's policies towards eunuchs and its implementation of them appear to have differed significantly under the various emperors. The most obvious and essential similarity which marked the reigns of the three emperors, K'ang-hsi, Yung-cheng, and Ch'ien-lung, was a clear understanding of the abuses of the eunuchs in the Ming period and a determination to avoid a repetition. All three also exhibited a certain contempt for the eunuchs, although none ever seems to have thought of driving them from the palace. In terms of administrative psychology, however, their attitudes seem to have differed significantly. The views of the K'ang-hsi and Ch'ien-lung Emperors appear quite similar in this regard, but the attitude of Yung-cheng appears to have been distinctive.

K'ang-hsi, the earliest of these three emperors, was closest in time to the Ming experience, and this influenced his views. Once he remarked to his ministers that

> when I assumed the throne it was only twenty years after the end of the Ming Dynasty. I employed eunuchs and officials who had served under the Ming Emperor Shen-tsung. They told me about the events of the late Ming . . . how the eunuchs exercised power and the emperor refused to meet with his ministers . . . The eunuch's character is different from

that of normal people. Eunuchs are only good for performing menial tasks within the palace and nothing else.[82]

At another point he compared the wasteful extravagance of
the Ming court with the frugality of his own household administration:

> The court expenses of the Ming were extremely wasteful. One
> day's expenditures of the Ming court would be enough to
> last us for one year. Ming court expenses for cosmetics were
> 400,000 taels and for provisions several million taels [yearly].
> In the Ming period the number of palace maids reached 9,000
> and the number of eunuchs 100,000. . . Today, however,
> there are not more than 400 to 500 concubines and eunuchs
> combined.[83]

The Ch'ien-lung Emperor echoed the same thoughts about the
Ming and earlier dynasties. He criticized, for instance, the inclusion
of a book with the title "History of the Palace in the Ming Dynasty"
in the library of the Yang-hsin Hall. "The actions of the eunuchs
in the Ming dynasty are not worthy of publication," he claimed,

> especially since the eunuchs of the Ming dynasty caused such
> great harm to government. Eunuchs such as Wang Chen, Liu
> Chin, and Wei Chung-hsien used their positions as heads of the
> Directorate of Ceremonial to usurp power. . . When I read of
> the widespread abuses of the Ming eunuchs, I feel a profound
> revulsion.[84]

Later, in 1769, he became furious at the type of education
eunuchs received at the Eunuch School (Ch'ang-fang kuan-hsueh)
established in 1696. He asserted that "literacy only made it easier
for eunuchs, such as those in the Directorate of Ceremonial in
Ming times, to satisfy their own greed and ambitions. What harm
is there in eunuch illiteracy?" he asked rhetorically. "All they need
to be able to do is recognize a few characters and that's all."[85]

The policies and attitudes of K'ang-hsi and Ch'ien-lung suggest that the main thrust of their eunuch administration was preventive, while its overall tone was coercive or punitive rather than persuasive. Thus, these emperors' policies often consisted of directives to Nei-wu-fu or assistant chief eunuchs to tighten their supervision of the eunuchs or orders prohibiting the eunuchs from committing certain acts. The primary function of the Nei-wu-fu in this regard was to discover and punish misconduct or, better yet, prevent it from taking place at all. In these circumstances avoidance of reprimands and punishments, rather than imaginative and innovative fulfillment of their tasks, was probably the eunuchs' principal concern. Generally, however, people in bureaucratic-type organizations perform most efficiently when they are motivated by normative and material incentives rather than punitive ones.[86] Personnel who feel an emotional or economic sense of identity of interest with an organization perform better than those whose actions are determined by the desire to avoid punishment. One might, therefore, surmise that the coercive nature of control and motivation in the administration of eunuchs in the reigns of K'ang-hsi and Ch'ien-lung kept them from abusing their positions, but at the expense of efficient administration.

It is interesting to note that the emperor who went furthest in attempting noncoercive management of the eunuchs was Yung-cheng, sometimes thought of as a despot. The term "despot" seems to imply that the ruler uses his absolute power to compel immediate and complete compliance with his directives. In practice, however, the rulers most effective in gaining compliance with their orders are most often those who are liberal rather than disciplinarian.[87] They try to nurture voluntary obedience through a sense of social obligation in their subordinates by favoring them in unexpected ways. Furthermore, they employ diffuse sanctions which increase the dependency of subordinates on superiors, but at the same time allow the subordinates to internalize the principles of administration and thus escape feelings of dependency.

The Yung-cheng Emperor seems to have made more of an effort than his father or his son to use such favors and diffuse sanctions to elicit better service from the eunuchs. His primary means of increasing the eunuchs' sense of obligation to him was to favor them by establishing a loan fund in order to help them meet unexpected expenses and by providing shelter and stipends for them in their old age. He also tried to appeal to the eunuchs' sense of self-respect by allowing them to bow, rather than kneel, when the ground was muddy.[88] In his orders to the eunuchs berating them for poor performance or for committing misdeeds, he reminded them of their moral indebtedness to him and implied or stated that it was ungrateful of them to misbehave. He made effective use of diffuse sanctions, such as the re-establishment of a rank system and the institution of categories of performance for rewarding eunuchs, so that his decisions on advancement, demotion or rewards could be made objectively.[89] He also clarified and made more equitable the punishments for eunuchs. These measures— essentially a combined stick-and-carrot policy—may well have promoted a greater sense of self-esteem and solidarity among eunuchs as well as greater efficiency in performing their tasks. For these reasons it may seem appropriate, in speaking of his policies towards eunuchs, to characterize the Yung-cheng Emperor as a keen student of human nature and a skillful administrator rather than as a willful despot.

Chapter III

THE SOCIAL ORGANIZATION OF THE
IMPERIAL HOUSEHOLD DEPARTMENT'S BONDSERVANTS

The Nei-wu-fu's banner organization, which derives from the Manchu heritage, has few parallels in Chinese history. The social status and the functional role of the bondservants, however, resemble similar groups in Chinese society, both of earlier times and of the Ch'ing period. The unusual nature of bondservant status, in particular, should be examined in the context of the Chinese conception of bondage in earlier times and in the Ch'ing era. An examination of other aspects of the social organization of the Nei-wu-fu bondservants, such as social structure, social mobility, and government service, may then serve to place the Nei-wu-fu in the general context of Ch'ing society and government.

The Nature of Bondage in Chinese History and in the Ch'ing

The Pre-Ch'ing Background
Perhaps the most vexing question concerning the social aspects of the Imperial Household Department is the meaning of the word *pao-i*. This is a Manchu word literally translated as "household person" and sometimes rendered as "slave." However, the standard foreign work on Ch'ing governmental institutions translates the term as "bondservants."[1] The *pao-i*, then, were in some form of bondage and occupied, in theory, an inferior and subordinate position in Ch'ing society.

Slavery existed in Chinese society from early times, but the origin of slaves is uncertain. In earliest times slaves may have been mostly war captives, but later conquest dynasties introduced the concept of productive slavery.[2] At least from Han times onward, however, Chinese slavery was a milder form than that prevalent in ancient Rome or Germany, for Chinese law always perceived of the slave as "half man and half object" (*pan-jen pan-wu*), rather

53

than as a mere chattel.[3] In accordance with this concept, slaves in certain situations seem to have been viewed, on the one hand, as private property no different from cows or horses.[4] They could be partitioned by a father among his sons and could be the object of robbery.

On the other hand, slaves in China acted as individual person-alities recognized by the law. They owned property and could buy their freedom or make money for themselves and for their masters.[5] In the Yuan period especially, slaves owned other slaves and prob-ably owned real property besides. Slaves also assumed and paid their own debts. Their persons were protected by law so that an armed robber who killed a slave would receive the same punishment as if he had killed a commoner. A person who committed a tort against a slave, however, received a lesser punishment than for the same offense against a commoner. The family relationships of slaves were recognized; marriage and the relationship of parent to child, in particular, were protected. Slaves often had surnames and, in any case, their identity was recorded in registers kept by local government officials. Slaves, of course, not only enjoyed the pro-tection of the law, but were also subject to its sanctions, and the punishment they received was generally harsher than that for commoners. Slaves could utilize the judicial system to litigate against each other and to assert a claim to freedom, although they were generally not allowed to denounce their master unless he was plotting a rebellion against the dynasty.

The legal status of the Chinese slave, then, seems to have been comparatively high. In fact, a European legal scholar writing in 1810 said:

> It is observed, indeed, that the slavery which is recognized and tolerated by the laws of China is a mild species of servitude and perhaps not very degrading in a country in which no con-dition of life appears to admit of any considerable degree of personal liberty and independence.[6]

In accordance with this view of the different nature of bondage

in Ch'ing China and the West, we follow other scholars[7] in employing the term "bondservant" to describe the Nei-wu-fu *pao-i* in
order to avoid any misunderstanding arising from the connotations
of the word "slave" in English.

Bondservants in Ch'ing China

Since the Ch'ing dynasty adopted the Ming legal code almost
in toto, the legal position of bondservants during the Ch'ing period
in general resembled that of bondservants in the Ming and earlier
periods. The social function of bondservants, as opposed to their
legal status, was another part of the heritage which the Ch'ing in-
herited from the Ming. In the early Ming era, changes in local government burdened officials with a large number of tasks which they
were unable to fulfill by themselves. As a result, a system of employing private secretaries—and probably bondservants—to act as
aides and agents in the management of government work arose and
continued throughout the dynasty.[8] In the military field bondservants assumed a key role from the late sixteenth century as
aides-de-camp to high military commanders.[9] In the economy in
general bondservants occupied key positions as commercial representatives and managers for the richest traders in China, the Hui-
chou merchants.[10] These bondservants were most common in the
prosperous Yangtze delta where they grew so rich and haughty
that efforts by their masters to control them led to a revolt in the
early seventeenth century. Agricultural serfs or slave-like tenant
farmers whose condition was less favorable than that of the commercial bondservants also existed, but were not the basis of the
agricultural labor force. In Ming times, it seems, bondservants fulfilled important social and economic functions in various aspects
of government and society.[11]

The role of bondservants in the Ch'ing dynasty, however,
was not an exact replica of what it had been in Ming times because
of the Manchu heritage. As noted above, the Jurchen tribes employed
Chinese agricultural slaves as early as the fifteenth century, and by
the late sixteenth century a Chinese visitor observed that all the
Manchu military commanders had both field and house slaves.

Later, as the Manchus conquered areas with large Chinese populations, they absorbed some educated men like Ning Yuan-wo who were familiar with history and literature and, although bondservants, achieved positions in civil government in the 1620s.[12] These Chinese bondservants played an important role in the flourishing commerce between Inner Mongolia, Manchuria, and China and, centered in Kalgan, were entrusted with thousands of taels by their masters and escorted on their travels by *pao-i* officials.[13]

The bondservants of Manchus also took part in military campaigns at various times with their individual masters or in *pao-i* units, and were freed from bondage for exceptional acts of courage or bravery. Originally, it seems that a bondservant who denounced his master for any serious crime which was later proven was emancipated.[14] Later, the scope of the rule was restricted to include only the crimes of insubordination, rebellion, and illegal hunting and trading.[15] The state, however, punished masters who killed their bondservants without good reason and at times redistributed or freed bondservants when it seemed in its best interests.[16] The state also emphasized its own interests in allowing *pao-i*, the imperial bondservants, to take examinations for entrance into the emergent public bureaucracy as early as 1629.[17] These features of bondage during the conquest may be owing in part to the fact that the interests of the bondservants and the state largely coincided in a period of severe manpower shortage. The similarities of this Manchu attitude towards bondage to the traditional Chinese view of slavery, however, may in part be the result of the conscious adoption of Chinese philosophy and institutions by the Manchus in the 1630s and 1640s.

Yet certain substantive differences persisted. An unusual exchange between the Yung-cheng Emperor and the grand secretaries in 1727 over the proper punishment for a Chinese bondservant who killed his Chinese master illuminates the basic differences between bondage among the Chinese and among the Manchus. First, the emperor noted that the Manchus observed a strict separation and distinction between master and bondservant.[18] The Chinese, on the other hand, treated their bondservants carelessly so that bondservant and master were almost indistinguishable in their conduct, and the bondservants began to foster desires for freedom. Declaring that bondage should be immutable, Yung-cheng asked the grand secretaries how to punish the arrogant bondservants of the Chinese so that they received the same stiff punishment as those of the Manchus. The secretaries replied with a lengthy discourse on the different nature of Chinese and Manchu bondage. Among the Chinese the numbers of hereditary slaves (*shih-p'u*) and people in bondage with a notarized sales contract (*yin-ch'i suo-mai*) were very few, while the numbers gained through sale by an unnotarized contract (*pai-ch'i suo-mai*), through the practice of "submitting oneself to another" (*t'ou-k'ao*), and through marriage to a slave (*chao-p'ei*), were very great. They proposed that all Chinese people in bondage should be registered with local officials, as Manchu bondservants were, so that they could punish them with the same severity as they did their Manchu equivalents, that is, having their faces tatooed and exiling them to areas 2,000 li from their homes to do hard labor for life.

The secretaries distinguished these bondservants from two other groups of unfree people: those indigent folk who indentured themselves through a contract for a period of years (*tien-shen, tang-shen ping li yu wen-chüan*, also known as *chia-jen*) and the personal servants (*ch'ang-sui*) who attached themselves temporarily to Chinese officials in office in order to connive with the yamen runners, to demand and steal money until they were discovered or their master left office, whereupon they sought another official to pledge themselves to. For both these groups the master was expected to decide on and mete out a suitable punishment; but if he met resistance, the secretaries suggested he could report malefactors to the officials for punishment. These proposals were accepted by Yung-cheng in the hope that they would curb the haughty ways of Chinese bondservants, indentured servants, and personal servants. Although these policies were not ultimately successful, they do indicate that Manchu bondservants differed from their Chinese counterparts in two ways: their condition was apparently hereditary and more stable; and the state played a larger role in controlling and punishing Manchu bondservants who were insubordinate.

Although the legal status of Chinese and Manchu people in bondage may have differed slightly before 1727, the functions they fulfilled in Ch'ing society in the seventeenth and eighteenth centuries were often identical. Differences in the roles Chinese and Manchu bondservants played probably stemmed from the different positions occupied by their masters in the bureaucratic or military hierarchy.

The bondservants and indentured servants of those Manchu and Chinese officials assigned to military and civil posts in the provinces engaged in various activities. They carried correspondence and gifts back and forth between the emperor and their masters, extorted sums from the postal stations, and caused such disorder that efforts were made to limit strictly the number of bondservants and indentured servants officials took with them to the provinces.[19] In the local area where their master served, they often exploited their control over access to him by collecting sums of money to see him from all commoners and lower officials.[20] They also acted as their master's agents in helping him to carry out the many tasks that often demanded simultaneous action. At the customs bureaus where the master supervised the main office and his bondservants or indentured servants managed the smaller subordinate bureaus in the same area, the latter were constantly embezzling funds and making illegal demands on merchants for extra contributions.[21] Governors and governor-generals stationed their indentured servants in the capital city of the province (*tso-sheng chia-jen*) and allowed them freedom to exploit any opportunities they saw for making wealth through commerce or influence peddling. These indentured servants acquired such illicit authority that they became widely known as "officials" (*t'ang-kuan*). Those with a knack for business operated rice and silver shops, sold salt, jade, silks, and porcelain in the provinces where their masters served.[22] Some of them, such as a certain Li Ch'ao-tso, who owned two estates and a total of 250 rooms,[23] accumulated considerable property.

The bondservants and indentured servants of Manchu officials who served in Peking and entered the Forbidden City were involved in different kinds of misdeeds. Yung-cheng, for instance, criticized the boisterous conduct of the bondservants who accompanied their masters into the Forbidden City to report to him.[24] He also criticized Manchu high officials for sending their bondservants outside the city to buy up the limited supply of charcoal in the surrounding countryside where it was cheaper. In 1724 he imposed a fine of two months' salary on the master of a bondservant who was found gambling. Later in the century, in 1775, eunuchs apprehended a thief jumping down from a wall inside the inner palace. Interrogation revealed that he was a Manchu and the indentured servant of an official who often brought him into the palace in the course of fulfilling his duties. He was familiar with the layout of the palace grounds and had entered them this time on the pretext that he was a workman.[25]

The relationship of master and bondservant or indentured servant did not remain unchanged over time. One significant change came through the case of Fo-lun. Fo-lun was a Nei-wu-fu *pao-i* who, in 1757, served as the manager of the Imperial Mausoleum (Ling-ch'in shih-wu ta-yuan) and exercised authority over the woodsmen (*shu-hu*) who resided on the grounds and cared for the trees.[26] Fo-lun had an indentured servant named Wang Hung, but did not supervise his actions carefully. As a result Wang formed acquaintances with the woodsmen and began to conduct financial dealings with them. At times he borrowed money from them. Sometimes he tried to demand money from them. Eventually, his demands led to an altercation between him and a secretary named Kan-fu in which Wang was killed. The Board of Punishments recommended to the emperor that Kan-fu be given one hundred blows with a bamboo rod and handed over to the Nei-wu-fu to deal with according to the precedents. Ch'ien-lung evidently felt that the precedents did not adequately deal with this case. He ordered that from then on any official who allowed his indentured servants to borrow or lend money would be severely punished. In legal literature this case came to stand for the principle of strict liability, that is, that the master of an indentured servant or bondservant would

be punished whether or not he was aware of the indentured servant's or bondservant's illegal activities.

The application of strict liability to masters of bondservants
was a change from the Ming code, which had been followed in the
early Ch'ing. It had provided no punishment for a master who was
not aware of his bondservant's crimes, and a leading Ch'ing legal
scholar criticized this new rule of Fo-lun's case for being too harsh
towards masters.[27] Two factors probably prompted this change to
a harsh rule. First, the emperor probably felt a need to make masters
more responsible for the acts of their bondservants and indentured
servants in order to reduce crimes committed without the consent
or knowledge of the master. The assumption behind this reasoning
was that the indentured servants' or bondservants' misdeeds arose
from their own cupidity. Ch'ien-lung, in fact, once claimed that
the misconduct of the indentured servants stemmed in large part
from their inferior and base nature and their ability to deceive their
masters.[28] Second, the imposition of strict liability can be seen as
a means of attacking the problem of those indentured servants
and bondservants who engaged in corruption not for themselves
but at their masters' orders. As the official Shin-chu said in 1759,
in discussing the corruption of Li Yung-piao, a Nei-wu-fu *pao-i* and
former superintendent of the Canton Customs, "When an indentured servant makes illicit demands, it is really his master who does
it."[29]

*The Banner Organization and the Relation of the Imperial Bond-
servants to the Emperor*

This general account of the legal status of bondservants and
their functions in the Ch'ing period provides an appropriate background for viewing the functions and position of the Nei-wu-fu
pao-i. Although the imperial bondservants resembled indentured
servants and other bondservants in Ch'ing society, they did differ
in two significant ways. First, the Nei-wu-fu *pao-i* were socially
organized according to the eight-banner system. Second, the
emperor for them assumed the dual role of master and head of
state.

The basic nature of the eight-banner system has been described above. In certain respects, however, the *pao-i* banner organization differed from the model of regular banner organization. Each of the *pao-i* banners had five *ts'an-ling* units, but none of the *pao-i ts'an-ling* seems to have contained five *tso-ling*, although some contained a combined total of five *tso-ling* and *kuan-ling* in 1739. The dates for the establishment of the various *tso-ling* and *kuan-ling* indicate that the banners reached this size only after a protracted development starting in the 1620s and extending until 1695. Of the fifty-three *tso-ling* and *kuan-ling* units for which dates of origin are available, for instance, twenty-seven, or over one-half, relate to the period after 1661 when the Nei-wu-fu was re-established. It seems, then, that the basic core of the *pao-i* banner, a combination of at least twenty-nine *tso-ling* and *kuan-ling*, dates from the beginning of the dynasty, while significant additions were made later in the seventeenth century. Still smaller undersized *tso-ling* were added in the mid-eighteenth century.[30]

Another significant difference between the *pao-i* and regular banner system was in the leadership of the *tso-ling* and *kuan-ling* units. Unlike the other banners, the *pao-i tso-ling* and *kuan-ling* units displayed "almost no hereditary succession,"[31] perhaps because the upper three banners were owned by the emperor, while the whole or parts of the lower five banners were owned by the *beile* and other Manchu nobles.[32] The emperor, as owner, could determine succession in the top three banners, while in the other banners succession was hereditary through the *beile* and Manchu nobles. This not only shows the greater degree of control over these units, but indicates as well that the *pao-i* banner organization, in terms of succession, resembled a primitive bureaucratic, rather than feudal hereditary organization.

Tenure for the leaders of *tso-ling* and *kuan-ling* was often for life, but was not hereditary. Of the total of 526 replacements of these officials which took place before 1739, 295 were for reasons of death.[33] Only 13 replacements were due to retirement, sickness, or old age, so a sizable proportion of the others must have held on to their positions while they were quite old. These figures suggest a combination of bureaucratic and hereditary elements—appointment was similar to that in a bureaucratic organization, but tenure was similar to that in a hereditary system. One of the implications of this unusual situation for administration may have been a weakening of control. It seems doubtful that these senile officials were able to manage the *pao-i* banner sub-units as effectively as fully bureaucratic personnel who would have been retired as their age advanced.

The second most common cause of replacement for the leaders of the *tso-ling* and *kuan-ling* was for implication in malfeasance or corruption (*yuan-shih*). These cases numbered 107 or about 20 percent of all replacements. In general it seems that inefficiency or senility was tolerated, but malfeasance or corruption was not. The incidence of dismissal for the latter causes varied widely from unit to unit. In the fifth *ts'an-ling* of the plain yellow *pao-i* banner, for instance, implication in corruption or malfeasance was the cause for 25 percent of the replacements, while in the third *ts'an-ling* of the bordered yellow *pao-i* banner the same was true for only 9 percent of all replacements. The other main causes for replacement were transfer (*tiao-yung*), implying that the *tso-ling* and *kuan-ling* leader was sent to another position of approximately equal rank, and promotion (*sheng-jen*) implying a movement upward. The fact that transfers were twice as frequent as promotions (20 percent to 10 percent) may suggest that positions as leaders of *kuan-ling* and *tso-ling* were not generally a stepping-stone to higher office. Other reasons for replacement were transfer of a leader to another banner, to work in the household of a prince or princess, and release from *pao-i* status.

The importance of this semi-bureaucratic banner organization lay in its function as a means of social control over the *pao-i*. Before 1757, as noted above, masters were punished for the crimes of their bondservants if they knew of them. Ignorance of a bondservant's misdeeds was generally accepted as sufficient excuse for the master to escape punishment.[34] In 1679, for instance, bondservants who occupied mountain passes and river crossings and relied on their masters' authority to cheat and oppress merchants were beheaded, but their masters were deprived of their official positions only if they were aware of their bondservants' conduct.[35] In the case of the Nei-wu-fu *pao-i*, both before and after 1757, it would have been impractical and unacceptable politically for their master (the emperor) to be punished along with them for their misdeeds. Thus, when Nei-wu-fu *pao-i* committed crimes, they themselves were, of course, punished. In addition, however, it was not their true master, but only their *tso-ling* and *kuan-ling* leaders who were punished for failing to restrain the *pao-i* from antisocial behavior.

The control of the *pao-i* through the eight-banner organization made their status as bondservants anomalous, because bondage, like slavery, is essentially a definition of the conflicting claims of the master and the state over the bondservant. Slavery, the most extreme form of bondage, exists where the state leaves the slave completely to the will of his master, while slavery shades into serfdom and lesser forms of bondage as the state interferes more in the relationship between master and slave in order to protect its own interests and those of the slave. In the case of the Nei-wu-fu, the emperor was at the same time the highest representative of the state as well as the master of the *pao-i*. Thus, a clearly expressed clash of interests between the state and the master of the *pao-i* could never occur as in the relationship of other masters to their bondservants.

The general social organization of the Nei-wu-fu *pao-i*, on the one hand, was partly bureaucratic, partly hereditary, and the *pao-i* were responsible to banner leaders rather than to the emperor directly. In this regard the Nei-wu-fu *pao-i* were similar to state slaves. On the other hand, since the emperor represented the interests of the state, there was no institutional check on his use of bondservants. The *pao-i*, then, were a resource the emperor could avail himself of to accomplish for him tasks similar to those performed by indentured servants and other bondservants for their masters, but without any corresponding sanctions for such peculation by proxy. Needless to say, such a situation left much room for abuse.

The Decline of Martial Heritage among the Imperial Bondservants

The banner system was primarily a form of military organization, and the *pao-i*, therefore, were not strangers to the martial traditions of the Manchus. Although references to the use of *pao-i* in battle are not common in the early period, the fact that they were granted freedom if they were first to scale the enemy's barricades suggests that they did in fact take part in the campaigns during the conquest.[36] After 1644 only a few references can be found to the employment of *pao-i* military forces, as in 1674 in the rebellion of the three feudatories.[37]

After the conquest, the *pao-i*, like the Manchus, disregarded military affairs, looked for official sinecures, and adopted a comfortable civilian mode of life. One example of this can be seen in the practice of "wearing armor" (*p'i-chia*), that is, taking the role of a foot soldier. Originally one of every two or three men in the banners had to wear armor,[38] but as early as 1675 K'ang-hsi complained that the bannermen were forgetting the martial arts and devoting themselves to literature.[39] He inveighed against those Manchus who considered wearing armor as something to avoid, and used their indentured servants to take their places in the ranks. By 1724 the number of men obliged to wear armor had been reduced to only one in four or more in the regular banners, although there were more of these armor bearers in the *pao-i* banners.[40] At that time the majority of those wearing armor in the *pao-i* banners were the indentured servants of the high *pao-i* officials, such as Lai-pao.[41] Others were the adopted sons of *pao-i* or men taken at an early age by *pao-i* and raised by them like slaves to wear armor in their place.[42] The decline of interest in the martial arts among the *pao-i* and the substitution of bondservants in their place as armor wearers suggests a process of Sinicization. The *pao-i* gained status under Chinese values by directing their energies from military to governmental endeavors.

The Social Structure of the Imperial Bondservants

The people who constituted the Nei-wu-fu were not a homogeneous group. The Nei-wu-fu had a hierarchical social system which displayed great contrasts in social rank but also exhibited a certain amount of social mobility. The *pao-i* social structure reflected to a degree tendencies that were apparent in society as a whole due to the declining vigor of the ruling Manchu elite. No example could be more demonstrative of this decline than the fact that, by the early eighteenth century, some imperial clansmen had fallen to such debased status that they were reviled and abused by the lowest of eunuchs and generally treated like slaves.[43]

The Nei-wu-fu social structure can be divided into roughly four groups: the state slaves, the indentured servants of the *pao-i*, the majority of the *pao-i*, and a small *pao-i* elite. The first of these was the *hsin-che-k'u* (Manchu: *sin jeku*)[44] at the lowest rung of the Nei-wu-fu social ladder. The origins of this group are unclear. The *hsin-che-k'u* were a class of government slaves (*kuan-nu*) formed by Nei-wu-fu *pao-i* and bannermen who were punished for crimes by inscription into this class.[45] They seem to have been responsible to the Nei-wu-fu's overseers and to have performed the most menial physical tasks. Downward mobility from *pao-i* status into the ranks of the *hsin-che-k'u* was very rapid but, since inscription into this status was an unusual punishment (death or removal from office being more common punitive measures), the number of men degraded to their ranks was probably rather small. The chances for upward mobility were probably very slight, for it must have been difficult for a menial workman to display such unusual talents in his duties that he would be noticed and promoted. A few examples of such mobility, however, do exist. The maternal uncle of Prince Yin-ssu, Ko-ta-hun, for instance, originally was a *hsin-che-k'u*, under the management of a *pao-i tso-ling*, but later became the servant of a bannerman and then eventually a hereditary *tso-ling* official.[46] A more startling example is that of Lai-pao, a *hsin-che-k'u* who rose to the highest position in the Nei-wu-fu, that of Manager of the Imperial Household Department. His eventual fall, like his rise, however, was precipitous; in 1725 he was dismissed for malfeasance, given 100 strokes with the whip, and forced to wear the cangue for three months.[47] By Ch'ien-lung's reign the status of the *hsin-che-k'u* as a whole improved. In 1738, for example, they assumed the same status under the criminal law as the *pao-i*.[48]

Next above the *hsin-che-k'u* in status were the indentured servants and slaves of the *pao-i*. They occupied much the same relationship to their masters as did the personal house slaves and indentured servants of the banner troops (*ch'i-hsia p'u-pei, ch'i-hsia chia-jen*) to their masters, or the indentured servants of Chinese officials to their masters.[49] In fact, they are mentioned together with the bondservants of Manchu and Chinese officials in descriptions of extortion and other illegal activities in both the seventeenth and eighteenth centuries.[50] It was these bondservants who acted as the commercial agents of the most prominent *pao-i* mentioned below who served in the customs bureaus, the salt monopoly, and the manufactories.

The condition of these indentured servants and slaves, for the most part very miserable at the beginning of the dynasty, showed gradual improvement in later times. With these indentured servants, as with others, the Chinese state interposed itself between master and slave and acted to ease the condition of bondage. Prohibitions dating to the beginning of the dynasty prevented the sale of slaves to another banner and the sale of separate members of a slave family.[51] In 1673 the killing of a *pao-i*'s slaves to accompany their dead master to the grave was outlawed, and in 1727 the relatives of an indentured servant killed by his master were granted freedom.[52] In 1739 a statute that called for the return of a slave girl who married without her master's consent was amended so that any slave girl who married in this fashion would not be returned, but merely fined.[53] Although the status of these *pao-i* slaves and indentured servants as a whole was improving, it is hard to find evidence that any of them individually raised themselves to the rank of *pao-i* or served as officials. The few of them that served *pao-i* masters who received lucrative posts in the provinces, however, were undoubtedly able to enjoy a certain amount of physical comfort and to accumulate sums of money.[54] Some of them even had slaves of their own.[55]

The masters of these indentured servants and slaves, the *pao-i* proper, formed the great majority of those people who served in the Nei-wu-fu or were under its jurisdiction. Most of the *pao-i* were the direct descendants of Chinese, Manchus, and Koreans who had entered *pao-i* status in the seventeenth century, but small numbers of entertainers, actors, and craftsmen entered the Nei-wu-fu in the eighteenth century when they were sent to serve the emperor.[56] The *pao-i* were, by definition, the emperor's bondservants who were enrolled in the upper three banners. Thus, the Nei-wu-fu and the *pao-i* of the upper three banners were very close to being synonymous, but were in fact not so. The Nei-wu-fu employed a few non-*pao-i* officials in the ranks from the department director up, so the bureaucrats who worked in this bureaucratic organization were, strictly speaking, not exclusively *pao-i*. On the other hand, many *pao-i* did not serve in the Nei-wu-fu or any other position, but were simply "idle." Furthermore, a few *pao-i* from the upper three banners were appointed to positions in the state bureaucracy. Many of these positions had financial connections with the Nei-wu-fu, but others, such as that of district magistrate,[57] did not. Institutionally, then, the distinctions between the Imperial Household Department as a bureaucratic organization and as a social grouping are fine indeed.

Above the majority of *pao-i* stood a small *pao-i* elite consisting of those imperial bondservants favored with appointments to high positions in the Nei-wu-fu in Peking or to substantial financial positions in the provinces. Sources do not allow a quantitative study of entry and exit into this *pao-i* aristocracy, but several examples suggest that families were able to maintain elite status for only one or two generations. Perhaps the most illustrious example of *pao-i* cultural distinction, financial success, and prolonged government service is the Ts'ao family described in Jonathan Spence's *Ts'ao Yin and the K'ang-hsi Emperor*. Another *pao-i* family that gained much notoriety in the later part of the eighteenth century was the Kao lineage, described below, which spanned three generations and was linked by marriage to other bondservants of the elite, such as Chi-ch'ing, Chi-hou, and Shu-wen.[58] These two examples suggest that the fragility of the personal links to the emperor and the unabashed corruption of the *pao-i* officials were key elements in their precipitate fall.

While they enjoyed the favor of the emperor, members of the *pao-i* elite were able to amass considerable sums of money. The Soochow Manufactory and Hu-shu Customs Superintendent Hai-pao, for example, had property valued at 100,000 taels in 1740[59] not including opera performers and dozens of singing girls whom he had purchased on the pretext of presenting them to Ch'ien-lung, but whom he had ensconced in his own mansion.[60] Later in the century the activities of Kao Heng and Kao P'u and the creation of the secret accounts bureau leave no doubt that the *pao-i* elite of that time accumulated considerable wealth as well. That these imperial bondservants could accumulate fortunes was no surprise, then, and least of all to Ch'ien-lung himself. When the *pao-i* Chi-ch'ing, the Liang-huai salt censor, was denounced for his wealth in 1740, Ch'ien-lung came to his defense, telling the critics of Chi-ch'ing that it was not unusual for a smart *pao-i* to become rich and that Chi-ch'ing, in fact, had been wealthy even before his appointment.[61]

The affluence of the Nei-wu-fu *pao-i* invariably led them into contacts with merchants. Indeed, so close were the relationships between the Liang-huai salt merchants and certain *pao-i* that Chi-ch'ing suggested in 1748 that the merchants pay off fines which the *pao-i* owed the state.[62] Ch'ien-lung's rejection of this proposal did not mean that merchants did not help out the *pao-i* in other cases. The *pao-i* Ch'üan-te, for example, borrowed 20,000 taels from lumber merchants while he was a customs superintendent,[63] and the illustrious merchant Chiang Ch'un and others spent 600,000 taels in purchasing jade and other valuable goods for the Liang-huai Salt Censor I-ling-a, another *pao-i*.[64] In certain cases *pao-i* were linked to merchants not only by their financial ties, but also by marriage. Chi-ch'ing is one example of a *pao-i* related to merchant families by marriage.[65]

While there were social divisions among the *pao-i*, they all enjoyed the same privileged legal status. They were not allowed to intermarry with the regular eight banner personnel[66] and, until

1737 separate groups of *pao-i* within the Nei-wu-fu were not even permitted to intermarry.[67] In the Nei-wu-fu administration, as in Ch'ing government as a whole, no distinction existed between judicial and administrative duties, so the Nei-wu-fu exercised both these functions over the *pao-i*. Thus, the Nei-wu-fu's own Judicial Department handled most judicial matters arising among the *pao-i*, although serious cases were subject to review by the Board of Punishments. Cases involving *pao-i* and commoners called for joint deliberation by a mixed court composed of members of the Nei-wu-fu's Judicial Department and the appropriate civil judicial authorities. The punishments inflicted on *pao-i* were generally lighter than those imposed on commoners. Exile or banishment was commuted to whipping and to wearing of the cangue, and convicted *pao-i* did not have their faces tattooed. Furthermore, certain privileges applied to imperial bondservants who served as Nei-wu-fu officials. If they performed badly, they were only fined instead of removed from their positions.[68] Over time, however, the privileges of the *pao-i* were whittled away, and by the beginning of the nineteenth century they were in almost the same position as commoners. In 1788, for example, Nei-wu-fu officials lost the privilege to commute their punishment to fines.[69] Those who had commended their lands lost the right to have their judicial cases tried by the Nei-wu-fu's Judicial Department, the estate stewards lost the privilege of the commutation of punishments, and local officials were given greater authority to search their houses and sentence them for misdemeanors. These changes may well evidence a desire to tighten administration over the *pao-i* in order to curb their disruptive and criminal behavior.

The Examination System

Although the Nei-wu-fu offered the *pao-i* other forms of advancement, the traditional means were also available to the imperial bondservants. Since Sung times entry into the civil service was by examination. As noted above, the *pao-i* of the three upper banners were permitted to take examinations for government service even before the conquest of China. This privilege, however, did not extend to all groups of *pao-i*, for the privilege of sitting for the exams was granted, for example, to the stewards of the Nei-wu-fu fruit orchards only in 1711.[70] In fact, certain agricultural workers on some of the Nei-wu-fu estates were never allowed to take the exams. In general, however, it seems that most of the *pao-i* from the upper three banners were entitled to take the exams. It is impossible to know how many *pao-i* took advantage of this privilege, which was not extended to other bondservants, but the number of *pao-i* who passed at the highest level, the *chin-shih*, may have been less than a half dozen for the seventeenth and eighteenth centuries.[71]

Several reasons might explain this low number of successful *pao-i chin-shih*. One factor may have been that, from at least 1725, conscientious *pao-i* were recommended for posts inside and outside the Imperial Household Department by the Nei-wu-fu managers.[72] Since this other avenue of advancement was open, *pao-i* may have been reluctant to spend the effort necessary to prepare for the *chin-shih* exams. Another circumstance, which was undoubtedly decisive for some *pao-i*, was the fact that, from 1670, the sons of *pao-i* who held a position of Rank 1 were allowed the *yin* privilege of hereditary succession, while one son of a father who attained a post of Rank 4 to Rank 2 was allowed to assume the status of a *chien-sheng*.[73] Furthermore, the purchase of the *chien-sheng* degree and of official positions started in 1675.[74] *Pao-i* with sufficient funds were allowed to take advantage of this procedure to gain entrance to the regular civil bureaucracy. These hereditary privileges and the opportunity to purchase a degree or position probably satisfied the sons of many *pao-i* officials and dampened any ambitions they might have had for success through the examination system.

A rare source from the late eighteenth century illuminates some of the details of the purchasing of offices by *pao-i*. This work is a list of the sons of all officials (not exclusively *pao-i*) who had gained the right, generally by purchase, to occupy a civil post and were awaiting actual appointment to it.[75] The total number of officials' sons was 4,483, and the number of different types of posts they had acquired the right to occupy was 63. However, more than 74 percent of them were awaiting appointment to the eleven most popular types of positions.[76] The *pao-i* from the upper three banners constituted only a small proportion of the total number of officials' sons listed, 110 out of 4,483, or little over 2 percent. The number of *pao-i* who attained positions such as District Magistrate (6) or Sub-Assistant Salt Controller (3) was very small. The one position for which the *pao-i* were waiting for appointment in large numbers (86 men or 78 percent of the *pao-i* listed) was that of clerk, *pi-t'ieh-shih*. The *pao-i*, in fact, constituted 16 percent of all expectant clerks in the list. The reason for the popularity of this position among the *pao-i* is that it was open only to Manchus (including *pao-i*) and closed to Chinese.[77] The monopoly granted to bannermen (including *pao-i*) in positions as clerks was a deliberate policy of favoring these groups as against the Chinese and became an important means of entrance into the civil bureaucracy for Manchus and *pao-i*.

Exactly how all the *pao-i* on this list came to secure appointments as clerks is not known. The fact that over 80 percent of the *pao-i* mentioned possessed the *chien-sheng* degree suggests that attainment of this degree was the primary qualification for most of the *pao-i* for appointments. There were three possible ways by which a *pao-i* could attain the *chien-sheng* degree: purchase, hereditary privilege, and successful performance on the civil service examinations. From the small number of *pao-i* holders of the *chin-shih* degree, which was only given upon passing the examinations, it appears, by analogy, likely that few *pao-i* attained the *chien-sheng* degree by passing the exams. Purchase of the *chien-sheng* degree, however, was widespread at this time, and some Nei-wu-fu *pao-i* could have taken advantage of their *yin* privilege to gain the *chien-sheng* degree. The Nei-wu-fu *pao-i* contained in this list, then, probably consisted mostly of purchased and hereditary *chien-sheng*. Of these two types of *chien-sheng* it seems that the purchased were far more common. In the list the hereditary *chien-sheng* seem to be referred to by the term *yin-sheng*, while those who purchased the degree are referred to only as *chien-sheng*. The number of *pao-i* denoted as *yin-sheng* was two. Since this is less than 3 percent of the *pao-i* on the list, the hereditary *yin* privilege seems not to have been an important means of appointment to the post of clerk.

It seems, then, that some *pao-i* were able to purchase degrees, pass exams, or use their hereditary privileges to gain access to the general civil bureaucracy and gain status and prestige in the traditional Chinese manner of government service. Some of the *pao-i* who were able to do this may have come from the most humble circumstances, but the evidence on the purchase of degrees suggests that it was mostly the *pao-i* elite who occupied positions in the civil bureaucracy.

Distinctive Modes of Social Mobility

One of the most unusual forms of upward mobility for the *pao-i* of the upper three banners was through the service of a daughter in the Forbidden City. Within the palace there were essentially three types of women: 1) nurses and wet nurses, 2) concubines and empresses, and 3) palace maids.

The nurses (*pao-mu* and *shih-mu*) and the wet nurses (*ju-mu*) of the emperor's sons provided a rare but sure means of upward mobility for a *pao-i* family. When the Manchu Imperial Family first started to employ nurses and wet nurses for their sons is unknown, but it was probably well before the conquest. In 1661 the first regulations on the selection of nurses and wet nurses were promulgated. The palace overseers were to send suitable women to the palace where the eunuchs would select them.[78] Those chosen were provided with other wet nurses for their own children and were paid eighty taels for their services. Later, in 1729, they were given a monthly salary of two taels and twenty pecks of rice.

The first reference to a wet nurse is to that of Fu-lin, who was born in 1638 and became emperor in 1644. His wet nurse was the wife of a bordered yellow banner *pao-i* named Man-tu-li. This *pao-i* had gained a reputation for military prowess by capturing single-handedly twenty boats from the enemy in campaigns against Korea and thirty boats in battle against the Ming forces.[79] Perhaps it was as a reward for his feats that his wife was chosen as Fu-lin's wet nurse. Later, because of his wife's service, however, he was rewarded with a hereditary military rank, and in 1652 he and his family were released from *pao-i* status. The nurse of the following emperor, K'ang-hsi, was the daughter of a Nei-wu-fu *pao-i* of the Sun family. She later left the palace and was married to the *pao-i* official Ts'ao Hsi, father of Ts'ao Yin.[80] The emperor had great affection for her and visited her in person to offer his condolences when her husband died in 1684. The nurse of K'ang-hsi's son, the Yung-cheng Emperor, was the mother of the Nei-wu-fu Minister Hai-pao, who owed his prominence to his mother's position.[81] Although Ch'ien-lung later discovered that Hai-pao had embezzled over 200,000 taels while serving as Soochow manufactory superintendent, he pardoned him because of his mother's close relationship to Yung-cheng.[82] Although the names of Ch'ien-lung's and Chia-ch'ing's nurses and wet nurses are not known, they were well provided for. The wet nurses and nurses received 1,000 taels, some land, and honors, such as the right of succession by male relatives to a Grade 7 honorary title, for their labors.[83]

The close ties between the emperor and his nurse may well have been owing to the strict rules and proper decorum which prevented young princes from forming close relationships with their mothers. The last emperor of the dynasty writes fondly of his own wet nurse in his autobiography:

> The only person in the palace who could control my cruelty was my nurse, Mrs. Wang. Although she was completely illiterate and incapable of talking about the "way of compassion and benevolence" or illustrious sovereigns and sage rulers of history, I could not disregard the advice she gave me. . . In my mind others were only my slaves or subjects. In all my years in the palace I was only reminded by my nurse's homely words that other men were the same as myself. . . I grew up in my nurse's bosom, being suckled by her until I was eight, and until then I was as inseparable from her as a baby from its mother. When I was eight the High Consorts had her sent away without my knowledge. I would gladly have kept her in exchange for all four of my mothers in the

palace. . . I see now that I had nobody who really understood
humanity around me once my nurse had gone. But what
little humanity I learnt from her before the age of eight I
gradually lost afterwards.[84]

The nurses and wet nurses, of course, were not the only ones
who enjoyed the emperor's favor. Service in the Forbidden City
as a palace maid provided the daughters of *pao-i* with the chance
of promotion to concubine or even empress and thus served as a
possible avenue for *pao-i* mobility. Almost all women who entered
the palace (except the nurses, wet nurses, and the daughters of
Manchu nobles) started out as palace maids performing light, but
menial, tasks. Some of these caught the emperor's eye and were
elevated to the rank of concubine or even empress. Most of them,
however, seem to have spent their time in the palace as mere
attendants.

Early in the dynasty the selection of Chinese women into the
palace was prohibited, and the palace maids were chosen only from
among the daughters of Manchu bannermen and *pao-i*.[85] From 1661
the manager of every *pao-i kuan-ling* was to send registers containing the names of all maids twelve years old to the Accounts Department which forwarded the lists to the head eunuchs.[86] In the
eighteenth century only Nei-wu-fu girls of thirteen and banner girls
of fourteen years were eligible.[87] Palace maids who reached the age
of twenty-nine were sent home, but their parents were responsible
for sending other girls to take their places.[88] In order to prevent
any family from gaining undue influence in the inner palace, under
no circumstances was a sister or niece of the empress or the emperor's mother allowed to enter the palace as a maid, but relatives
of concubines could become maids with Ch'ien-lung's permission.[89]

The lot of the palace maids was not altogether a happy one.
In 1681, for example, K'ang-hsi upbraided them for their lack of
good manners and ordered the eunuchs to investigate and punish
them for their boisterousness.[90] In the eighteenth century Ch'ien-
lung complained that the maids in the En-yu Temple were so lazy
that he himself had to go and offer up incense in their place.[91]

Other evidence, however, demonstrates that genuine concern was at times shown for the welfare of these maids. In 1685, for example, K'ang-hsi criticized the Nei-wu-fu for placing the *chi-cheng-fang*, the hospital for palace maids, outside the palace and ordered them to find a more convenient location within the palace grounds.[92] Late in the year 1700 he demanded that, since the girls coming to the palace for possible selection as palace maids were mainly from poor families, they be taken to warm quarters and fed with hot soup and rice when the weather was cold.[93] Ch'ien-lung took various measures to ease the expense of sending girls to the palace for possible selection as palace maids. Those girls who were not chosen were expressly permitted to marry, just like the palace maids themselves who now returned home from the palace at the age of twenty-four.[94]

Since the number of women selected to be concubines was only a small percentage of the women in the palace, and the daughters of *pao-i* were only a part of the girls serving in the palace, the number of *pao-i* women who rose to the ranks of concubine or higher should not have been very great. Accordingly, for the period from 1662 to 1796, there were about half a dozen *pao-i* women of varying social backgrounds who achieved prominence. In fact, one of them, K'ang-hsi's Imperial Concubine of the Third Rank of the Wei clan was originally the daughter of A-pu-nai, a *hsin-che-k'u*.[95] Her position helped her father advance well beyond his lowly status—he was elevated to *pao-i* status, became a Nei-wu-fu manager and the leader of a *kuan-ling*. Other examples seem to be those of the Chia-ch'ing Emperor's Concubines of the Third and Fourth Ranks of the Hou and Shen clans, who entered his household during the Ch'ien-lung period while he was still a prince.[96] The fathers of these two concubines cannot be positively identified as *pao-i*, but they may well have been—they served as Director of the Palace Stud and as honorary (*chih-hsien*) Nei-wu-fu manager respectively.[97]

More famous were two of Ch'ien-lung's Concubines of the First Rank. One of them, of the surname Kao, entered Ch'ien-lung's residence when he was the heir apparent. Her father was the famous official Kao Pin, a *pao-i* of the bordered yellow banner, but he and the rest of his family were freed from *pao-i* status in 1735 because of his daughter's rank as Imperial Concubine of the Second Rank.[98] Kao Pin had served in several Nei-wu-fu posts before 1735, but no doubt his daughter's position greatly aided his advancement. In later years he reached the pinnacle of the regular bureaucracy assuming the position of Grand Secretary. The other Concubine of the First Rank carried the surname of Chin. Her father was a Korean *pao-i* of the plain yellow banner who served as Ch'ang-lu Salt Censor and as Director of the Palace Stud.[99] Her older brother Chin Chien had a brilliant career—after his younger sister had given birth to three of Ch'ien-lung's sons.[100] He held various posts in the Nei-wu-fu and in 1772 was put in charge of compiling the Imperial Manuscript Library. Later he served as President of the Board of Works and the Board of Civil Appointments.

Daughters of *pao-i* not only reached the rank of Imperial Concubine of the First Rank; two of them actually attained the title of Empress. The first became an empress posthumously. She was from the Wei clan, the granddaughter of the Nei-wu-fu manager Wu-shih-i of the plain yellow *pao-i* banner. Her father, Ch'ing-t'ai, was a palace overseer who later received the title of Duke because of his daughter's position. She was elevated to Imperial Concubine of the First Rank in 1765, four months before she gave birth to Ch'ien-lung's fifteenth son, Yung-yen.[101] She became Ch'ien-lung's favorite concubine and presided over a cultural salon at her residence in the Summer Palace.[102] She died in 1775, but in 1795 when Yung-yen was designated heir apparent, she was posthumously elevated to the rank of Empress. The next year Yung-yen was enthroned and is known as the Chia-ch'ing Emperor.

The second *pao-i* daughter to become an empress was of the Hetala clan, daughter of the Nei-wu-fu manager Ho-erh-ching-o and a member of the plain white *pao-i* banner.[103] Her father was also a lieutenant-general and later received the honorary title of Duke. Unfortunately little information on the life of the empress herself is available. She gave birth to Yung-yen's second son in 1782.[104] It is unclear what rank she held at this time but, when

Yung-yen became Emperor in 1796, she was immediately raised
to the position of Empress. Her reign as Empress, however, was
brief, for she died the next year. Still, her son, Min-ning, so impressed his father that he was secretly chosen as heir to the throne
in 1799. This decision was later made public in 1820, shortly before he ascended the throne under the reign title Tao-kuang.

These examples suggest that the daughters of high *pao-i*
officials had a better chance of rising to the rank of Empress, but
that, in general, the daughters of even the humble *pao-i* had the
chance of becoming an Imperial Concubine.

Service in the Nei-wu-fu

The richest and most prominent *pao-i* may have come to their
positions through hereditary privileges, purchase of office, or connections of female relatives within the palace, but service in government or the Nei-wu-fu administration was the true mark of
success for *pao-i*. The first step in a brilliant career for the Nei-wu-
fu *pao-i* was good performance at one of the schools set up especially for them. After finishing studies, the young *pao-i* were
granted positions in the lower ranks of the Nei-wu-fu bureaucracy,
such as clerks. Movement upwards within the Nei-wu-fu may have
been slow, but seems to have been almost automatic at the lower
levels. It was particularly difficult, however, for *pao-i* to proceed
beyond the middle ranks of the Nei-wu-fu bureaucracy into the
top positions. In part this was because of the smaller number of
positions above Rank 5b, that of Assistant Department Director.
Also, these positions, as opposed to the lower posts in the Nei-wu-
fu, were not a monpoly of the *pao-i* from the upper three banners,
but were occupied by various Manchu officials who had earned the
emperor's confidence. This was true before 1661[105] and afterwards,
especially in the eighteenth century for the post of manager of the
Imperial Household Department.[106] While it is difficult to determine
the exact status of all those who were Nei-wu-fu managers, it seems
likely that, in the eighteenth century at least, about half of the
normal quota of four or five managers were not of *pao-i* status.
One example of a Manchu official is Fu-heng of the bordered

yellow banner. He was a younger brother of Ch'ien-lung's first empress and one of his closest advisors as Grand Secretary from 1748 and as Nei-wu-fu manager from 1742 until his death in 1770. Another example is that of the notorious Ho-shen, a Manchu of the plain yellow banner, who served as Nei-wu-fu manager from 1776 until 1796.

The most prominent among the *pao-i* seem to have served not only in the Nei-wu-fu, but to have been assigned to lower posts in the provinces for a trial period after distinguishing themselves in the Nei-wu-fu bureaucracy. The career of the *pao-i* I-la-ch'i illustrates this point. He was a Nei-wu-fu *pao-i* with some prior experience in administration in the Nei-wu-fu before receiving short-term appointments as an "Imperially Commissioned (*ch'in-ch'ai*) Nei-wu-fu Assistant Department Director" sent out to the provinces to investigate specific problems.[107] He then received an appointment as Fukien Salt and Postal Taotai (*yen-i-tao*) early in Yung-cheng's reign. This appointment may have been due in part to the recommendation by the Governor-General of Kwangtung, Yang Wen-ch'ien, who praised him in a memorial as "honest and direct" (*lao-shih*). Yung-cheng added to this the rescript "This is a good man,"[108] and, when he appointed I-la-ch'i, Yung-cheng warned the other officials in Fukien that it would be a great mistake for them to think that the appointment of a *pao-i* meant that they could connive together with him to their own advantage.[109] Later reports indicate that I-la-ch'i performed his duties in Fukien with "a correct attitude and a pure heart." Although he had still not accustomed himself to all the duties of a provincial official, he did well by working hard. I-la-ch'i performed well enough in this "experimental appointment"[110] to merit advancement to the post of Salt Censor of Anhui and Kiangsu in 1728.[111]

This promising career, however, was not without its darker side. When I-la-ch'i thanked Yung-cheng for his promotion to Salt Censor in 1728, the emperor replied that, "If you purge yourself completely of your shameless and base *pao-i* habits, you can become a great official."[112] Later, however, Yung-cheng praised his work as a censor, telling him that, "I am delighted with your memorials. . .

I have other sources of information on what is happening (in Soochow), but none of them is as detailed as your reports."[113] In 1730 the emperor had to remind him not to be too harsh, because, "if you are too harsh in carrying out your duties [as a censor], then you will create resentment which will make it impossible for you to perform your job."[114] When I-la-ch'i served as Liang-huai Salt Censor the emperor again reminded him, "If you don't put aside your base *pao-i* habits, you will never be more than a petty little fellow."[115] Later, in 1731, Yung-cheng lost his patience with I-la-ch'i and wrote to him commenting on his desire to come to Peking, "There is no way that an ungrateful and perverse character like you could be changed by any moral instructions from me. There is no need for you to come to the capital for an audience."[116]

While I-la-ch'i was not allowed to go to the capital, his career was not gravely affected by the emperor's rebuke. Some years later, under the Ch'ien-lung Emperor, he received an appointment as Superintendent of the Huai Customs Bureau. There he showed his realistic grasp of the essentials of administration by persuading Ch'ien-lung not to push for the abolition of the small illegal exactions which the yamen underlings pinched from the merchants when collecting taxes.[117] While he was willing to look the other way when the yamen underlings took their due, he would not tolerate interference with tax collection or false accusations of illegal taxation by local bullies.[118] Both these measures seem to have favorably impressed Ch'ien-lung, as did his discovery of the improper tax exemptions his predecessor as superintendent had granted.[119] When his term expired he was transferred to the post of Ch'ang-lu Salt Censor where he fulfilled his duties by carefully reporting to the emperor the measures he was taking to cope with the drought that had struck the area.[120] While these policies gained Ch'ien-lung's approval, his report on the reasons why the excess customs revenues had declined did not. In late 1746, I-la-ch'i memorialized to Ch'ien-lung telling him that the excess revenues at the customs bureaus under his jurisdiction had declined because a lack of rain in early spring had lowered the water level in the various rivers used by merchants to ship their goods. Ch'ien-lung, noting that rainfall had been adequate in I-la-ch'i's area, concluded that he was concealing the true reasons for the shortfall in revenues and chastized him for his prevarication.[121] Finally, when I-la-ch'i's performance failed to improve, Ch'ien-lung ended his career by dismissing him with the comment that, "I-la-ch'i is very mediocre and lazy. The office of Ch'ang-lu Salt Censor is too much for him. Remove him from this post and order him to work in the construction office at the Summer Palace."[122]

I-la-ch'i's career was similar to that of other elite *pao-i*. They were able to occupy some of the most weighty fiscal positions in the empire, and at times were very effective administrators, but they never completely discarded the corrupt habits they acquired as bondservants and as lower officials in the Nei-wu-fu. The Ch'ien-lung Emperor continued to appoint them to these posts to increase his control over economic resources, but he despaired of ever reforming them. As he said to Yin-chu, the *pao-i* Superintendent of the Huai Customs Bureau in 1778, "I see that you *pao-i* will never change your base manner. What can I do? What can I do?"[123]

Chapter IV

THE FINANCIAL FUNCTIONS
OF THE IMPERIAL HOUSEHOLD DEPARTMENT

The Nei-wu-fu's financial functions covered a wide range of
activities involving many aspects of fiscal and commercial policy.
The sub-department most concerned with these activities was the
Department of the Privy Purse. Aside from the landed estates and
the ginseng trade, which were associated with the Nei-wu-fu by
historical ties, the financial functions of the Nei-wu-fu were often
carried out by individual *pao-i* officials serving in key financial
posts which were not officially subordinate to the Nei-wu-fu. Thus,
in financial terms the Imperial Household Department was less
important as a bureaucratic organization than as a social group
which provided a reservoir of *pao-i* officials sent out by the emperor to manage certain financial matters. In the following discussion, however, both official and informal activities which
illuminate the unusual nature of the Nei-wu-fu are included.[1]

The Department's Vaults

The Nei-wu-fu treasuries were located mainly within the
Forbidden City and generally in the outer, rather than inner, palace.
The major coffers were: the Bullion Vaults located in the Hung-i-ko
of the T'ai-ho-tien, the Fur Store to the south of the Silver Vaults
and in the eastern section of the Pao-ho-tien, the Porcelain Store
beside the T'ai-ho-tien, the Imperial Wardrobe just south of the
Silver Vaults, and the Tea Store to the west of the T'ai-ho-tien.[2]
All these vaults were part of the Department of the **Privy Purse**.
Other vaults, which were subordinate to the overseers, were the
Vehicle Store (Ch'e-k'u) by the western creek inside the Forbidden
City and the Copper Store (T'ung-ch'i-k'u) to the west of the Chung-
ho-tien. Still other coffers were part of the Imperial Armory. These
were the Armory Store (Chia-k'u) located just south of the T'i-jen-
ko and also outside the palace's east gate, the Carpet Store (T'an-k'u)

located east of the T'ai-ho-men and outside the palace, and the Southern Saddle Store (Nan-an-k'u) located east of the T'ai-ho-men and outside the palace. The Storage Room for Musical Instruments (Yü-yueh-k'u), under the supervision of the workshops of the Imperial Household Department, was just inside the eastern gate of the Forbidden City. Completely outside the Forbidden City on a local street was the Office for Collecting Rent of Confiscated Property (Kuan-fang-tsu-fang) which was part of the Accounts Department.[3] In addition to these separate treasuries in the capital there were also another treasury at the Summer Palace outside Peking and grain storehouses in Jehol and Mukden (modern Shenyang).[4]

The specified procedures for opening the six vaults of the Privy Purse were designed to prevent oversight and corruption. A total of five officials, a current and an expectant inspector and three storehouse keepers, proceeded to the vault together and opened it with a key which the inspector and two storehouse keepers had procured from the guards on duty at the Ch'ien-ch'ing Gate.[5]

The inspectors and storehouse keepers were sub-officials directly in charge of the treasuries. Starting in 1684 they were selected from among the pool of *kung-sheng*, licentiate holders, *sheng-yuan* holders, privates of the Guard Division (Hu-chün), and idle bannermen who had passed a qualifying examination.[6] This development was probably linked with the creation a year later of the School on Prospect Hill, which trained Nei-wu-fu bond-servants for employment as inspectors and storehouse keepers.[7] In 1728 the Yung-cheng Emperor established the more advanced School at the Palace of Universal Peace exclusively for the sons of Nei-wu-fu *pao-i*, and a year afterwards the qualifications for the posts of inspector and storehouse keeper were raised and differentiated from those of the clerks and other sub-officials.[8]

From 1729 on, the inspectors and storehouse keepers were chosen from the ranks of those who could write Manchu well, but could not pass the translation exams or exams in both Chinese and Manchu.[9] The formal qualifications of the inspectors and the storehouse keepers were essentially the same throughout the eighteenth century. Their school curriculum seems to have been largely literary, perhaps simply reading and writing, with no specialization. The inspectors and storehouse keepers thus received the same education as the scribes. In fact, many who received positions as inspectors or storehouse keepers were probably aspiring scribes and translators who could not pass the exams at a high enough level to realize their ambitions. This tendency probably grew stronger as time went on, for, although the formal qualifications did not change, competition for posts became greater because of the increasing numbers of *pao-i* and improved educational facilities. As the pool of qualified applicants grew, entrance examinations were given less frequently. The holding of exams was limited to once every three years in 1743, every five years in 1746, and the number of students taking them to 200.[10] Although within the limits of the *pao-i* status the inspectors and storehouse keepers for the Nei-wu-fu treasuries seem to have been chosen on the basis of merit, this was not true for some. Those who worked in the Yuan-ming-yuan vaults were chosen partly from the sons of wealthy families after 1749.[11]

One difficulty in the administration of the treasuries was the lack of any provisions for the rotation or exchange of the sub-officials. As these lower officials accumulated long years of bureaucratic tenure, supervision and inspection became more difficult. In 1768, therefore, the Ch'ien-lung Emperor took measures to counteract this trend. Asserting that the Nei-wu-fu personnel in the six treasuries were too familiar with each other and were conniving together to cover up malfeasance, he undertook the unusual step of ordering that an assistant department director for each treasury must come, not from the Nei-wu-fu, but from each of the six government boards.[12] This practice was further refined in later years to limit the terms of these outside officials in the Nei-wu-fu vaults to three years in order to prevent their forming close relationships with the *pao-i*. In addition, in 1774, the Nei-wu-fu managers and Nei-wu-fu censors were ordered to take turns each year in supervising the administration of the treasuries.[13]

The qualifications for inspectors and storehouse keepers were rising in the eighteenth century, but it is difficult to judge whether administration of the storehouses improved accordingly. Although some corruption was evident in the management of the storehouses,[14] large-scale peculation was more evident in other Nei-wu-fu offices.

The Department's Landed Estates

One aspect of the Imperial Household Department's economic activities which had close links with the development of Manchu society and the conquest of China was the system of landed estates managed by various sub-departments. Imperial estates (*kuan-chuang*) had existed previously in the Sung period and in the Ming period after 1464 as well. In the sixteenth century the Ming imperial estates covered 3,750,000 mou (6.6 mou = 1 acre) in the area near Peking and a century later were used by the Manchu conquerors in forming the imperial estates which came under the control of the Nei-wu-fu.[15] Historically, however, the Imperial Household Department's landed estates may derive more directly from the policy of encouraging or even capturing and forcing Chinese peasants to cultivate the fields in Manchuria.

The oldest Nei-wu-fu estates were formed in Manchuria before the conquest of China and were called "[estates] outside the passes" (*kuan-wai*). The later estates "within the passes" (*kuan-nei*) were concentrated around Peking. Those in Manchuria were scattered throughout the provinces of Kirin and Liaoning, although many were concentrated around the city of Mukden. What made the estates of the Imperial Household Department different from those of previous dynasties were the institutions of "commendation" (*tai-ti t'ou-ch'ung*) and capture (*fu-huo pu-lu*).[16] In the formation of the imperial estates the practice of commendation was most important, for it seems that the greater part of the estates was formed by Chinese who voluntarily surrendered or "commended" their lands to the Manchu conquerors. Under this process the owners of the land delivered their lands to the Nei-wu-fu, took on Nei-wu-fu banner status, and rented their land from the Imperial Household Department in lieu of paying taxes.[17] There were two advantages in this procedure for the Chinese: by commending their land they could insure the security of their property and their persons in a time of turmoil and at the same time gain for themselves the privileges of Nei-wu-fu status. The practice of commendation was limited only to the areas where large-scale encounters of Ming and Manchu forces took place, and for this reason was limited to areas in Manchuria and near Peking. The imperial estates were, therefore, restricted to these same lands. Furthermore, the estates created by the process of commendation were not a few large plots, but many small scattered holdings.[18] The practice of commendaton was prohibited in 1646 and 1647, so later additions to the Nei-wu-fu estates came through confiscation rather than commendation.[19]

Of course, once established, the estates did not remain stable for the whole period from 1662 to 1796. In the eighteenth century a number of impoverished bannermen and *pao-i* sold (*tien-mai*) estate lands, but the state repurchased them and reconverted them into estates. Of more importance, strong pressures were working in the eighteenth century to enlarge the extent of the estates. Uncultivated lands were opened and some private lands were confiscated, both adding to the number of Nei-wu-fu estates. A comparison of available figures from the years 1764 and 1818 indicates that the total area of the imperial estates more than doubled from 1,327,280 mou to 3,577,275 mou.[20] Most of this increase seems to have come from increases in estates in the metropolitan area (from 322 to 539) and in Chin-chou (from 211 to 296). The greater part of this increase probably came from the incorporation into the registers and organization into new estates of lands which the cultivators had opened by their own efforts. Still, even in the eighteenth century the Nei-wu-fu estates did not occupy a large area by national standards. At that time they constituted only .54 percent of all cultivated land in China.[21]

The estates included many different types of land usage. In Manchuria, for instance, there were four different grades of grain estates from 3,900 mou to 5,400 mou in Chin-chou, orchards in

Sheng-ching of 70 to 210 mou, and in the Peking area of 100 to 5,000 mou, 55 apricot orchards, various indigo, salt, and hunting estates in Liaoning and Kirin.[22]

The different Nei-wu-fu estates were handled by various sub-departments. Those near Peking were subordinate to the Office for Collecting Rents of Imperial Lands (Yin-liang chuang-t'ou-ch'u), those in Feng-tien were managed by the Sheng-ching Imperial Household Department and the Chin-chou Estate Office (Chin-chou chuang-t'ou ya-men), those in Kirin by the Office of Wula Hunting (Ta-sheng wu-la tsung-kuan ya-men) or the local lieutenant general (*tu-t'ung*).[23] In fact, however, the estates were run by the local stewards (*chuang-t'ou*). These men were supposed to collect only taxes, but they exercised broad authority over the management of the estates, since the Nei-wu-fu was uneager or unable to exercise a tight control over stewards through the transmission of orders from the capital or other locations where the responsible bureaus were situated. At the beginning of the dynasty, it seems that some of the estates were formed from lineage groups who commended their lands as a whole to the Nei-wu-fu and chose their elders as a rent collection agent.[24] The Manchus took advantage of the lineage organization to impose rent quotas on the members of the estate and appointed the leaders as estate stewards. In other cases, the post of steward was given to the wealthier landowners who had entrusted their lands to the Manchus. The position of steward was hereditary, but succession passed through the nuclear family and not through the lineage as did the status of cultivator (*chuang-ting*).[25] In the case of stewards, great efforts were made to preserve family continuity—even to the extent of a steward's widow adopting a son to provide a successor.[26] The status of cultivators was allotted to the lineages in all estates and, although their status was fixed, changes in the distribution of rent according to the number of cultivators were allowed at times to reflect changes in the relative position of the various lineages located in an estate.

The organization of the estates allowed the stewards great power over the slave cultivators, and they used it to enrich themselves. Most often the abuses of the stewards did not come to light because Nei-wu-fu officials covered them up or because local government officials were reluctant to intervene. One scandal which reached the ears of the emperor concerned stewards on the estates in the metropolitan area who amassed considerable wealth by oppressing the cultivators. They engaged in illicit mining operations through their indentured servants which netted 40,000 to 50,000 taels a year.[27] Loaning out money at exorbitant rates, they expropriated the wives and children of those who were unable to repay and swaggered about the estates with entourages of fifty to sixty followers, imposing summary punishment on those that opposed them. By Yung-cheng's calculations their property amounted to several hundred thousand items.[28] These stewards were discovered, investigated, and secretly reported to the emperor by the provincial governor, Li Wei-chün, but were later handed over to the Nei-wu-fu for punishment. The fact that the Nei-wu-fu was not instrumental in discovering these abuses may have in part resulted from the scant supervision over stewards. According to Yung-cheng, however, it was also because scheming stewards always had contacts with "powerful forces in the inner palace" (nei-t'ing shih-yao).[29]

The Imperial Household Department's main interest in the estates was in the income it received from them in kind and in silver. The chief responsibility of the stewards was to collect the annual rent quotas from the cultivators. The official regulations explaining the management of the estates describe in meticulous detail the policies designed to encourage the stewards, out of fear or self-interest, to fulfill their quotas. No information, however, exists on the social or political role the stewards were supposed to play on the estates. Until 1685 a steward on the grain estates who overfilled the quota by one picul was rewarded with almost half an ounce of silver, while one whose collection of rent was one picul under the quota received two strokes of the whip.[30] The punitive features of this system were later abolished, but the rewards for overfulfillment of quotas continued as a stimulus for the conscientious or exploitative. In 1711 three Nei-wu-fu officials were sent out to help supervise and take responsibility for the sending of the grain to the storehouses.[31] The situation seems to have been similar on the other estates, such as the so-called "silver estates" which gave rent in money instead of in kind. In 1726 officials in charge of collecting the rents there were given twenty lashes of the whip if their rent collections were 10 percent below the quota.[32] On these estates, it seems, the stewards were not entrusted with the task of collecting rents alone, but received help from lower officials sent out from the capital. The importance attached to the fulfillment of the quotas can be seen as well in the fact that, although great emphasis was placed on the continuous transmission of the post of steward in one family, stewards were dismissed for rent arrears.[33]

Originally the purpose of the Imperial Household estates was to supply provisions for the emperor, his household, and for the officials and bannermen and their families associated with the Imperial Household Department. Thus, in the seventeenth century, most of the rents were in kind. In the eighteenth century, however, a broad and consistent movement towards the commutation of rents in kind into silver can be seen in almost all the imperial estates. This tendency started in the grain estates, for instance, in 1723, when the Nei-wu-fu was ordered to depute two officials to collect half an ounce of silver for every picul of grain instead of the grain itself on the estates near the capital.[34] The next year the grain estates in Manchuria were ordered to convert their "extra" grain into rice at the rate of two piculs of rice for every one of grain. In 1739 the metropolitan estates' quota of millet stalks was converted to silver.[35] A large part of the conversion into silver was sent to the Department of the Privy Purse in Peking. The change in the total income of the Nei-wu-fu from the imperial estates reflects the tendency towards monetization. In 1764, for instance, the income was 164,818 piculs of grain and 28,555 taels of silver, while by 1818 it was 42,671 piculs of grain and 140,674 taels of silver.[36]

The estate economy of the Nei-wu-fu in the eighteenth century expanded its area and enlarged its monetized income. While the total income due to the Nei-wu-fu was growing, the actual amount received is harder to estimate. Figures suggest that the increasing monetization was accompanied by large deficiencies in rent payments. The back rents due in 1767, for instance, amounted to 23,000 taels, while by 1801 they had risen to 53,100 taels.[37] In short, the imperial estates provided food supplies as well as an income of silver to the Imperial Household Department, but, although the estates were expanding and the total income from them was rising, they did not constitute a major source of income. Administratively the estate system had an authoritarian organization which placed real power in the hands of the stewards and allowed them to enrich themselves as long as they fulfilled their quotas.

The Ginseng Trade

In the early seventeenth century the trade in ginseng was probably the major source of income, aside from booty, for Nurhachi's treasuries. Although the Chinese had used ginseng for medical purposes for centuries, in the Ming period the demand grew while supply shrank. The medical practices of the Jurchen and Mongols in the Chin and Yuan periods spurred consumption, which increased considerably from Sung to Ming times. At the same time the traditional sources of ginseng within China proper (the T'aihang Mountains in eastern Shansi province) were approaching exhaustion. As a result of these developments Chinese traders eagerly sought ginseng from new sources of supply in Manchuria.[38]

After the conquest of China, ginseng was an essential commodity in Chinese trade with Manchuria, and the Nei-wu-fu played a major role in the sale of this highly prized medicine. Prior to the conquest of China and in the early years of the dynasty, each of the eight banners had specific areas reserved to it for the collection of ginseng, and stiff penalties were imposed on those who violated restrictions by taking ginseng from areas assigned to others.[39] At this time, groups of slaves of the various princes and ministers and groups of bannermen were the principal diggers of this root. Needless to say, the collection of ginseng was closely tied to the banner organization and the imperial estates. Communications between the emperor's household officials in the capital and the stewards on the imperial estates in Manchuria indicate that in 1651, for example, 25 *tokso*, or estates, were to provide 5.4 pecks of grain to each of 620 *pao-i* and bannermen recruited from the various *niru* which belonged to the emperor.[40] These expeditions to dig ginseng seem to have been large gangs of a hundred or more bond-servants, recruited from the banner organization, led by banner officials and provisioned by the banner and imperial estates.

The banners' monopoly on gathering and supplying ginseng continued until the middle of the K'ang-hsi period. The first major change came in 1684 when a system of patents was established to facilitate the apprehension of illegal diggers, and new taxes were imposed on the extra-quota ginseng brought through the pass at Shan-hai-kuan.[41] A total of 3,019 patents were issued by the Board of Revenue, but no quotas were attached to them. The new tax probably went to the Board of Revenue, while the ginseng went to the princes, banner leaders, and the Imperial Household Department. In 1701, however, the Nei-wu-fu assumed general control over the digging of all ginseng and the opening up of new areas to exploitation.[42] The basic organization of ginseng gathering did not change, but revenues may now have gone to the Nei-wu-fu. The total amount of ginseng or funds from the ginseng trade entering the Nei-wu-fu at this time, however, is unknown.

The structure of the ginseng monopoly changed fundamentally in 1709. The link between the imperial estates and ginseng gathering was severed when the Manchu diggers received five taels of silver in lieu of provisions of grain from the estates.[43] Also in 1709 a quota system began which would supply 100,000 ounces of ginseng yearly. Since the price of an ounce of ginseng varied from 8 to 23 taels of silver,[44] the value of the yearly quota was between 762,000 and 1,848,000 taels. From this total the finest 1,600 ounces were for the emperor's use, and another 14,400 ounces were destined for the Nei-wu-fu's tea store to serve as imperial presents to loyal and meritorious officials. The remaining ginseng was split into three parts: two parts were given to the Board of Revenue which delivered them to the Superintendent of Customs at the Ch'ung-wen Gate for sale and conversion to silver, and one part was given to the diggers of ginseng as wages.[45] The Board of

Revenue may have sent the silver gained from the sale of ginseng to the Nei-wu-fu's bullion vaults, following the example of expropriated goods, which were sold at the Ch'ung-wen Gate with the proceeds going to the Imperial Household Department. As early as 1709 some of the extra ginseng from the Nei-wu-fu's Tea Store was delivered to the Nei-wu-fu manufactory superintendents, such as Ts'ao Yin, for sale by them.[46] The proceeds from these sales went, at least in part, to the Nei-wu-fu's Department of the Privy Purse.[47]

In 1730 another reorganization of the trade took place. This change severed the connection between the banners and ginseng gathering and authorized merchants to hire gatherers on the open market. The merchants received 10,000 patents and were obliged to deliver 16 ounces of ginseng for every patent, but 6 of these ounces were returned to them to provide for capital investment.[48] When this experimental scheme was abolished in 1744 because of widespread corruption, these 6 ounces were sent to the Nei-wu-fu to hire ginseng diggers. Sources from 1745 and later also mention "ginseng for public expenditures" (kung-yung shen) and "official ginseng" (kuan shen) as going to the Nei-wu-fu "as in previous times."[49] It seems likely, then, that from the 1730s the Nei-wu-fu received the gross income from the ginseng trade of 160,000 ounces of ginseng, of which about 60,000 ounces went to pay for ginseng gatherers.

About mid-century still another change took place in the procedure for selling ginseng. This concerned ginseng the emperor did not need for himself or for gifts to others. Previously this extra ginseng had been sold at the Ch'ung-wen Gate, but now princes and high officials received permission to buy up this surplus.[50] Since this procedure was considered a "charity measure" (hsu-shang), it seems likely that the prices they paid for the ginseng were well below the market price and enabled them to make a fat profit on resale. This policy was later extended in 1757 to provide for the routine sale of surplus ginseng through the Nei-wu-fu officials in the manufactories, the Liang-huai and Ch'ang-lu salt monopolies, and the Canton customs bureau.[51] This procedure served the

Nei-wu-fu in two ways. First, the money paid for the ginseng by the princes and others went to the Nei-wu-fu's Department of the Purse, and in later years any funds received over the set price of 18.7 taels of silver per ounce of ginseng went to provide free meals for Nei-wu-fu clerks and vault inspectors. By 1770 these funds had reached 30,000 taels per year. Second, the policy of allowing Nei-wu-fu managers and later *pao-i* the profitable privilege of acting as ginseng brokers was a means for the emperor to reward a few favored bondservants.

From the above figures it is not inconceivable that the gross income of the Nei-wu-fu during the mid-eighteenth century from the ginseng trade may have exceeded 1,000,000 taels annually. And this was not all. The Imperial Household Department's Tea Store also received ginseng from the department's own estate workers in the Wula district who were under the supervision of the Department of the Household Guard and the Imperial Hunt (Tu-yü-ssu). By the end of the century, however, the Nei-wu-fu's income from ginseng seems to have declined considerably. At that time collection of ginseng became more difficult, corruption grew, the Nei-wu-fu had to extend loans of up to 30,000 taels to the diggers, and quotas went unfilled.[52]

Commercial Operations and the Copper Trade

The Imperial Household Department's commercial activities, like its role in the ginseng trade and its management of the imperial estates, date from the early years of the dynasty. This role in commercial activity derives from the alliance between the Manchu conquerors and certain Chinese merchants from the early years of the dynasty. In a fashion similar to the Mongols four hundred years earlier,[53] the Manchu imperial household found it very advantageous to cooperate with and support certain merchants by licensing them and granting them loans and other privileges.

The Fan lineage provides a concrete example of this cooperation.[54] When the Manchus entered the passes to conquer China, the merchant Fan Yung-tou, who engaged in trade along the border, enjoyed a reputation for trustworthiness and integrity.[55] The Shun-chih Emperor ordered him to come to Peking for an audience and offered him a position as an official, but Fan refused the post, saying that he knew nothing of government affairs. He accepted, however, a house in Kalgan and the privilege of becoming a Nei-wu-fu broker who provided money and pelts from his border trade for the emperor's personal treasury. His son Fan San-pa followed in his footsteps, but his eldest grandson, Fan Yü-pin, achieved wider fame as a trusted and influential Nei-wu-fu merchant of the eighteenth century whose career spanned three reigns and extended to such disparate activities as the ginseng trade, military supplies, the salt monopoly, and mining.

The first mention of Fan Yü-pin's commercial activities dates from the Yung-cheng period. He participated in the mining boom in Hunan in the 1720s[56] and received the title of Director of the Nei-wu-fu's Imperial Stud in 1729. In the years from 1721 to 1732 he supervised the shipment of more than 1,000,000 bushels of grain to the northwest for the campaigns against the Eleuths.[57] In 1730 the Shansi Censor Tsung Yun by coincidence encountered some of Fan's subordinates. In his travels about the province he had stopped at a tavern where he spotted a suspicious group of men who seemed to be traveling together. When asked who they were, they replied that they were employees of a nonexistent Nei-wu-fu "tax department." They said they worked at Fan Yü-pin's offices and had received a commission to deliver confidential messages and carry out secret business in Shansi. Tsung inquired further and discovered that the secret business of these men was purchasing camels for military supplies, but that they had made a detour to Ning-wu because Fan Yü-pin had ordered them to deliver a letter to his relative, the Governor of Shansi, Shih-lin.[58]

Connections with the Nei-wu-fu and the regular bureaucracy,[59] however, did not prevent business reverses caused by the sudden conclusion of the war in the northwest. These cost Fan 2,620,000 taels in 1731, but he was still able to carry on his commercial activities, acting as a rice broker supplying the military encampments and the banner rice bureaus in the early years of the Ch'ien-lung Emperor's reign.[60] In 1738 he received permission to buy

ginseng in the Ussuri region as part of the reorganization of the
ginseng trade mentioned above. After considerable portions of the
copper quotas had remained unfilled for several years, the copper
trade was also reorganized in 1738, and soon after Fan Yü-pin
became the leading copper merchant.

Originally in 1645 the copper required by the Board of Revenue
for making coins and by the Board of Works for construction came
from purchases made by the superintendents from Chinese merchants at four of the customs bureaus nearest the capital.[61] Later,
in 1647 and 1650, the number of bureaus using part of their revenues to purchase copper and the quotas were both increased, but
the failure of the customs bureaus to provide enough revenue to
meet the demands for copper led in 1664 to the use of 164,510
taels from the salt revenues from Ch'ang-lu for purchasing copper.[62]
This precedent was cited after 1679 to justify the use of salt
revenues from the Liang-huai, Liang-che, and Ho-tung areas. The
increasing demand for copper finally led in 1699 to a new policy
of opening up sea trade with Japan in order to purchase Japanese
copper. At the request of the Nei-wu-fu the copper quotas for six
of the customs bureaus, a total of 1,938,970 catties in the Yangtze
basin, were handed over to "Nei-wu-fu merchants" from Kalgan
to collect and sell to the customs superintendents at a price of one
and one-half cash per catty.[63] In 1713 the amount saved by allowing the Nei-wu-fu merchants to act as brokers was estimated at
50,000 taels, and additional revenues from the salt administration
were entrusted to them as advances to aid them in purchasing
copper.[64] The Board of Revenue and the Board of Works seem to
have been satisfied, even pleased, with the handling of copper
quotas by the Nei-wu-fu merchants. Two years later, however, it
appears that, because of considerable debts which they were unable
to pay off, the Nei-wu-fu merchants' role in the copper trade was
severely restricted.[65] These developments were undoubtedly linked
to the new system of permits the Japanese put into effect in 1715
and the consequent decline of the Fukienese merchants who had
monopolized aspects of the trade up until that time.[66]

These "Nei-wu-fu merchants" may have included members of

the Fan lineage, but in any case they were probably from families, like the Fan, who had received licenses from the Nei-wu-fu at the beginning of the dynasty. The term "Nei-wu-fu merchants" would seem, then, to refer to those merchants who were old and reliable friends of the Nei-wu-fu *pao-i* and had been cooperating with them for generations. Institutionally, however, the term may have had a narrower meaning. It seems that the merchants who took part in the copper trade had to be sponsored (*pao-chieh*) by a Nei-wu-fu *tso-ling*. "Nei-wu-fu merchants" in this context may simply refer to those who were able to gain sponsorship by a *tso-ling*.[67] In practice, there may have been no difference in these two putative groups, for it was probably the merchant families whom the emperor had designated as Nei-wu-fu brokers generations before who were most likely to secure sponsorship by the Imperial Household Department. These "Nei-wu-fu merchants" clearly, then, were not Nei-wu-fu *pao-i* but commoners. What distinguished them from ordinary merchants, of course, was their tie to the Nei-wu-fu. If one judges from analogy with the situation a few years later, it seems likely that the "Nei-wu-fu merchants" received capital from the Nei-wu-fu and played a managerial role, while the Fukienese and, later, Kiangsu and Chekiang merchants employed their own capital and actually carried on the commerce.

In any case, changes in the administration between 1738 and 1745 led to a new framework for commerce which gave the Fan lineage a hereditary monopoly on the leading role in the copper trade.[68] The position they occupied was that of "state merchants" (*kuan-shang*) who received loans for operating capital of up to 650,000 taels a year from the Nei-wu-fu.[69] Undoubtedly Fan Yü-pin's experience in the Yunnan copper industry and his lately acquired status as a Ch'ang-lu salt merchant made him a likely candidate for the position. In addition, Fan himself hoped that participation in the copper trade would allow him to earn enough to pay back his accumulated debts of 1,140,000 taels to the state from his other commercial activities.[70] The fact that he was able to pay off this sum within six years testifies to the economic power he wielded.

The "state merchant" did not himself make the voyage in the convoy of sixteen ships which left the Yangtze delta laden with silks and medicinal products each year for Nagasaki.[71] Rather he supervised and directed the trade, pooling his capital with the "quota merchants" (*o-shang*) and hiring others to handle the actual conduct of commerce.[72] The "quota merchants" were a group of twelve traders from the lower Yangtze basin, who used their own capital to take part in the copper trade.[73] From the 1740s until well into the nineteenth century the "state merchants" and the "quota merchants" dominated, if not monopolized, the Nagasaki trade which brought to China between 1,000,000 and 2,000,000 catties of copper every year.[74]

The Fan lineage's participation in the copper trade and other commercial activities was, of course, not limited to Fan Yü-pin. After his death his second son, Fan Ch'ing-chu, temporarily succeeded him in his role in the copper trade in the middle of the century.[75] Soon afterwards, however, his first son, Fan Ch'ing-hung, took over the duties of "state merchant" and in 1764 received a Nei-wu-fu loan of 132,000 taels.[76] During the 1750s and 1760s both sons served in official positions which complemented and enhanced their commercial activities. Both, for example, served as department directors in the Board of Revenue, and Fan Ch'ing-hung at one point held the post of Ning-po and Shao-hsing Intendant which entailed management of the Chekiang Customs Bureau and the "quota merchants."[77] Since officials were prohibited from engaging in commercial activities while in office, the Fan brothers probably used their indentured servants to carry on business activities for them during their stints of government service. While Fan Ch'ing-chu held the post of department director, for example, he deputed his indentured servant, T'ao Lung, to manage the purchase of glass from the English trader James Flint.[78] Further, in 1757 when Ch'ien-lung decided to open up a Nei-wu-fu managed trade at Urumchi in cloth produced by the imperial manufactories, he chose Fan Ch'ing-hung to supervise it because of his broad knowledge of commercial matters and his close connections with the Nei-wu-fu.[79]

Fan Ch'ing-hung and Fan Ch'ing-chu were followed as "state merchants" in the mid 1770s by a cousin, Fan Ch'ing-chi, who never served as an official.[80] This nephew of Fan Yü-pin had been involved in the copper trade for many years and received the privilege of transporting salt in 1764 in order to funnel the money he made in that lucrative business into the less profitable copper trade.[81] By 1783, however, Fan Ch'ing-chi's poor management of his salt interests and the corruption of his son, Fan Li, brought on debts of 1,300,000 taels, most of it probably owed to the Nei-wu-fu.[82] As a result, Ch'ien-lung transferred his salt interests to ten other merchants and his role as "state merchant" in the copper trade to another Ch'ang-lu salt merchant, Wang Shih-jung,[83] while the real estate in Kalgan and salt lands near Peking which had belonged to Fan Yü-pin were taken from Fan Ch'ing-chi and given to Fan Yü-pin's grandson, Fan Chung-ch'i.[84] Fan Ch'ing-chi's remaining property was expropriated and passed to the Nei-wu-fu, and an additional fine of 80,000 taels was paid off by contributions from other merchants.

The Fan lineage's dominance of the copper trade came to an end in 1783, but it lost the last of its major sources of wealth in 1796 when the salt properties which Fan Chung-ch'i had received from Fan Ch'ing-chi passed to the Nei-wu-fu because he was unable to pay off the debts on them.[85] The reasons for the fall of the Fan lineage seem varied. The extravagance of the members of the lineage, inordinate demands by the state or the Nei-wu-fu, the declining value of copper cash, and a lower number of members in influential positions in the bureaucracy all played a part.[86]

The Customs Bureaus

The Imperial Household Department was closely connected with commercial enterprise, not only through its relations with the ginseng and copper trade, but also through its role in the collection and storage of the commercial taxes levied on merchant goods at several key communications and market areas located mainly in the Yangtze and Pearl River deltas.[87] The main tax bureaus which were connected with the Nei-wu-fu were those at

Kalgan northwest of Peking, at the Ch'ung-wen Gate in the capital,
at Kiukiang in Kiangsi province above the Yangtze from Nanking,
at Hangchow, at Hu-shu near Soochow, and at Canton.

Perhaps the most unusual of these tax bureaus was the one in
Canton because it played a vital role in foreign commerce. Although
the Europeans made periodic attempts to establish firm commercial
relations at other ports, from 1685, when Chinese ports were opened
to foreign commerce, until 1760, when foreign trade was limited
to Canton, Western trade was concentrated mainly in Canton.[88]
The superintendent of trade at Canton, then, managed most foreign
sea trade before 1760 and all of it after 1760. Foreign ships trading
along the coast of Chekiang in 1755, for instance, procured "permits" from the *pao-i* superintendent in Canton.[89]

The Customs Bureau of Canton assumed definitive form in
1685 when K'ang-hsi settled a dispute between the Board of Rites
and the Board of Revenue by reconciling the tribute system with
foreign trade. He declared that only three tribute ships from each
foreign country would be exempt from taxation—all others would
have to pay taxes.[90] The small local fishing boats and Chinese
coastal trade were not taxed, so this bureau's revenue probably
came exclusively from foreign trade. The original tax quota at the
bureau seems to have been 91,744 taels, but it was reduced to
83,362 taels in 1688 and further to 48,412 in 1699.[91] This regular
quota generally rose in the eighteenth century, however, passing
from 43,750 in 1727 to over 1,000,000 taels by the end of Ch'ien-
lung's reign.[92] Aside from the regular quota, which was supposed
to be determined by the number of foreign ships arriving in Canton
and the quality of the goods, two other exactions were placed on
the trade. These were the extra taxes and the illegal demands or
"squeeze" by the superintendent, his indentured servants, and clerks.[93]
The origin of these two exactions is hard to date, but the latter
probably existed from 1685, although the first recorded dates for
both are in the reign of the Yung-cheng Emperor. In 1727, for
example, the regular quota was 43,750 taels, while the extra tax
quota amounted to 48,000 and the illegal squeeze to 38,000 taels.[94]
The squeeze, of course, went to the pockets of the superintendent,

his indentured servants, clerks, and lesser workmen connected with the trade. The regular quota was sent to the provincial treasury, but the excess quota was forwarded to the "Inner Board," that is, the Imperial Household Department.[95]

The changing quotas and a paucity of statistics make it difficult to supply precise comparative estimates for the Nei-wu-fu's income from the excess customs taxes in the eighteenth century. Originally there were no quotas for the extra taxes, but in 1749 Ch'ien-lung redefined them as a standard item of taxation. He also provided that the extra tax receipts for 1735, the last year of Yung-cheng's reign, amounting to more than 1,600,000 taels from twenty customs houses, should serve as the basis for the quota of extra taxes.[96] The offices at Hu-shu, Huai-an, Kiukiang, Fukien, and Canton supplied over half the total. Within thirty years this system was abandoned for yet another under which the lowest amount of extra taxes delivered during the three previous years served as the lower limit of receipts a superintendent was responsible for fulfilling.[97] Under this policy of 1777 the previous quotas became an absolute minimum which could be exceeded but had to be fulfilled. The minimum yearly income for the Imperial Household Department from excess taxes in the last quarter of the century, then, should have been at least as high as the quota for 1749 and perhaps considerably higher.

The delivery of funds from the Canton customs to the Privy Purse from at least as early as 1727 may have been linked to the appointment of Nei-wu-fu personnel as superintendents.[98] The superintendent, or "Hoppo" as he was known to the Europeans, was the official in charge of managing the foreign trade at Canton. The position of superintendent existed as a distinct position from 1685, but was bestowed at times on the Kwangtung governors. The governor served as superintendent in the first half of the eighteenth century and for various short periods towards the end of the century.[99] The length of tenure of office for individual superintendents in the eighteenth century was irregular. Some, such as Te-k'ui, served many years (eight consecutive years and eleven years altogether), while others held the post for only a few months.[100]

The first appointment of Nei-wu-fu officials as superintendents at the customs bureaus is hard to pinpoint. A list of the superintendents of Canton from 1685 to 1796 is available, but biographical information, including the possible Nei-wu-fu status of these officials, is difficult to obtain. No Nei-wu-fu personnel seem to have served as superintendents at Canton in the K'ang-hsi period, and biographical data have not yielded any proof of service in the Yung-cheng period. Of the twenty-six men who served as superintendents from 1736 to 1796, data are available on the backgrounds of twelve.[101] Of this dozen, seven served as concurrent or acting superintendents. Five of these were "Manchu." None of the seven, however, can be affirmatively identified as Nei-wu-fu *pao-i*. Of the other five, three were certainly of Nei-wu-fu status, while one was probably a Nei-wu-fu man and the last was possibly a Nei-wu-fu *pao-i*. The diversion of funds of the Canton Customs Bureau to the Imperial Household Department began probably at the same time—or perhaps even earlier than—the appointment of Nei-wu-fu personnel to the office of superintendent. In any case, the Imperial Household Department was directly involved in the foreign trade at Canton in the latter half of the eighteenth century through revenues and personnel.

The situation at other customs bureaus was probably similar. It seems that the excess quota taxes from many, perhaps all, of the other bureaus went to the Imperial Household Department after the first quarter of the eighteenth century. Two bureaus that are representative are those at Kiukiang and Chekiang (known as Che-hai). The former had the second largest regular quota (153,889 taels) in the mid-eighteenth century, while the latter, with a quota of 32,158 taels, was typical of the small bureaus.[102] At both these offices Nei-wu-fu officials received appointments as customs superintendents considerably earlier than at Canton. The earliest use of the Nei-wu-fu *pao-i* in Chekiang, for instance, was in 1692, while at Kiukiang it was approximately 1704.[103] Appointment of Nei-wu-fu personnel, however, seems to have been somewhat erratic at both these posts from these first years. From 1692 to 1733 fourteen out of sixty superintendents at Che-hai can be positively identified as belonging to the Nei-wu-fu. At Kiukiang only ten of the fifty-four superintendents from 1704 to 1796 can be affirmatively identified as imperial bondservants. The number of *pao-i* superintendents in the latter half of the eighteenth century may have been much larger than these figures suggest, however, for the lists of officials in local gazetteers often designate the Nei-wu-fu *pao-i* simply as "Manchu" or "Han-chün" (Chinese who surrendered prior to the conquest of China proper). Up until the beginning of Yung-cheng's reign, it seems clear that superintendents were chosen from among the assistant department directors and department directors of the various governmental offices in Peking (the six Boards, the Nei-wu-fu, the Court of Colonial Affairs, and the Court of the Imperial Stud), and that officials from the Nei-wu-fu served as superintendents only slightly more often from 1704 to 1723 than, for instance, officials from the Board of Revenue. During Yung-cheng's reign the bureau was managed mainly by local officials, while Nei-wu-fu *pao-i* again were appointed early in Ch'ien-lung's reign. These facts suggest that the appointment of superintendents to the various customs bureaus seems not to have been the exclusive domain of the imperial bondservants. However, the *pao-i* did play an important role in the collection and handling of large sums of money.

The customs offices not only provided the Nei-wu-fu's treasuries with considerable revenues; they also provided the *pao-i* superintendents with an opportunity to fill their own pockets. From early in the eighteenth century measures were taken to deal with this problem. When the Yung-cheng Emperor assumed the throne, for instance, he transferred responsibility for customs to the provincial governors in order to eliminate the rampant corruption by Nei-wu-fu *pao-i*.[104] He soon was forced to withdraw this measure at least for certain bureaus, however, because provincial officials were too busy or too far away to take on the additional task of managing the bureaus.[105] For the remainder of his reign, both provincial officials and Nei-wu-fu bondservants served as superintendents.

Failing to discover a better strategy, the Ch'ien-lung Emperor followed these same tactics. Soon after the death of his father some officials advocated the appointment of bannermen, including imperial bondservants, while others suggested employing only local officials. Ch'ien-lung refused to commit his name to any set policy, insisting that it would take time to develop an effective plan that would preserve imperial control over the bureaus, yet eliminate large-scale embezzlement which both deprived the public fisc and the privy purse of revenues and placed an undue burden on commerce.[106] The remaining years of his reign bear tribute to the difficulty, indeed the impossibility, of this task. After twelve years of trying without success to reconcile these conflicting goals he admitted in 1748 that there simply was no solution to the problem.[107] He came to accept the endemic corruption at the bureaus as the product of human foibles to which the bannermen and, in particular, the imperial bondservants were all too susceptible. He mused about the difficulty of recruiting truly honorable men and wondered who would not be corrupted by the large sums of money passing through the bureaus. The censors and other officials would in time, of course, denounce the misdeeds of embezzlers, but they could never predict which potential customs superintendents would give in to temptation. In 1762, when an egregious case of peculation by an indentured servant of the Superintendent Anning, a Nei-wu-fu *pao-i*, came to light, Ch'ien-lung threatened to stop using Nei-wu-fu personnel as superintendents altogether. But he never implemented such a change of policy.[108]

The impossibility of eliminating corruption at the customs bureaus or the impracticalities for his own purposes of dismissing all the Nei-wu-fu customs superintendents did not prevent Ch'ien-lung from seeking measures to reduce the losses to him and to the public treasuries. He took various measures throughout the eighteenth century to curb corruption. At Canton, for instance, procedures for measuring, recording, and reporting tax revenues were revised numerous times after 1726, when it was discovered that the Superintendent Yang Wen-ch'ien had embezzled 60,000 taels.[109] In 1735 double bookkeeping was prohibited, while in 1748 the various accounts in the registers were revised, and in 1750 the superintendents were ordered to report tax receipts together with the governor-generals. In 1759 efforts were made to prohibit the unofficial exactions known as *kuei-li*, and from 1787 special tax registers sent from the capital had to be used to record receipts.[110]

None of these measures was successful in curbing corruption because the superintendents operated only as a part of a system of squeeze which extended from the superintendents and their bond-servants to the highest Nei-wu-fu officials in Peking. Each link in this chain exploited those below and was, in turn, squeezed for profit by those higher up. Still, a clever superintendent could manage to make a small fortune for himself from the customs bureau and, if he was lucky, it would not be expropriated by the emperor. This was why Ts'ao Yin and Li Hsu in the early eighteenth century made repeated, but unsuccessful, efforts to convince the emperor to allow them one of the lucrative customs posts.[111] The exactions of the Hoppo were noted by foreigners at Canton and were one of the causes of the chronic lack of capital among the Cohong merchants.[112] The mention as early as 1728 of an irregular item called the "Nei-wu-fu Managers' Item" (*Tsung-kuan nei-ssu teng-hsiang*) among the illegal exactions at Canton indicates that the Imperial Household Department's managers were gouging the superintendents who themselves were busy filling their own pockets at the expense of the foreigners.[113] Towards the end of the century the superintendents sent large bribes and gifts not only to the Nei-wu-fu Manager to Ho-shen, but also made "voluntary contributions" of tens of thousands of taels to the emperor himself.[114]

The Salt Monopoly

The Imperial Household Department played a major role in the management of the salt monopoly as it did in the customs bureaus. Indeed, the Nei-wu-fu's ties with the salt industry were even closer than with the taxation of trade.

As with the tax bureaus, the link between the Imperial Household Department and the salt monopoly was the appointment of Nei-wu-fu *pao-i* as officials to oversee activities and to forward part of the revenues to the privy purse.[115] Unfortunately, information on the background of the various men who occupied positions of authority in management of the salt monopoly is difficult to obtain. In the three largest salt-producing areas (Liang-huai,[116] Liang-che, and Ch'ang-lu) the extant lists of salt censors classify many Nei-wu-fu *pao-i* as simply "bannermen," making it impossible to identify many possible *pao-i* in these lists without independent confirmation—which is very difficult to obtain. The Liang-huai gazetteer, for instance, gives the status of Ts'ao Yin and Li Hsu, two of the most notable *pao-i*, as simply "bannermen," although it does specify others, such as Chi-ch'ing as being *pao-i*.[117] It is at least clear, however, that bannermen (including Nei-wu-fu *pao-i*) had an almost total monopoly on these posts. At Liang-huai, for example, the clear preference for bannermen officials began in 1684. From that date until 1796 the total number of bannermen officials was forty, while the number of Chinese was only six.[118] In the special post of salt supervisor (*tsung-li yen-fa ta-ch'en*), established in 1731 at Liang-huai, thirteen bannermen as opposed to four Chinese served.[119] At Liang-che the trend towards non-Chinese officials began in 1688 and continued until the end of Ch'ien-lung's reign with fifty-eight bannermen and seventeen Chinese serving.[120] At Ch'ang-lu the predominance of bannermen began in 1701 and continued with the appointment of forty-seven of them and only two Chinese.[121]

Information in other sources supports the assertion that, for the later eighteenth century at least, these "bannermen" officials were in reality Nei-wu-fu *pao-i* in at least two locations. In Ch'ang-lu the salt censors serving from 1769 to 1795 can be positively identified as *pao-i*, as can those serving in Liang-huai from 1770 to 1796, except for the years 1776 and 1781. Nei-wu-fu *pao-i*, then, commanded a strong, if not dominant, position in the salt administration from the late seventeenth century and a near monopoly by the late eighteenth century.

How much of the revenues from the salt monopoly these imperial bondservants sent back to the treasuries of the Nei-wu-fu is a difficult question. Surplus funds seem to have been collected from as early as the 1690s for use by the Nei-wu-fu's manufactories and other purposes.[122] In the early eighteenth century these amounted to about 500,000 taels per year, and these "surplus" funds were collected even while the regular quota went unfulfilled.[123] Illegal exactions probably accompanied the collection of the surplus funds from the beginning. The Yung-cheng Emperor discovered in his first year on the throne that the "customary leakage" (lou-kuei) in the accounts of the Kwangtung Salt Administration included the sum of 2,000 taels of silver which was "forwarded to the Nei-wu-fu for the use of the managers of the Imperial Household Department."[124]

Large amounts of authorized receipts entered the coffers of the Nei-wu-fu from about mid-century. In 1748, for example, 50,000 taels received yearly by the Liang-huai Salt Administration from the sale of copper were diverted from the Board of Revenue.[125] At the same time, another 100,000 taels in excess funds at Liang-huai, which had previously been spent on administrative expenses (pang-t'ieh), were forwarded to the capital for the Nei-wu-fu's use. The Ch'ang-lu Salt Administration also began to send 50,000 taels a year which it saved on these same costs to the privy purse. In 1749 a new source of income appeared: the Nei-wu-fu acquired government salt certificates (yin) authorizing it to sell salt in the Chi-an area of Kiangsu.[126] These certificates had originally belonged to a senior vice president of one of the six boards named Yung-shou, but the Yung-cheng Emperor had transferred them in 1726 to his loyal half-brother Yin-hsiang, Prince I, and later, in 1739, these certificates were entrusted to Liang-huai salt merchants to manage.[127] After 1749 these merchants, who received operating capital from the Nei-wu-fu, took turns using these certificates and others the Nei-wu-fu had acquired.[128] In 1763, for example, the income to the Imperial Household Department from the Chi-an certificates was 52,400 taels.[129] Besides this the Imperial Household also received 800 taels in rents from land and houses (t'ien-fang tsu-yin) which were connected with the salt administration.[130] Later years reveal an increasing number of small miscellaneous sums, such as 800 taels for the meals taken by secretaries (shu-li), 5,207 taels for the clerks, and indefinite sums such as "money for expenses" (ching-fei yin), for "delivery" (chieh-fei yin), and the money "saved from porters' costs" (*chieh-sheng ch'e-chiao yin*) at the Liang-huai salt monopoly.[131] It would be very difficult to estimate the total income of the Imperial Household Department from salt revenues during the latter half of the eighteenth century, for, while the Nei-wu-fu was generally adding new sources of revenue, some old sources were being diverted.[132] From the figures above it seems likely, however, that its income exceeded 250,000 taels per year near the end of the century.

Of course, not all funds designated for the privy purse actually reached their destination, for the salt censors, like the customs superintendents, were able to embezzle sizable sums during their terms of office. The salt censors accumulated substantial amounts of money by pressing the salt magnates for entertainment and contributions, while these large salt merchants, in turn, squeezed money from the smaller traders. The salt censors, however, had to remain in the good graces of the emperor and their superiors in the Imperial Household Department, so they often cooperated with the salt merchants in sending special gifts and contributions to the capital.[133] Such gifts could not, however, excuse gross corruption such as that of Kao Heng, the Liang-huai Salt Censor in the 1760s.[134] The *pao-i* salt censors, like the customs officials, were involved in the major underhanded financial dealings brought to light in the Secret Accounts Bureau and the investigation of Ho-shen's property described below.

Loans by the Department

One of the most intriguing aspects of the Nei-wu-fu's financial operations was the granting of loans to salt merchants and others in order to earn interest. This procedure may well have begun in the K'ang-hsi period at the time of the first appointments of Nei-wu-fu officials to positions in the salt administration and the imperial manufactories in the late seventeenth century.

The first mention of these loans appears in a memorial of Li Hsu, the Superintendent of the Imperial Manufactory at Soochow in 1700. He informed the emperor that he had learned of his generosity in loaning funds from his personal treasury to Nei-wu-fu

pao-i at low rates of interest so that they could invest the money
and earn enough above the interest they owed the emperor to make
a considerable profit.[135] Li requested a loan of 100,000 taels, but
mentioned that, since he was stationed in Soochow, far from the
capital, it would be difficult for him to make the monthly payments on the loan that were the usual procedure and asked for
permission to make the payments of 11,000 taels on a yearly basis
to the provincial treasuries which would forward them to the
capital. The emperor suggested that Li direct any inquiries concerning the Nei-wu-fu to the managers of the Imperial Household
Department. While the ultimate decision on this request seems unclear, Ts'ao Yin in the following year was able to borrow over
30,000 taels, interest free, from the Department.[136]

Later, other larger loans were made to individuals and groups.
A few years after his first request, Li Hsu made another proposal
for a loan from the privy purse to the Liang-huai salt merchants.
Stating that they had completely paid off the previous loan from
the Nei-wu-fu, he requested a loan of 120,000 taels for them.[137]
K'ang-hsi, obviously annoyed at this request, replied that it was
ridiculous to claim that the merchants had completely paid off the
previous loan. He refused to give them another loan and told Li
not to bring up the subject again. By 1704, however, the emperor
seems to have reversed himself, granting an extremely large loan
of 1,000,000 taels to these very Liang-huai salt merchants.[138] At
this time Ts'ao Yin, an Imperial Household Department *pao-i*
serving as Superintendent of the Imperial Manufactories at Soochow,
reported to the emperor that actually the merchants who were
supposed to get the loans only received 800,000, while the rest
was handed over to imposters.[139] As a result, Ts'ao Yin, who seems
to have had a role in distributing these funds, tried to make the
Liang-huai merchants mutually responsible for loans they received
from the privy purse. Under this policy, if one merchant could not
pay back his part of the loan or if part of the funds were improp-
erly distributed, then all the merchants would have to contribute
to make up the loss. Later, in the Yung-cheng period, very large
sums were loaned to the Yang-chou salt merchants. Before 1727,

for example, the salt merchant Huang Kuang-te had borrowed and repaid 400,000 taels from the privy purse.[140]

The primary purpose of the loans for the Imperial Household Department seems to have been to earn a steady income from the interest and to provide thereby for certain yearly expenses the department incurred. The department first determined the amount of income it needed each year for certain expenses, then, figuring interest at 10 percent per year, the department calculated the amount of capital it would have to give to the merchants to receive the amount of income in interest it desired. In 1765, for instance, a loan of 10,000 taels was made to generate funds for the carriages necessary for the emperor's travels.[141] Later, in 1770, Ch'ien-lung ordered the Liang-huai Salt Censor Li Chih-ying to deliver the 100,000 taels from the funds received yearly by the Nei-wu-fu from the Liang-huai salt administration to merchants to earn interest of 10 percent per year. The interest income was distributed as rewards (*shang*) for meritorious service of the Artillery and Musketry Division (Huo-ch'i-ying).[142]

From the merchants' point of view this investment of operating capital was most welcome. At one point Ch'ien-lung had leaned towards abolishing these loans, but the Liang-huai merchants pleaded that he continue them. Later, in 1794, Ch'ien-lung reproached Cheng-jui, the Ch'ang-lu Salt Censor, for his pro-merchant bias and reminded him:

> Originally it was the merchants themselves who sincerely requested that the Nei-wu-fu loans be made to them. This was not at all a case of officials forcing them to take the loans. The loans were given as a result of the merchants' own efforts to secure them. Besides, the amount of profit to the Nei-wu-fu treasuries is only the interest payments of ten percent, which is very little. If the merchants were to take loans on the open market, how could they get such low interest rates? This shows that the merchants have profited very much by these loans.[143]

This indignant rebuke may contain a large element of truth, but the Nei-wu-fu's income from interest on invested funds did not always come from money in its own treasury. In 1748, for example, the Grand Secretary Chang T'ing-yü suggested that the yearly extra taxes of 100,000 taels from Liang-huai and 50,000 taels from Ch'ang-lu for the cost of gifts during Ch'ien-lung travels be handed over to merchants to earn interest of 15 percent. The interest would be added to the capital and the interest thus compounded with capital at the end of five years would total over 1,000,000 taels.[144] From this amount, 600,000 would then be left with the Liang-huai salt merchants to earn interest while the remaining 400,000 would go to the Ch'ang-lu salt merchants for the same purpose. The total yearly interest from these two investments of 180,000 would go to the Nei-wu-fu for rewards (*shang-lai*). The Liang-huai Salt Censor Chi-ch'ing, a Nei-wu-fu *pao-i*, opposed this plan, saying that there was no "surplus" available. However, the merchants themselves were eventually willing to contribute 100,000 taels every year to earn interest which would be added to capital. At the end of five years there would be 600,000 taels which would form a sum of capital from which interest would be earned each year and sent to the Nei-wu-fu. In 1750 interest was set at 10 percent.

At times the loans took the form of rewards for favors or good administration. This was the case of a loan of 300,000 taels to the colorful Liang-huai salt merchant Chiang Ch'un (also known as Chiang Kuang-ta) in 1771.[145] Only one-tenth of the interest on this loan was delivered to the Nei-wu-fu, while the rest was collected and used by Chiang. In 1774 Chiang modestly feigned that he was receiving too much interest and offered to give 10,000 of the 26,000 taels he received yearly in interest to the Nei-wu-fu for public expenses.[146] Chiang Ch'un probably was able to secure such a favorable loan because he was on good terms with Ch'ien-lung. He also was an unusually prosperous merchant—one of the "head merchants" (*tsung-shang*) who were chosen from among the richest salt magnates to bear financial responsibility for the merchants as a whole. He owned a famous garden (the K'ang-shan-yuan), but after his death in 1789 it fell into disrepair when his son Chiang Chen-hung met financial reverses. Ch'ien-lung ordered the salt merchants to contribute 50,000 taels to buy the garden and to give it to Chiang Chen-hung. At the same time he told the Nei-wu-fu to loan Chiang's son another 50,000 with the interest going to the Privy Purse.[147]

Although the loans to salt merchants may have been the largest loans given out by the Nei-wu-fu, they were by no means the only ones. For example, in the early 1700s, it was the custom for the emperor to grant loans of 4,000 taels to the inspectors at the manufactories for them to invest in business enterprises as they wished.[148] Later, the emperor made special efforts in 1742 to aid the lower officials and sub-officials in the Nei-wu-fu by small loans of 20 taels, for instance, for those who earned a salary of 4 taels.[149] The purpose of these loans, however, was less to earn interest than it was to benefit the indigent *pao-i* who received them, so they were often superseded by outright grants of "rice money." At times even large grants of money were made, such as those of 10,000 taels to the guards at the Ch'ien-ch'ing Gate, 20,000 to each of the three upper banner guards, 20,000 to the overseers, and 20,000 to the Nei-wu-fu officials in 1729 to invest in real estate or business as they saw fit and to earn interest—for themselves.[150]

The Imperial Household Department was not the only institution that used its funds to earn interest through investments with salt merchants. The Imperial Clan Court (Tsung-jen-fu) also engaged in these operations in the eighteenth century as did the governor-generals and governors of provinces in the lower Yangtze with funds from provincial treasuries.[151] The transactions in the Liang-huai salt area, however, show the amount of loans from the Nei-wu-fu (at least 1,400,000 taels) far exceeded the amount from either the Imperial Clan Court (440,000) or the provincial treasuries (490,000).[152]

The Imperial Manufactories

A financial function of the Nei-wu-fu which originated not from the dynasty's Manchu heritage but from the substitution of the Imperial Household Department for the eunuch bureaus of the Ming period was the management of the imperial manufactories. These offices, located in the three lower Yangtze cities of Nanking, Hangchow, and Soochow, were huge enterprises which employed thousands of workers to produce silks and textiles sent to the Nei-wu-fu's silk store and imperial wardrobe for the emperor's personal use and for presentation to foreign tributary envoys.[153] Administration of the bureaus was confused in the early years of the Ch'ing period—in the 1640s an official from the eunuch-operated Inner Board of Works managed the manufactory at Soochow, but an official from the Board of Revenue handled affairs at the manufactory in Nanking.[154] In 1661, however, when the Nei-wu-fu was re-established, the K'ang-hsi Emperor decided to subordinate the manufactories to it and to fill the vacancies in the textile administration at all three sites with Nei-wu-fu *pao-i*.[155] Thus, throughout the seventeenth and eighteenth centuries, the manufactories were closely tied to the Nei-wu-fu, both institutionally and through personnel.[156]

The financial arrangements at the imperial manufactories were originally relatively simple, but they became complex in the eighteenth century. At first, wealthy families in the lower Yangtze were made responsible for the production of a certain amount of cloth, which entailed hiring labor, buying the thread, and arranging for manufacture.[157] These arrangements broke down early and were followed by a succession of measures that provided for the investment of funds in the manufactories for production expenses by the national treasuries, the provincial treasuries, the salt monopoly, and the customs bureaus. During K'ang-hsi's reign the state took over the manufacturing, so state funds were spent in the various stages of production. Funds for salaries of the workmen came from the Board of Revenue, while funds for other purposes came from the Board of Works and,

later, from the provincial treasury. In 1705 on the recommendation
of Li Hsu and Ts'ao Yin, however, the major funds for the Soochow
and Nanking manufactories were no longer taken from the provincial
treasury, but from the surplus funds of 210,000 taels yearly from the
Liang-huai Salt Administration.[158] Only a few years later this policy too
was abandoned. In 1722 the Board of Revenue ordered the Liang-
huai Salt Censor not to release any more funds for the manufactories because of the delays in delivery. Instead, in 1723 it was
decided that not only the money for the workmen's salaries
(57,753 taels), but also the 227,620 taels for purchasing and administrative expenses would come from the provincial treasuries.[159]
The Liang-huai surplus funds from then on went to the Board of
Revenue in the capital. At least part of the expenses of the manufactories were met by funds from the customs bureaus in addition
to those from the provincial treasuries. It was probably for this
reason that during Yung-cheng's reign the customs office at Hu-shu
was merged with the Soochow Manufactory.[160] Probably at the
same time two other customs bureaus were joined to the Hangchow
manufactory. In 1793, however, when the Hangchow manufactory
was merged with the Liang-che Salt Administration, these two
customs houses became independent again.[161]

During the greater part of the eighteenth century, then, the
Nei-wu-fu was not contributing funds directly into the imperial
manufactories, but its officials at the manufactories, the customs
bureaus, and the salt monopoly were managing the large sums
necessary for the production of imperial textiles. The imperial
manufactories need not be seen merely as a financial liability,
however, for from at least mid-century their products were sold
in operations which probably netted the Nei-wu-fu not insubstan-
tial sums. This trade seems to have begun in 1757 when Ch'ien-lung
recruited Fan Ch'ing-hung and Fan Ch'ing-k'uang to manage this
officially sanctioned commerce between the Chinese, who sold
textiles, tea, and horses, and the Moslems, who sold camels and
goats.[162] While the textiles bartered by the Chinese probably came
from the imperial manufactories during the first months of trade,
they certainly did from 1758 on.[163] In 1777, for example, 11,000

bolts of silk and other textiles were shipped to Sinkiang and the Ili region for sale.[164] The other goods sold by the Chinese side in this trade also seem to have come from the Nei-wu-fu.[165] As we might expect, Ch'ien-lung deputed Nei-wu-fu *pao-i* to supervise this substantial commerce[166] and the profits from this trade probably went to the Nei-wu-fu, although at times they were used to provide for provincial expenses.[167]

Although the manufactories were located in the lower Yangtze, the Imperial Household Department in Peking exercised control over financial aspects of the manufactories. In the later seventeenth century, various financial activities carried on by the manufactories, such as selling government grain stores to reduce grain prices on the open market, had to be reported in registers sent to the Nei-wu-fu at the time of the sale.[168] In 1745 this procedure was further refined so that at the end of each year the manufactory superintendents made up two registers, one of which was sent to the emperor or the Board of Revenue, and another was sent to the Privy Purse so that Nei-wu-fu officials could conduct a thorough check of the year's finances.[169] When new expenditures arose, such as transportation costs for the buyers sent out from the Nanking and Soochow manufactories to purchase silk, they were added up at the end of the year and reported to the Nei-wu-fu to guard against squandering or pilfering. These measures suggest that the manufactory superintendents, like the customs officials, were interested not only in producing textiles, but in lining their own pockets.

Expropriation

Another source of wealth for the Nei-wu-fu was confiscation of the property of officials whose crimes merited severe punishment, such as death or exile. Before the conquest of China, Nurhachi at times took away troops and property from military commanders and distributed them as if they were his personal property. After 1644 this practice was reinforced by the Chinese tradition of delivering confiscated goods to the personal treasury of the emperor.[170] As might be suspected, the greater part of the expropriated items was not money, but other forms of personal and real property.

Often the property itself was taken into the treasuries of, or placed under the management of, the Nei-wu-fu. This was the case with the homes and estates of officials receiving punishment. In the early days of the conquest, some of the property accumulated through expropriation probably consisted of abandoned dwellings. Later, however, all of it seems to have come from the punitive confiscation of officials' property. In any case, early in the dynasty all "state residential property" (*kuan-fang*) was entrusted to the Imperial Household's overseers to administer, to repair, and, most important, to collect rents, which went to the Nei-wu-fu's Privy Purse.[171] Some of the residences in the Nei-wu-fu's inventory were converted into tributary hostels, but most of the Nei-wu-fu's real property was kept and leased out to earn income. Among the most profitable of these enterprises were the pawn shops.[172] In 1754 ten of them had resources totaling over 388,000 taels.[173] Originally the bondservants of punished officials were assigned to various Nei-wu-fu estates as cultivators, but after 1727 they were sold on the market at the Ch'ung-wen Gate and the money received was forwarded to the privy purse.[174] This measure may suggest a trend away from the appropriation of the confiscated goods themselves towards a conversion of the goods into money. In fact, however, sale and conversion into money seem to have been the accepted procedure for most personal property, at least from the early years of the K'ang-hsi period.

The income from confiscations would be difficult to ascertain, and in any case it varied in different periods according to the number and size of the scandals which led to confiscation. Fortunately, we have records on the confiscation of what was the largest political fortune of the eighteenth century, that of the imperial favorite Ho-shen.[175] Originally a young and obscure Manchu guard stationed at the Ch'ien-ch'ing Gate, he skyrocketed to fame and wealth when the emperor took him into his favor after 1775.[176] His banner status was elevated from plain red to plain yellow and he was appointed to a variety of high civil positions, such as grand councilor, and

rewarded with special privileges, such as permission to ride horseback in the Forbidden City. In 1776 he was also appointed a
manager of the Imperial Household Department, even though he
did not possess *pao-i* status. His power penetrated both the public
and private sectors of the court and he amassed a private fortune
by demanding bribes from officials eager to keep in the good graces
of the emperor. Among the officials most anxious to curry favor
with the emperor were the *pao-i* profitably engaged in large-scale
corruption in the salt monopolies, the customs bureaus, and the
imperial manufactories. Another feature that further increased
Ho-shen's power over the *pao-i* was his position as Nei-wu-fu
Manager in charge of the Secret Accounts Bureau, for this enabled
him to quash a demand for a contribution or to mitigate payment
procedures.[177]

The case of Cheng-jui illustrates the system of payoffs to
Ho-shen current at the end of Ch'ien-lung's reign. Cheng-jui was a
Nei-wu-fu *pao-i* who had served as Superintendent of the Hangchow,
Nanking, and Soochow manufactories, as Superintendent of the
Huai-an Customs Bureau and as Salt Censor of the Ch'ang-lu and
Liang-huai salt monopolies.[178] Towards the end of Ch'ien-lung's
reign he owed large amounts to the Secret Accounts Bureau for
embezzlement of government funds while in office. Although he
had difficulty in paying up these arrears, he was able to purchase
an official post for his son and to pay large bribes to Ho-shen.
Ho-shen, however was not satisfied with the expensive gifts and
the 200,000 taels in silver that Cheng-jui had presented to him and
demanded another 200,000. After Ho-shen's death Cheng-jui was
able to relate the full story to the Chia-ch'ing Emperor, who exclaimed:

> [Cheng-jui] wanted to win favor [with Ho-shen] through
> bribes and presents and planned to gain his protection in
> order to remain for a longer period as salt censor in the Liang-
> huai Salt Administration. He thought that he could use these
> bribes to fill his own pockets. According to the law he should
> be executed and his property confiscated.[179]

The emperor, however, commuted his punishment to work as a manual laborer and to the contribution of funds as redemption.

After Ho-shen had committed suicide at his orders, the Chia-ch'ing Emperor, in carrying out the investigation of Ho-shen's property in 1799, told the Nei-wu-fu ministers not to bother about the case of T'ai-fei-yin, a general commandant of the gendarmerie in Chin-chou who had given government estates to Ho-shen as presents. "As for sending gifts [to Ho-shen]," he said, "surely the officials in the salt administration, the manufactories, and the customs bureaus did most of this."[180] No doubt the emperor meant specifically the *pao-i* officials, for in an earlier rescript he mentioned his suspicion that Ho-shen's contributions to the imperial wardrobe really came not from Ho-shen, but from the "*pao-i* officials who wanted to make up their deficits or even to gain merit."[181]

This investigation of Ho-shen's property which the Chia-ch'ing Emperor launched in 1799 uncovered a great private fortune accumulated by the types of bribes and squeeze from the Nei-wu-fu *pao-i* described above. The Nei-wu-fu, which recorded and expropriated Ho-shen's property, estimated that it consisted mainly of 33,551 ounces of gold, 3,014,095 taels of silver, 12 pawn shops, 1001 rooms and buildings leased, and 126,600 mou of land leased out and worth 203,300 taels.[182] The money and the real property both were taken over by the Nei-wu-fu. Thus the major part of Ho-shen's wealth went to the Nei-wu-fu, although some miscellaneous items, such as the theatre costumes from his residence at Jehol, were sold and the receipts given to the Jehol district treasury.[183]

Ho-shen's fortune also included the property of his indentured servants. This also was confiscated. His senior henchman was an indentured servant Liu Ch'üan whose property included 109 ounces of gold, 15,924 taels of silver, 90 strings of cash (*ta-chih-ch'ien*), loans of 12,770 taels of silver, and income of 26,000 taels of silver from his two money-changing shops, his pharmacy, and his accounts office (*chang-chü*). Ho-shen's other indentured servants and even eunuchs (Ho-shen took former palace maids as his concubines) also owned property and engaged in commercial activities.[184]

While confiscations provided an irregular source of income for the Nei-wu-fu, large scandals, such as that of Ho-shen, could provide the Imperial Household Department with a substantial amount of money and property. Of more significance, perhaps, the confiscation of Ho-shen's property indicates that the Nei-wu-fu *pao-i* were involved in a large-scale and pervasive system of corruption in which the *pao-i* officials exploited their positions in the manufactories, salt administration, and customs bureaus to enrich themselves while at the same time they were exploited by Ho-shen, a Nei-wu-fu manager in the capital.

The Secret Accounts Bureau

One source of income for the Nei-wu-fu's treasuries which indicates the inner workings of the department is the contributions made to the Privy Purse by Nei-wu-fu officials and others to atone for their oversights or misdeeds in office. Registers of these accounts were kept in a Secret Accounts Bureau (Mi-chi-ch'u) attached to the Grand Council, which reviewed the reports of the accounts prepared by the managers of the Imperial Household Department. The origin of these contributions is uncertain, but the surviving documents date from the period 1786 to 1795. These archives may have originated about the middle of the eighteenth century, but the earliest reference to them is in 1776.[185] These contributions were not the same as the fines deducted from officials' salaries. Such fines were levied by the Board of Revenue.[186] The special contributions mentioned in the Secret Accounts Bureau were part of the personal relationship between the emperor and his *pao-i* and other high officials, which was institutionalized through the Nei-wu-fu. The accounts were recorded and collected by the managers of the Imperial Household Department, and the funds received, with few exceptions, were paid into the coffers of the Department of the Privy Purse.

At first glance the nature of these transfers of money is not altogether clear. The documents themselves speak of the officials' "taking an active role" (*tzu-hsing*) in reporting their transgressions to the emperor and their "willingness" (*yuan*) to pay thousands of taels to him as a form of repentance. The term most commonly encountered in the accounts is *i-tsui-yin* which seems to mean that the guilty official has "deliberated" about his "crimes" and has proposed payment of a certain amount of "money" as punishment. Other terms refer to "money in recognition of guilt" (*jen-tsui-yin*), "punishment money" (*fa-yin*), or "money in redemption of guilt" (*shu-tsui-yin*).[187]

Although these payments were made with the active partici-pation of a willing official, the emperor—or Ho-shen—seems, in fact, to have prompted them into action by suggesting that they should make some gesture to atone for their behavior. For example, Ho-shen, after reviewing the misdeeds of one of the *pao-i*, the Salt Censor at Ch'ang-lu named Hsi Ning, wrote to him saying that he should voluntarily make a contribution to the Privy Purse as a measure of atonement.[188] It seems likely that when the emperor knew of or had some well-grounded suspicions of an official's mis-conduct, he told the official to confess and repent. Perhaps an artful official himself would at times voluntarily report his misdeeds in the hope that his confession would mitigate the punishment due him from an impending disclosure of his malfeasance.

Although the significance of this bureau was more than merely symbolic, the number of officials making contributions and the number of accounts were not extremely large. The cumulative reports for 1786, 1788, 1795, and 1796, for example, list an average of twenty-three accounts and a slightly higher average of officials. The average amount of the contribution for an official was about 64,000 taels in 1786-1787 and about 79,000 in 1795-1796.[189] The median contribution for the four years, however, was almost 200,000. The majority of the payments, then, were in the few tens of thousands of taels, while a small number of payments reached hundreds of thousands of taels. The largest payments, as we might suspect, came from *pao-i*, such as Li Chih-ying, for his role in the Canton customs office or Ch'üan Te for his administra-tion of the Liang-huai salt monopoly. The offices held by the officials contributing lesser sums are not always indicated, but positions such as Superintendent of Imperial Manufactories at

Soochow, Nanking, and Hangchow, Manager of the Imperial Household Department, Ch'ang-lu and Liang-huai Salt Censor, and the
Superintendents at the Customs Offices at Kalgan and at Canton
are mentioned specifically. The names of Cheng-jui and Fan Ch'ing-
chi also appear. It seems that the archives of the Secret Accounts
Bureau, then, record the contributions or fines of the most favored
and wealthy of the Nei-wu-fu *pao-i*. Lower officials did not occupy
positions of authority which would enable them to appropriate
large amounts of money to their own use. Of the highest *pao-i*
officials, it seems that only the most egregious peculators were
urged to atone for their misdeeds by contributions.

The most skillful financial manipulators among the *pao-i*
may have been able to accumulate substantial fortunes, but they
were not always willing or able to raise the funds for their promised
contributions. In fact, for *pao-i* officials the contributions were
most often pledges of funds, with the payment delayed over a
number of years, rather than immediate transfers of money. The
reports by the Nei-wu-fu from the Secret Accounts Bureau are
really mainly listings of contributions pledged years before but
greatly in arrears. In 1787, for example, of the total of twenty-
seven entries only three had been fully paid up, while fifteen had
been partly paid, and for nine no funds at all had been received.[190]
The records for the year 1796 indicate that, from the second month
of 1795 until the eighth month of 1796, the amount of funds
pledged was 120,000 taels, while the amount actually received was
76,585 taels.[191] The yearly inflow of money, it seems, was not
very large in comparison with the total debt.

The delays in payments may have been the result of several
circumstances. In the first place, no penalties were assessed for
delaying payment, nor do any seem to have been proposed, although it was, of course, in an official's own best interest to try
to make efforts to pay up the amount he had promised. It was
probably in an effort to correct prior lax procedures in enforcing
payment that the Nei-wu-fu managers in the 1790s ordered that
the banner officials from the banners of the delinquent contributors be informed of the arrears in order to put additional pressure

on them to pay up.[192] Another force encouraging delay seems to
have been that the officials invested the funds they pilfered from
the public treasury or from the Privy Purse in real property which
they were reluctant to sell in order to raise the funds necessary to
fulfill their pledges. In 1782, for instance, Hsi Ning made a pledge
of contributions to atone for this inability to make salt merchants
repay their loans. He pledged the sum of 80,000 taels with payments to be made twice a year for eight years. From 1783 to 1787
he complied with this schedule by selling much of his property and
even his wardrobe. In 1788, however, the Nei-wu-fu managers
reported that he still owed 30,000 taels, but the only property he
had left was his residence, worth only 6,000 taels. As a result, he
could not meet his payment. By coincidence, however, Hsi Ning's
nephew, Shu-lin, happened to be in Peking at the time and offered
to donate 6,000 taels from his salary every year in order to help
his uncle pay up his debt. This amount combined with the sale
proceeds of Hsi Ning's house would be sufficient to erase the
amount owed within four years.[193] Another example of the forced
sale of property is that of San-pao, who pledged 110,000 in 1781
and handed over 72,500 by 1786, but had to sell his land and
buildings to raise the remaining 37,500 in 1787.[194]

The information from the Secret Accounts Bureau comple-
ments the evidence from other sources on the role of the Nei-wu-fu
and its officials in the salt administration, customs bureaus, and
imperial manufactories and Ho-shen's role at court. The network
of graft and squeeze, it seems, enveloped not only the *pao-i* officials
in the provinces and the Nei-wu-fu managers in Peking, but also
included the emperor himself. Ch'ien-lung, in particular, used the
Nei-wu-fu to mulct the most prosperous and corrupt of the *pao-i*
through contributions to the Secret Accounts Bureau as a lesser
alternative to outright confiscation of their wealth.

The Tribute System

Another source of wealth for the Imperial Household Department was the presentation of tribute gifts by foreign envoys. Ch'ing
China carried on diplomatic relations through a system of tributary

missions which invariably brought gifts for the Chinese emperor.
From the T'ang dynasty on, these gifts were considered not as
public income, but as a part of the emperor's personal fortune.[195]
For the Ch'ing rulers this probably represented also a continuation
of a Manchu practice current in Nurhachi's time. Accordingly, upon
the conquest of China in 1644, it was decreed that the Residence
for Foreign Tributary Envoys (Hui-t'ung-kuan) should make a
report on the goods brought to the capital to the Board of Rites
and then ship the goods to the Nei-wu-fu.[196] Elephants were handed
over to the Imperial Equipage Department, horses to the Imperial
Pasturage, knives and deerskins to the Imperial Armory. Since these
latter two offices were subdivisions of the Imperial Household
Department, it is clear that the Nei-wu-fu and its sub-offices received all tribute goods except elephants, and sulfur, which was
not even shipped to the capital but reserved for use in the provincial treasuries. The Nei-wu-fu's virtual monopoly on tribute goods
was weakened after 1716, however, when some cumbersome tribute
goods from Annam were transferred to the provincial treasury of
the border province of Kwangsi.[197] Still, throughout the eighteenth
century, all tribute gifts with these minor exceptions, went into
the emperor's personal treasuries.

The actual economic costs and benefits of the tributary system are difficult to estimate. A balance sheet for the system would
contain essentially three items. The presents received by the Chinese
emperor were assets, while the value of the goods given in return to
the foreign envoys and the transportation costs were liabilities.

The transportation costs included shipment from the foreign
country to the border, and shipment from the Chinese border to
the capital. The former were paid by the country bearing tribute.
The latter were paid for, in the first instance, by the local Chinese
government officials and postal system, but later the Nei-wu-fu
seems to have reimbursed them for these costs.[198] The same was
true on the return trip from Peking home. These transportation
expenses may have been substantial in certain cases, but would be
extremely difficult to measure.

The goods exchanged at court either came from or went into

the Imperial Household's treasuries. The various workshops of the Nei-wu-fu manufactured the presents of fur, cloth, leather, porcelain, and jewelry. The vague descriptions in the available sources of the value and numbers of gifts given and received make impossible a precise analysis of the cost or benefit to the throne of the exchange of tributary gifts with all countries. A careful study of Sino-Korean tribute relations concludes, however, that the exchange was very favorable to the Chinese emperor and very unfavorable to the Koreans.[199] At the beginning of the nineteenth century, for instance, the value of the Korean tributary gifts sent to the imperial coffers was about 80,000 taels, while the gifts from the Chinese emperor's personal treasury to the Korean king and to the members of the Korean tributary entourage were valued at approximately 29,000 taels.[200] From this example it would seem that the exchange of tributary gifts, while functioning as a vehicle for the conduct of international relations, also contributed to the emperor's personal fortune.

The Nei-wu-fu's financial role in the tributary system, as in other commercial enterprises, such as the salt monopoly and the customs bureaus, was accompanied by the appointment of *pao-i* from the Imperial Household Department to take part in the management of these activities. The Nei-wu-fu first assumed a role in the management of the tributary envoys when they were ordered to accompany all Europeans who came and went from the court in K'ang-hsi's reign.[201] This measure was probably related to the special relationship the Jesuits enjoyed with the K'ang-hsi Emperor, who placed them under the care of the Nei-wu-fu's Department of the Household Guard and Imperial Hunt while they lived in Peking.[202] The practice of sending *pao-i* to escort Europeans continued into Yung-cheng's reign, when abuses by the *pao-i* caught the emperor's attention.[203] The Ch'ien-lung Emperor followed this precedent,[204] and during his reign the Nei-wu-fu even received similar duties in regard to other countries. In 1790 the Imperial Household Department was entrusted with escorting all foreign envoys, except those from Korea, who would, as before, be handled by officials from the Board of Rites.[205] The original order of 1790 listed only Annam,

Burma, Siam, and Laos, but this was later extended to include all foreign countries except Korea. It was probably in accordance with this order that Ch'ien-lung commanded the Nei-wu-fu *pao-i* Cheng-jui to take care of the arrangements and look after Lord Macartney on his famous mission to Peking in 1793.[206]

In addition to receiving tribute goods and sending out officials to oversee the visits by foreign envoys, the Nei-wu-fu also played a role in the lodging of the tributary envoys and the storing of their goods while they were in the capital. In 1644 the Ming Residence for Foreign Tributary Envoys (Hui-t'ung-kuan) was re-established and served as the quarters for tributary envoys until 1724 when the Koreans were granted separate quarters in the Kan-yü by-street (Kan-yü hu-t'ung).[207] By 1737, however, these quarters had become too inconvenient, so the building was given to the Board of Works and the Koreans' hostel was changed to a house owned by the Nei-wu-fu near An-ting Gate (An-ting-men).[208] Seven years later the Board of Rites declared that the facilities for foreign envoys were insufficient.[209] It reported that, if two missions from different countries happened to arrive at the same time, friction might develop between them if they were housed in one building. While considering the possibility of lodging one of the missions in a temple, it rejected this proposal because it would have been unseemly to station the necessary guards outside a temple. Finally it appealed to the Nei-wu-fu to designate one or two other buildings that could be used as tributary hostels. The department responded by taking thirty-seven rooms in a house it owned near the Cheng-yang Gate (Cheng-yang-men) and combining them with the location at Kan-yu by-street and another near the Yü-ho Bridge (Yü-ho-ch'iao) to make new quarters for the Residence for Foreign Tributary Envoys. In 1748, however, the use of the An-ting Gate location as an envoy hostel was discontinued and it was returned to the Nei-wu-fu.[210]

The Department's Expenditures

The different expenditures of the Imperial Household Department were almost as varied as its many sources of income. Since the main purpose of the department was to sustain the emperor and his household in imperial fashion, vast amounts of money and goods were deployed to this end. In addition, however, the coffers of the Nei-wu-fu were available for other uses. In this manner they differed from the treasuries of the Board of Revenue which were under the control of the regular civilian government officials, their use limited by the need to overcome opposition of the entrenched bureaucratic machinery to unorthodox ways of handling funds. Although the Imperial Household Department had fixed expenditures too, the management of its funds gave more opportunity for the use of the emperor's discretion. The fixed expenditures of the Nei-wu-fu included expenses for maintaining the department's many bureaucratic sub-offices and operating expenses for the palace. Special expenses included such items as the Ch'ien-lung Emperor's southern tours, which were supposed to be fully financed by the Nei-wu-fu but were not.[211]

One of the large elements in the budget of the Nei-wu-fu was repair and construction of the palace. From the beginning of the dynasty special officials patrolled the palace grounds looking for worn-out tiles and other details in need of repair.[212] While constant repairs must have demanded substantial amounts of money, it was construction of new palaces or the refurbishing of old ones that required enormous sums. At the beginning of the dynasty the amounts spent on construction were not as large as might be expected. On the one hand, much of the palace remained intact from the Ming period. On the other hand, in the early years of the dynasty vast sums were not as available as they were later. In any case, the memory of the Ming excesses in this aspect of government was very clear in the minds of the old officials who had served in Ming times, and opposition to large expenditures on the emperor's private life was strong. In fact, the wasteful spending of some eunuchs in proposing additional buildings within the Forbidden City was one of the issues that rationalized the re-establishment of the Nei-wu-fu in 1661.[213]

Expenditures for work on the palaces became significant only in the eighteenth century. The reign of the K'ang-hsi Emperor saw

the beginning of a growth in construction. The Summer Palace was
an example of this. The Yung-cheng Emperor continued these expenditures cautiously, but his successor, Ch'ien-lung, was extrava-
gant.[214] Extremely detailed estimates made by the Nei-wu-fu officials in 1772 and submitted to him for his approval indicate that
the refurbishing of the Ning-shou-kung in the inner palace would
cost over 800,000 taels.[215] By 1775 the estimate had increased to
over 860,000 taels.[216] This project involved over 59,000 artisans
and required the resources of the various vaults of the Privy Purse,
such as the bullion vaults and the porcelain store, as well as those
of the Board of Revenue for 75,000 catties of copper in 1773.[217]
Many of the other construction projects, of course, were not of
this scale. Many, such as the repair of the Ying-t'ai-tien, which cost
9,556 taels, and of the Pao-yuech-lou, which cost 64,300 taels, required only a few thousand or ten thousand taels.[218] But all these
expenditures, however small, were justified and explained in
detailed lists giving the amounts of materials needed and their cost.
Ironically, precise figures for the cost of the most expensive projects of the Nei-wu-fu, such as the construction of the famed
Summer Palace and gardens, are not available. Construction of this
great architectural undertaking started in 1710, but expansion and
additions were in progress continuously throughout the Yung-
cheng and Ch'ien-lung reigns.[219] One author has estimated the cost
of simply repairing the gardens for the period 1710 to 1860 at
180,000,000 taels.[220] The costs of construction would no doubt
increase this figure substantially. Since large projects involved the
Board of Works too, however, it is impossible to know exactly how
much of the expenses for this construction came from the Nei-wu-
fu. Still, any substantial part of such expenses would constitute a
tremendous sum of money.

The emperor not only used Nei-wu-fu funds to care for himself; he used them to aid others. Thus its expenditures included
rewards and charitable expenses. Before 1662 the private coffers
of the emperor were opened to provide for afflicted people in areas
of distress during times of famine or other natural disaster. This
practice was continued after the re-establishment of the Nei-wu-fu

in 1661, as, for instance, in 1679 after an earthquake in the capital when K'ang-hsi released 100,000 taels from the Nei-wu-fu vaults to be distributed to those belonging to the banners (four taels for each room), to commoners (two taels per room) and to impecunious relatives of the dead for burial expenses (two taels for each corpse).[221] Another expenditure by the Imperial Household Department was rewarding victorious generals for their military feats. In 1676, for instance, K'ang-hsi rewarded the General-in-Chief Chao Liang-tung with 100,000 taels to be distributed to him and his troops for their part in the suppression of the rebellion of the three feudatories.[222] Gifts presented to foreign tributary envoys, as mentioned above, came from the Nei-wu-fu coffers, but were usually goods rather than money. Certain occasions stirred the emperor to send certain goods from his privy purse to one of his officials. In 1689, for instance, K'ang-hsi, hearing that the former Minister of the Board of Civil Appointments, A-erh-to, had fallen ill, ordered the imperial physician to look after him and sent him some of his own clothing and ginseng.[223] The Ch'ien-lung Emperor gave away Nei-wu-fu real estate as rewards[224] and granted generous sums for the funerals of favored officials. In 1766, for instance, he ordered the Nei-wu-fu to take 300 taels to prepare a funeral for a Westerner named Lang Shih-ning—the famous Italian painter Giuseppe Castiglione—[225] and in 1784 he spent 5,000 taels on the funeral of Fu-lung-an, his brother-in-law and former grand councilor.[226]

These miscellaneous expenses were current in all three reign periods from 1662 to 1796, but the mid-eighteenth century shows the addition of various new expenses. As the revenues from its various financial operations filled the vaults of the Nei-wu-fu, the emperor could afford to be more generous. Early in his reign Ch'ien-lung restored some of the practices from K'ang-hsi's reign which had been discontinued, such as giving support to the orphanages in the capital.[227] Later he added new items such as the grant of one tael for travel expenses to the daughters of Manchu and *pao-i* who came to the palace for selection as palace maids after 1737.[228] In addition, Ch'ien-lung established various charitable pensions for elderly or sick among the *pao-i* during the early years of his reign, and substantial amounts of clothing and rice were given to sub-officials.[229]

The expenditures of the Nei-wu-fu exhibit some of the same traits that characterized its income. The Ch'ien-lung period was a time of rising expenditures and increasing activity on the part of the Imperial Household Department. While the meticulous listing of expenditures for palace construction indicates an effort to prevent the improper use of funds, surely the growing expenditures benefited not only the emperor himself, but also the Nei-wu-fu *pao-i*.

The Department and the Board of Revenue

The Nei-wu-fu's expenditures for the emperor's personal benefit were to be expected. What is more interesting is that the department disbursed tremendous amounts for public projects as well. In the 1670s it employed funds to help pay for the expenses of campaigns against the three rebellious feudatories,[230] and during the first twenty years of Ch'ien-lung's reign it supported military operations and other public activities.[231] Indeed, the Ch'ien-lung Emperor exclaimed in 1759 that "for years" all expenses for war needs and military settlements (*t'un*) had come from the Nei-wu-fu.[232] The department continued to contribute to public projects in the latter half of the eighteenth century, spending, for example, 5,000,000 taels for construction of city walls in the lower Yangtze urban centers in 1765,[233] 1,500,000 taels for military expenditures in Yunnan in 1768,[234] and 400,000 taels for city wall construction in Chihli in 1781.[235] Through the greater part of the eighteenth century, then, it appears that the Nei-wu-fu was fulfilling some of the functions ordinarily reserved to the Board of Revenue and, accordingly, it should come as no surprise that the department had close ties to the board.

While many details on earlier years remain obscure, it is clear that during Ch'ien-lung's reign the Board of Revenue and the Nei-wu-fu exchanged funds. In the first half of the reign the flow of money was from the board to the Nei-wu-fu, while in the second half the funds went from the Nei-wu-fu to the board.[236] The hundreds of thousands of taels[237] or more which the board sent to the department in the 1740s and 1750s, for example, were used for the military expenses mentioned above. The reason for funding military operations from the Nei-wu-fu may have been related to the department's ties to merchants, such as Fan Yü-pin, who handled supplies, but the emperor's desire for closer personal control over the funds and the personnel handling them was undoubtedly a factor too.

By the 1760s, the flow of funds seems to have reversed. The first hint of a change came in 1763 when Ch'ien-lung, after promoting new sources of income for the department for many years, angrily rejected a proposal to forward some 290,000 taels earned as interest at the Kwangtung salt monopoly to the Nei-wu-fu.[238] Just a few years later, in 1766, he refused a suggestion that the increased revenue from the T'ai-p'ing customs in Kwangtung go to the Nei-wu-fu and ordered that they be sent to the Board of Revenue instead.[239] By 1768 the Nei-wu-fu managers were requesting permission to hand over 1,500,000 taels from their vaults to the Board of Revenue.[240] This flow from the department probably continued through the 1780s and 1790s. In 1784 Ch'ien-lung rebuked the Nei-wu-fu *pao-i* Ch'üan-te for having allowed the Liang-huai salt merchants to contribute 1,000,000 taels to the department when its vaults were well supplied and the moneys were needed for local expenses.[241] And in the 1790s the Nei-wu-fu lost its income from certain items in the salt monopoly which probably were diverted to the Board of Revenue.[242]

While the general outline of the relationship between the Nei-wu-fu and the Board of Revenue is clear, the fiscal significance of the transfers remains something of a mystery. The difficulty in appraising these developments is the lack of figures on the comparative size of the holdings of the board's and the department's treasuries at various times. The amount of funds in the board's vaults are fairly clear for the eighteenth century. When Yung-cheng took the throne, the national treasury held about 8,000,000 taels, but rose to over 60,000,000 taels during his reign.[243] At the time of Ch'ien-lung's succession, the amount in the vaults had declined to between 24,000,000 to 30,000,000 taels, but reached 70,000,000 by the 1780s. Unfortunately, however, analogous figures for the Nei-wu-fu are unavailable. Nevertheless, the above figures provide at least a basis for speculation about the relative size of the different treasuries and the reasons for the transfers of funds.

It seems clear that the reversal of the flow of the moneys in the late eighteenth century was not occasioned by any need of the Board of Revenue, for it had amassed large amounts of funds by this time. Nor does it seem probable that the Nei-wu-fu possessed more funds absolutely than the board and that the change was simply a means of balancing public and private assets more evenly. What appears more likely is that the Nei-wu-fu, although absolutely commanding fewer resources than the board, was considered relatively more prosperous in the late eighteenth century and was therefore obliged to share its wealth with the board. The previous grants of moneys from the board to the department for military expenses may have added to this sense of obligation. This is not to say, however, that other factors, such as the decline in military activity after mid-century, did not also play a role in this change. In fact, the relationship of the privy purse to the public fisc was probably influenced by a wide range of fiscal, military, and political concerns.

Chapter V

TWO ILLUSTRATIVE CASES

The two incidents described below may add substance to the generalizations about the *pao-i* in the Ch'ien-lung period. The first case is a lamentably brief sketch of a major scandal concerning the Nei-wu-fu's role in the management of palace affairs, in particular the problem of eunuch control. The second case concerns the conduct of Nei-wu-fu *pao-i* outside the capital in the provinces—in this instance a remote area of Sinkiang.

The Case of Kao Yun-ts'ung

During the seventh month of 1774, the Vice President of the Board of War, Kao P'u, a Nei-wu-fu *pao-i*, went to Jehol to have an audience with the Emperor.[1] When Ch'ien-lung asked him what matters of note he had observed or heard of lately, he replied that he had heard that a eunuch was divulging the contents of imperial rescripts. Ch'ien-lung was greatly surprised and pressed him for specific details of concrete evidence of such activities. Kao P'u's vague reply mentioned only a eunuch of short stature whose name he did not know. Later, when the Nei-wu-fu manager Fu-lung-an interrogated Kao P'u, he divulged that the officials Kuan-pao, Chiang Tz'u-ch'i, and Wu T'an had been discussing the contents of the various files kept on the officials who served as intendants and district magistrates. These records included the rescripts written by the emperor on the memorials of other officials which commented on the conduct of the intendants and district magistrates (*tao-fu*). The Yung-cheng Emperor had started the practice of keeping such files to provide himself and the grand secretaries with accurate information on the past performance of officials so that they could properly decide whether they were deserving of promotion or demotion.[2]

Further inquiries disclosed that the guilty eunuch worked in the "writing office" (*hsieh-tzu-ch'u*), probably the place where eunuch scribes reproduced imperial rescripts. This office was affiliated with the Inner Chancery of Memorials,[3] which handled communications from the boards and offices in the capital to the emperor as well as palace memorials (*che*)[4] brought to the Ch'ien-ch'ing Gate by the indentured servants of the governor-generals and governors in the provinces. These documents were first received by the officials of the Outer Chancery of Memorials (Tsou-shih kuan-yuan), who turned them over to the eunuchs of the Inner Chancery of Memorials (Tsou-shih t'ai-chien). Originally the Nei-wu-fu had a monopoly on the six posts in the Outer Chancery, but by this time officials from the general bureaucracy had come to occupy a few of these positions.[5] In order to prevent any illicit contacts between the eunuchs and the people on the outside Ch'ien-lung had ordered Ch'un-ning, a trusted member of his Senior Bodyguard (Yü-ch'ien shih-wei), to search out any abuses and report them to him.

A full-scale investigation under the emperor's supervision revealed mismanagement and lax control involving both Nei-wu-fu and regular government administration and showed the extent to which an enterprising eunuch could establish contacts outside the palace.

Of course, some contacts between eunuchs and officials were inevitable. The high officials who worked in the inner palace in such places as the Grand Council, the Mao-ch'in-tien, the Nan-shu-fang, and the Yueh-hua Gate had eunuchs present to wait on them and serve tea.[6] At various times these officials were accustomed to give them some money in consideration for this service, and the Ch'ien-lung Emperor, well aware of this practice, never questioned it. Contact by eunuchs with officials outside the palace or with lower officials who worked inside the palace, however, was strictly forbidden.

The investigation indicated that the guilty eunuch, Kao Yun-ts'ung, had several acquaintances among officials inside and outside the palace. For example, one Hui-ling, the son of the faithful official Na-yen-t'ai, worked in the Outer Chancery of Memorials, yet was a friend of Kao and sought favors from him.[7] For this he was later dismissed, given forty strokes with the bamboo, and ordered to repent by serving time in the *Nien-kan-ch'u* (literally "the pasting rod office"). Another acquaintance of Kao was Ni Ch'eng-k'uan, who worked in the Imperial Study (Shang-shu-fang).[8] He introduced Kao to a friend named Shen Pao. For this he was later dismissed and handed over to the Board of Punishments.

Perhaps the closest friend of Kao was Chiang Tz'u-ch'i, the son of the Grand Secretary Chiang P'u, who had only recently received an official post. Kao Yun-ts'ung's relationship with him dated back some years to a time when Chiang's father and older brother had served in the inner palace.[9] Therefore, in 1774, when Kao was cheated in certain real estate transactions, he asked the Grand Secretary Yü Min-chung to seek Chiang's help for him.[10]

When Ch'ien-lung learned of this, he was clearly upset:

> The various officials in the Nei-wu-fu work with eunuchs and have contacts with them. This is only natural. But if they speak one word about private matters, they should report it to me... Yü has worked at my side for years. How is it that he does not know the way I operate and wants to hide this matter from me? Yü works in the Grand Council as a Grand Secretary and speaks with me every day. Why didn't he tell me about this?[11]

Chiang Tz'u-ch'i's importance in the case, however, concerned not his friendship with Yü Min-chung but with another official, Wu T'an. It was Wu and Chiang who had connived with Kao Yun-ts'ung to disclose the files. Wu was an able official who had served in the Board of Punishments and as a Financial Commissioner,[12] and Ch'ien-lung had intended to employ him in the future as Governor-General of Kiangsu and even perhaps as President of the Board of Punishments. Wu's reason for plotting with Kao and Chiang to discover the contents of the imperial rescripts is unknown. His motivation puzzled Ch'ien-lung, who could only speculate that perhaps he had hoped to gain a rapid promotion by using the contents in some way. Perhaps the lack of clarity as to motive was one factor in Ch'ien-lung's releasing Wu and Chiang without further punishment, although ostensibly he did so because they had refrained from aggravating their crimes by taking bribes.[13]

Besides the above acquaintances, Kao Yun-ts'ung also had friends in the Nei-wu-fu. Most notable was Li Wen-chao, a Nei-wu-fu *pao-i* who had toiled for many years in the *ju-i-kuan*, the palace art studio.[14] Like other Nei-wu-fu officials at this time, he liked to strike up acquaintances with the eunuchs and apparently did so with Kao. Reviewing his years of diligent service in the *ju-i-kuan*, Ch'ien-lung appointed him as Canton Customs Superintendent in the third month of 1774.[15] As Li was preparing to leave Peking, Kao went to see him and asked him to take his brother, Kao Yun-hui, as his personal servant. Li agreed and left for Canton with Kao Yun-hui.

Kao Yun-ts'ung also arranged for positions in customs bureaus for his older brother, Kao Yun-chang, and another younger brother, Kao Yun-lung, through other friends.[16] Unfortunately, information is available only on the latter. In the spring of 1771, Kao Yun-ts'ung requested his friend, the Judicial Commissioner Yao Li-te in Lin-ch'ing department in Shantung, to recommend his younger brother, Kao Yun-lung, who was traveling in Shantung as a personal servant to one of the officials there. As a result of Yao's recommendation, Kao Yun-lung received a position in the customs bureau at Wei-chia Bay as attendant to the Department Magistrate Wan Mien-ch'ien.[17] During his stint at this bureau, Kao Yun-lung made friends with Wang Erh, the indentured servant of the official Hu Te-lin. After Wang was transferred to another post, Kao Yun-lung worked for Yao Li-te under the pseudonym Kao Sheng. In 1773 Yao recommended him to Hu Te-lin, then the Prefect of Tung-ch'ang,[18] who took him in on the strength of his connections with Wang Erh and Yao Li-te. Later Hu recommended him to Wang P'u, the Deputy Magistrate of Lin-ch'ing, who was under Hu's supervision. Wang, who did not know that Kao Sheng was Kao Yun-ts'ung's brother, employed him at the customs bureau at Wei-chia Bay.[19]

When the investigation of the case revealed these facts to

Ch'ien-lung, he analyzed the hiring of Kao Yun-hui in the following terms:

> The relatives of eunuchs should stay down on the farm and attend to agriculture or occupy themselves in a small business. If they become the personal servants of customs superintendents it can be for no other reason than that they want to demand money at the customs offices, to burden the merchants, and to steal taxes.[20]

The emperor was clearly furious with Li Wen-chao's hiring Kao Yun-hui:

> Li Wen-chao is a Nei-wu-fu official. I have just been kind enough to appoint him to the Canton Customs Bureau and yet he dares to communicate with eunuchs and accept their requests. This is outrageous. Have Li dismissed and have him come to the capital to be interrogated by the Nei-wu-fu managers.[21]

He also vented his anger on Ying-lien and Su-ho-te. "Ying-lien is a Nei-wu-fu manager and should know all that goes on in the palace. Su-ho-te has been working in the Grand Council for a year already. How is it that they don't know of this matter?"[22]

As for Wang P'u, Hu Te-lin, and Yao Li-te, Ch'ien-lung had them all dismissed. In addition, Yao was ordered to "take an active role in deliberating on his crimes," that is, make a contribution to the Nei-wu-fu's Secret Account Archives.[23]

Several other consequences followed from the misconduct of Kao and his friends. The most dramatic was Kao's beheading.[24] His property was confiscated by Ying-lien and, of course, turned over to the Nei-wu-fu. Furthermore, these punitive measures were accompanied by an institutional change in the Outer Chancery of Memorials. After 1774 only the communications from the Grand Council passed through the hands of the eunuchs in the Inner Chancery of Memorials. All other palace memorials (*tsou-che*) coming from various officials were to be received and transmitted by the officials of the Outer Chancery of Memorials. Even the communications from the Nei-wu-fu which dealt only with household matters were also to be transmitted to the emperor through the officials of the Outer Chancery. No palace memorials (except those from the Grand Secretaries) would be transmitted by eunuchs and, since officials would not have the chance to communicate with them, no confidential information would be disclosed.[25]

The Case of Kao P'u

One example of large-scale peculation by a Nei-wu-fu *pao-i* is that by Kao P'u (mentioned above), the Imperial Agent at Yarkand (Yeh-erh-ch'iang) in Sinkiang from 1776 to 1778. We are fortunate in having two collections of documents concerning Kao's illicit conduct which provide us with one of the most detailed views of eighteenth-century official corruption available in extant Chinese sources. The first source is the valuable and widely available "veritable records" for these years. More unusual and more informative are the almost one hundred memorials and rescripts concerning the investigation of Kao P'u's activities by provincial officials published in *Shih-liao hsun-k'an* in the early 1930s. These documents afford us the rare opportunity to observe how the Ch'ing bureaucracy, and especially the Nei-wu-fu *pao-i*, were operating in the late eighteenth century. The account that follows has been constructed by piecing together the complementary, and at times conflicting, testimony and reports of offenders and officials which appear mainly in *Shih-liao hsun-k'an*. While mention of these sources has been made in various articles, they have not been fully exploited.[26]

Kao P'u's Background

Kao P'u was a member of a very illustrious *pao-i* family of the bordered yellow banner. The origins of the family are unclear, but its rise to prominence in the eighteenth century seems to have been related to two developments. One was the administrative ability demonstrated by Kao Pin, one of its members who served well in several Nei-wu-fu positions before 1735. The other development was the selection of one of Kao Pin's daughters for service in the palace and her subsequent elevation to the rank of Concubine of the Second Rank in 1735. In this year Kao Pin, along with his immediate family, was freed from *pao-i* status. Afterwards he enjoyed a splendid government career, rising to the post of Grand Secretary and his daughter attained the rank of Concubine of the First Rank. One of Kao Pin's sons, Kao Heng, also served in high posts in government. He was Kao P'u's father.

Kao Heng's career presaged in certain respects that of his son. Although he enjoyed meritorious tenure in various government offices, including the post of Liang-huai Salt Censor, his career came to a sudden and violent conclusion. Unlike most government officials, Kao Heng did not gain entry into officialdom through the examination system. It appears that he never took the *sheng-yuan*, *chü-jen,* or *chin-shih* exams, but received his first appointment, that of a Secretary in the Board of Revenue, in 1740 through the *yin* privilege his father possessed.[27] Later he was promoted to Department Director, then to Superintendent of the Shan-hai-kuan Customs Bureau. At this latter post his conscientious attitude so impressed Ch'ien-lung that he gave him permission to deduct 4,000 taels of the excess revenues for his own personal use and to contribute another 14,000 from the same source to pay off debts his father owed the state.[28] Again in 1751 Ch'ien-lung allowed him to take 15,000 taels from the extra customs revenues and keep 4,000 for himself, while paying off the last of his father's debts with the rest.[29] Kao Heng continued his promising career as Ch'ang-lu Salt Censor and later, after an interlude as the Brigade General at Tientsin, as Superintendent of the Huai-an Customs. As superintendent he further ingratiated himself with the emperor by contributing funds to a project by local officials to teach the people of Hai-an how to produce cotton textiles.[30]

The death of his father in 1755 did not seriously affect his career. He took off three months and then took the post of Superintendent of the Kalgan Customs Bureau. After another tour of duty at the Huai-an Customs he achieved the most important position of his career, that of Liang-huai Salt Censor, in 1757. Here he further distinguished himself by impeaching the Inspector of

Salt Distribution, Chang Yung-kuei, a Nei-wu-fu *pao-i* whom Kao Heng himself had recommended, for his double dealing and poor administration.[31] In 1761 he became Acting Superintendent of the Imperial Manufactories at Soochow. In this position he received the first rebuke of his career for having yielded to a request by an official named Fu-te, who accompanied Ch'ien-lung on a southern tour, to sell 3,000 taels worth of ginseng for one of Fu-te's indentured servants.[32] Ch'ien-lung let the incident pass, however, with simply a reprimand and a warning. Kao Heng was allowed to stay on as Liang-huai Salt Censor. In subsequent years he regained the emperor's confidence by his efficient administration which saved money that could then be sent to the Nei-wu-fu[33] and by his forthright denunciation of the wrongdoings of other officials.[34] Most of all, Ch'ien-lung was pleased that Kao Heng had eliminated all the abuses long present in the Liang-huai salt administration.[35]

In 1765, when his cousin Kao Chin was promoted to Governor-General of Kiangsu, Anwhei, and Kiangsi, Kao Heng was transferred, under the law of avoidance, to the post of Acting Department Director of the Board of Revenue, where he gained further merit by capturing a eunuch who had stolen gold registers. Probably as a reward for this last accomplishment he received an appointment as Manager of the Imperial Household Department. In later years he became a lieutenant-general of the plain white Han-chün banner and later of the plain white Manchu banner.

Only in 1768, several years after Kao Heng had left the Liang-huai Salt Administration, did another side of his administrative activities come to light. In that year, P'u-fu, a Nei-wu-fu *pao-i*[36] who had succeeded Kao Heng at the salt monopoly, offered to send an extra 190,000 taels from the salt revenues to the Nei-wu-fu.[37] This aroused the suspicions of Yu Pa-shih, another imperial bondservant, who wondered where these funds would come from. Shortly afterwards, the newly appointed Kiangsu Governor, Chang Pao, followed up this lead by interrogating the head merchant Chiang Ch'un and others. After repeated questioning they finally admitted that for years Kao Heng had been concealing the actual revenues of the salt monopoly and, with the acquiescence of the head merchants, pocketing the difference. The total unaccounted funds came to more than 10,900,000 taels, while individual payments to Kao Heng by the salt merchants included some for 85,000 taels.[38] When this news broke, Kao Heng was immediately removed from his position and, later, after a full investigation substantiated the testimony of the head merchants, he was executed for embezzlement.

At the time of his father's death, Kao P'u[39] was serving as an assistant department director in the Board of Civil Appointments. Previously he had served a term as assistant department director in the Nei-wu-fu's Imperial Armory. In 1770 he received a joint appointment to the Store for Painting Materials (Yen-liao-k'u) and in the next year he was transferred to Kwangsi as a censor. While in this position he caught the attention of the emperor for his suggestion that the abuses of the sub-officials at the local government offices could be reduced by assuring that the secretaries (*shu-li*) were sent home when their term of duty was complete and that they did not return to the office on the sly for illicit purposes. Kao P'u later received appointments to positions as Metropolitan Censor and Shantung Grain Transport Censor (Hsun-shih Shan-tung ts'ao-wu). In 1772 he suggested enforcing strictly the limit of 126 piculs for local agricultural products on each grain transport ship. He feared that, if this restriction were not observed, the sailors would overload the boats with these goods and impede navigation. The Grand Councilors agreed with him and reimposed punishment on those overloading the ships. Later that year he was promoted to the post of Senior Vice President of the Censorate.

A short time later Kao P'u met the first serious reprimand of his career. In the ninth month of 1772, he did not take his place in the ceremony on the occasion of the lunar eclipse. The Ch'ien-lung Emperor noticed this and criticized him, saying:

> Even though Kao P'u is really quite young, I was particularly generous to him, promoting him in a most unusual manner because he had shown that he knew how to work hard. Previously I had had doubts about him because of his fondness

for levity and knew that at times he went beyond the bounds
of propriety, but how can he go so far as to shirk his public
duties? It seems that in performing his daily work before me
he gives the appearance of being diligent, but when he is out
of my presence he tries to take it easy. How can such conduct serve the interests of proper government administration?[40]

The Board of Punishments recommended that Kao P'u be demoted
one rank, but Ch'ien-lung relented and allowed him to remain at
his post, although he was nominally dismissed.

In 1773 he became Acting Senior Vice President of the Board
of Public Works and, later, of the Board of War. The next year he
devised and administered a plan under which those military and
civil officials serving in the military camps who had not applied in
time for honors would be allowed an extension for one year after
a victorious campaign. Soon afterwards he became a Senior Vice
President of the Board of War and a few months later reported to
Ch'ien-lung the divulgence of secret information by the eunuch
Kao Yun-ts'ung. While Ch'ien-lung was delighted that Kao P'u had
brought this situation to his attention, he criticized him as being
"an officious little man" and then continued:

If Kao P'u congratulates himself on his conduct and becomes
pleased with himself, this will confirm my opinion of him as
a man of little character. Moreover, if Kao P'u thinks that his
conduct in this affair so clearly demonstrates his rectitude
that he need not be cautious or fearful and can willfully engage in corruption, then let the fate of Kao Yun-ts'ung [i.e.,
execution] serve as an example of what will happen to him. I
will not show any mercy towards him in the future.[41]

In the short run this reprimand seems to have influenced Kao
P'u's conduct. His behavior in the following two years seems to
have been above serious reproach. Later in 1773, for example, the
Grand Secretaries approved an innovative suggestion by Kao P'u
for a change in the policy of grain sales from the banner grain
stores. His plan consisted of having officials in the Board of Revenue

in the capital review the prices at which the banner grain stores
were selling their grain through monthly reports and personal inspection. In 1776, after receiving a position as a banner captain,
Kao P'u became a deputy lieutenant general first in the bordered
blue Manchu banner and later in the plain white Manchu banner.
He also held a concurrent post of Acting Senior Vice President
in the Board of Rites.

Finally, in the tenth month of 1776, he received an order as
Department Director of the Board of War and Acting Department
Director in the Board of Rites to go to Yarkand in Sinkiang to
replace the imperial agent, Ma Hsing-a, who was to return to the
capital to take over Kao P'u's duties in the Board of Rites and the
Board of War.[42]

Kao P'u's Activities

Yarkand was a trading town located at the western end of the
Tarim Basin in Sinkiang near the present-day border with Afghanis-
tan to the west, Kashmir to the south, and Turkestan to the north.
Yarkand and other towns along the northern and southern rim of
the basin served as the administrative centers for Manchu rule over
the local Moslem population. Following the conquest by Manchu
forces in the 1750s, Sinkiang was not ruled by a regular hierarchy
of provincial officials but by several imperial agents stationed in
the various towns. Overall supervision and coordination of policy
in Sinkiang was the duty of the Chief Imperial Agent in Sinkiang
(Tsung-pan hui-chiang shih-wu ta-ch'en).[43] Although stationed in
the city of Wu-shih, on the northern rim of the basin, he was supposed to visit all the towns personally on regular tours of inspection. Below him were various imperial agents each of whom
managed the affairs of one town and the surrounding area with
the help of an assistant agent (hsieh-t'ung pan-shih ta-ch'en).[44]
In addition to these officials, each major town also had a Moslem
local governor (ak'im beg), and assistant governor (ishhan beg). The
begs were the representatives of the Moslem interests, but were
appointed by the imperial agent, with the approval of the emperor,
from among the cooperative local leaders.

The duties of the imperial agent seem to have consisted of overseeing matters in the town and preventing the occurrence of disturbances which might undermine or directly threaten Manchu hegemony in the Tarim Basin. Chinese green standard and Manchu banner troops were stationed in the various towns,[45] but the imperial agents, through cooperation with the *begs*, were expected to settle peacefully any dispute that might arise from friction between the Chinese-Manchu administration and the Moslem populace.

Yarkand was well known in Sinkiang as a major commercial center. Its bazaar, or Moslem market street, is reported to have been three miles in length, and its rice, grain, melons, and fruits were reputed to be the best in Sinkiang.[46] In addition, the surrounding area also produced sheepskins, Moslem cloth, gold, and jade, which merchants from across the border and from China proper came to purchase.

The Yarkand region possessed two major sources of jade.[47] One was the bed of nearby rivers where teams of twenty to thirty Moslems, under the supervision of an official and a soldier, waded shoulder to shoulder through the shallow waters feeling the riverbed with their feet to detect pieces of jade. The other source of jade was a mountain called Mi-erh-tai, a few hundred miles from Yarkand, where fine specimens of "mountain jade" (*shan-shih*) of five different hues and weighing up to 10,000 catties could be found in the highest, almost inaccessible, slopes. The Moslems mined this jade by riding up on agile yaks and using hammers and chisels to dislodge the clusters of jade which they then dropped down the steep slopes and later picked up at the foot of the mountain. In the 1770s the Imperial Agent in Yarkand generally sent from 7,000 to 10,000 catties of jade taken from these two sources to Peking, although there was no set quota.

All mining of jade except for purposes of shipment to Peking was prohibited.[48] In 1773, however, Ch'ien-lung approved a suggestion of the junior vice-president of one of the six boards, Ch'i-ch'eng-o, to expand the gathering of jade and to permit merchants and soldiers to buy on credit up to fifty catties each. The merchants purchasing this jade received government permits indicating that the jade was not contraband. Traders bought up about 60 percent of this production for local use, while the Moslem jade gatherers received the rest as compensation.[49] Later the limit on sales to merchants increased. For all jade the traders still received permits but, when they brought the jade from the increased quotas to the customs bureaus on their way back into China proper, the customs officials did not bother to verify that the amount of jade corresponded exactly with the number of permits. In some cases even merchants who had no permits at all slipped through.

Within a few years the sale of jade had reached substantial proportions. In 1775 alone Kao P'u's predecessor, Ma Hsing-a, sold over 10,000 catties of government jade to various merchants, including 4,200 catties to the Shensi trader Chao Chün-jui. Although Ch'ien-lung was aware of the general nature of these transactions, Ma and the assistant agent Shu-pao set low prices and manipulated transactions so that they could buy up the jade cheaply themselves or allow selected merchants to do so.[50] It seems, then, that by the time of Kao P'u's appointment the imperial agent in Yarkand was already involved in shady commercial dealings.

Kao P'u left the capital for his post in Yarkand sometime late in the eleventh month of 1776.[51] He was accompanied by an entourage of personal attendants including Hsiung-lien, his secretary, and Shen T'ai and Ch'ang Yung, his indentured servants. Hsiung-lien had originally been a soldier in the Chinese banner garrison at Chinkiang on the Yangtze below Nanking, but in 1762 he was permitted to abandon his banner status.[52] He went to the capital and became a commoner with residence in Ta-hsing district just outside Peking. He taught Manchu language for a while and then received a position writing out memorials for Kao P'u, who must have appreciated his work, for he gave Hsiung-lien money to purchase the *chien-sheng* degree. Afterwards Hsiung-lien worked as a scribe in the office for compilation of the Imperial Manuscript Library before joining Kao P'u to go to Sinkiang. Although the backgrounds of Shen T'ai and Ch'ang Yung seem more obscure than that of Hsiung-lien, their activities en route to Yarkand were more apparent than his.

As an official proceeding to a government post, Kao P'u enjoyed the right to use the facilities of the state postal system for
food, lodging, and horses. The administration of the postal stations
at this time was under the direct management of the local grain and
salt intendants (*liang-yen tao*) in most provinces and of the provincial judicial officer in Chihli Province.[53] Since these officials
were stationed in the provincial capital, they found it difficult to
oversee the network of postal stations, which extended throughout
a province, and shortcomings became apparent in the services provided by the stations. The most common deficiency, which led to
various abuses, was the lack of suitable horses. This was due to the
department and district magistrates' appropriation for their own
use of much of the funds apportioned for the expenses of fodder-
ing the horses. One frequent practice was called "relying on the
horses of a previous postal station" (*ta kuo-chan*), and consisted
of re-employing the horses of the previous postal station rather
than supplying fresh mounts.[54] Under these circumstances, the
local officials or their indentured servants willingly submitted to
extortion of a dozen or sometimes several dozen taels by any imperial commissioned official passing through, because these exactions were less than the amount they could gain from embezzling
the sums intended for the provisioning of straw.

Kao P'u's route led him southwest from the capital through
the city of Paoting and westward into Shansi. In addition to the
officially sanctioned amenities which Kao P'u and his retinue were
entitled to, Shen and Ch'ang demanded contributions of money
from the officials and sub-officials who managed the local postal
stations along the route. The first station outside the capital, that
in Liangsiang, was a very busy station, and therefore Shen and
Ch'ang did not dare ask for money for fear of being observed by
other officials.[55] However, when they arrived in Cho Department
about thirty miles from Peking they forced the department magistrate to hand over four taels to them. Farther on in An-su district
they extorted six taels.[56]

When Kao P'u and his entourage passed through Paoting,
about ninety miles from Peking, they stayed at the memorial hall

dedicated to the early Ch'ing official Yü Ch'eng-lung, because Tsingyuan district had no public hostel. The district magistrate's indentured servant, Li Yü, was at the postal station when Kao P'u arrived.[57] Shen T'ai appears to have asked Li and a companion a question or made some request of them, possibly in connection with the provisioning of horses for the next day's journey. When they failed to hear this request or ignored it, Shen T'ai came up to Li and berated them for their insolence, saying, "Are you pretending to be stupid?" (*Ni-men chuang hu-t'u ma*)?[58] Li paid no attention to Shen and went about his duties. Later, his master, the district magistrate Cheng Chih-chin, arrived and, as was his custom, arranged horses for the next stage of the officials' journey before returning to his office to take care of other matters.

Later that day at mealtime, Kao P'u, while dining in the postal station, complained to Li of the lack of fine bean sauce (*ch'ing-chiang*) and demanded that he procure some immediately. Li could not buy any at that time, so he mixed together brown sugar with salt water and sent this in to Kao P'u instead. When this concoction reached his lips, Kao P'u exploded, cursing Li for his laziness and ordering Shen to give him a good beating with a horse whip. Since it was winter, Li was wearing padded clothing and was not injured by the beating, but the next day he reported to his master what had transpired. Cheng, however, did not consider this incident worthy of mention to his superiors.

As Kao P'u's entourage approached the Shansi border, Shen and Ch'ang went ahead to the post stations in Cheng-ting and Huo-lu districts and extorted four taels from the officials in charge.[59] At the Tsingsing district post station, a chieftain of the native tribes of Ming-cheng in Szechwan who was going to present tribute at the court in Peking was present at the station, and an intendant (*tao-yuan*) came to send him off when Shen and Ch'ang arrived. Since Kao P'u did not stay over at this postal station, but merely changed horses, Shen and Ch'ang had no opportunity to make demands there. The postal stations in Shansi, however, provided them with better opportunities. In fact, as Kao P'u and his followers got farther from the capital, the amount Ch'ang and Shen were able to extort gradually increased to fifty or sixty taels from a single post station.[60]

In the fourth month of 1777, Kao P'u finally arrived in Yarkand. When he assumed his duties as imperial agent, one of those who came to pay him a courtesy visit was Chao Chün-jui, the Moslem merchant from Weinan County in Shensi who had bought a large part of the jade sold by Kao P'u's predecessor, Ma Hsing-a. Chao's father, Chao Chin-kuei, was a cobbler in the city of Su-chou (modern Kiuchuan) in Kansu who had adopted a young apprentice named Chin Pao who became Chao Chün-jui's younger brother.[61]

In the 1750s Chao Chün-jui engaged in business in various towns in Sinkiang such as Yarkand and Akosu. Sometime after 1755 he held the position of public lecturer on the sacred edicts (*hsiang-yueh*) in the city of Kuche on the northern rim of the Tarim Basin. During these years he opened a shop in Yarkand and began to buy jade, which he entrusted to his employees Yü Chin-pao, Hsu Tzu-chien, and others to transport to Soochow in the lower Yangtze. There they sold the jade and bought silks and tea which could be marketed in Akosu and other towns on the northern rim of the Tarim Basin where Chao maintained commercial contacts. During this time Chao was careful to cultivate good relations with the local Moslem *begs*. His success in establishing amicable relations with officialdom and his managerial skills assured the prosperity of these business operations which earned a handsome profit every year.

To maintain contacts and manage his business, Chao frequently made trips through Sinkiang and China proper. In 1777, for instance, he and Chao Shih-pao, an adopted son who helped him manage his far-flung commercial enterprises, made a trip to Soochow to collect debts.[62] In Soochow they stayed in the warehouse of a candle and charcoal shop owned by a man who stored the jade brought by Yü chin-pao and Hsu Tzu-chien on their trips to Soochow. Chao Shih-pao bought up 4,000 separate items, including silk cloth, purses, handkerchiefs, satin and velvet cloth, and more than ten baskets of tea leaves to take back to Sinkiang.

Chao Chün-jui's property holdings indicate the prosperity he enjoyed in these commercial dealings. In Weinan district he owned a large house of 24 rooms, shops with a total of 22 rooms, 78 mou of dry land worth 1,400 taels, 6 horses and mules, and assorted personal property.[63] In Yarkand, Akosu, and other towns in Sinkiang he had another home, a restaurant, 4 shops and 15 mules and horses. In Akosu he had 70 rented camels, and in Su-chou, 90.

During Kao P'u's first days in Yarkand, Chao came several times to present gifts of jade to him. Later he often went to Kao's office and passed the time there.[64] During Kao's first year of tenure, Chao took him on a trip to the Shih-san-t'ai region, probably to search for jade. These efforts to cultivate good relations with Kao P'u were undoubtedly related to Chao's desire to maintain his advantage over his competitors by retaining his role as the chief buyer of jade in Yarkand.

One of these competitors was Chang Luan, a merchant from northern Shansi who made Kao P'u's acquaintance in the tenth month of 1777. Chang was a *chien-sheng* holder in his thirties who lived together in Sha-hu-k'ou with his uncle and his older brother, who worked as a secretary (*shu-pan*) in the customs bureau there.[65] In 1768 Chang Luan had taken a position as a clerk in a cloth and variety shop called "The Three Righteous Principles" (san-i) in the town of Kuei-hua in Shansi.[66] Later his brother joined him as an employee in this same store, which was one in a chain of shops of the same name located in other towns, such as Akosu and Urumchi, and owned by the merchant Chia Yu-k'u, who was from the same district as the two Chang brothers.

Originally Chia and two partners had started the chain of stores with a joint pooling of capital in 1747, but later the other partners died, leaving Chia to handle all the business himself.[67] In these circumstances he was eager to find competent branch managers to aid him, so after a year's trial at the Kuei-hua store he appointed Chang Luan in 1769 to head the shop in Akosu. After a few years, however, Chang unexpectedly took more than 10,000 taels from the store's cash reserves, used this sum to buy up jade, and went off to Soochow. In 1775 he sent back over 9,000 taels, but Chia was not satisfied and went to Soochow to search for him. Finally he found Chang, who told him that he had sold the jade for a total of over 23,000 taels and had sent back three shipments of money to Chia, one of 9,000 taels and two of 5,500 taels.[68] The remaining 3,000 taels Chang said he would keep for himself as his profit. Part of this sum he may have used to purchase his *chien-sheng* degree. In any case, at this point—sometime in 1776—Chia, having realized that Chang was an unscrupulous fellow, severed all connections with him.[69]

In the second half of 1776 Chang Luan and his brother returned home and entered into a business partnership with their relative Jen Hsiao-tsai and the merchants Wei Ch'üan-i and Feng Chih-an. The first partner, Jen, was a relative from the same area as Chang Luan, who quit his job in the Sha-hu-k'ou Customs Bureau to take part in the joint business venture with the Chang brothers and the others.[70] The second partner, Wei Ch'üan-i, was a silk trader from Küwo District in southern Shansi,[71] who had formed a partnership in 1770 with a merchant from Kansu named Wei Chia-shih to ship Soochow silks to Kansu for sale.[72] In 1773 Wei Ch'üan-i, an only son, left his mother, wife, and adopted son[73] in his fifteen-room house in the village of Hsiao-nan-chuang and went to Soochow, where he rented a house and traded in silk, copper, porcelain, and jade. In the hope of siring a son, he took a concubine and did not return home. He first met Chang Luan in 1776 when Chang came to Soochow carrying a letter of introduction from Wei Chia-shih.[74] The third partner, Feng Chih-an, was a 29-year-old merchant from Fenyang district in southern Shansi.[75] He previously had done business with the Three Righteous Principles Shop in Sha-hu-k'ou and had acted as its agent in shipping goods to Yarkand. It was in this connection that he became familiar with Chang Luan.

The partnership formed at the end of 1776 between the Chang brothers, Jen, Wei, and Feng, consisted of contributions of 6,000 taels from the brothers jointly, 6,000 taels from Wei, and 1,000 taels from Jen.[76] Feng did not contribute any capital but was to receive a salary for his participation. The aim of this business venture was to buy jade in Yarkand and transport it to Soochow for sale. The money gained from the sale of the jade was used to buy silks which could be marketed in Kansu and Sinkiang. After setting up the partnership, Chang Luan and Feng went to Yarkand to arrange for the purchase of jade. In the first months of 1777 Chang's commercial dealings in Yarkand seem to have been mostly in silk, which he probably brought with him from Sha-hu-k'ou.[77] He must have sold a good deal of silk, for his interpreter, Ho-chin-erh, recorded debts owed to him by various Moslems for purchases of silk during this period which totaled almost 10,000 taels of silver. Significantly, O-tui, the Moslem *ak'im beg*, or local governor of Yarkand, owed almost 8,000 taels.[78]

While Chang was looking for jade in Yarkand in the tenth month of 1777 he made the acquaintance of Kao P'u.[79] By this time Kao P'u had accumulated over 2,800 catties of jade on his estate south of the city and wanted to market them. He requested Chang Luan to do this for him. Chang agreed, and they decided to divide the proceeds from the sale of the jade into seven shares of about 400 catties each. Kao P'u was to receive five shares, while Chang Luan was to receive two.

Kao P'u seems to have been reluctant to allow Chang Luan to ship the jade by himself; he probably wanted one of his associates to accompany the shipment for security reasons. In his discussion with Chang he arranged for his secretary, Hsiung-lien, to go along. When Kao P'u told Hsiung-lien that "I have collected some jade which I want taken to Soochow to be sold," Hsiung-lien repeatedly entreated Kao P'u not to carry out the plan. Hsiung-lien, however, was indebted to Kao P'u for loaning him 360 taels to purchase a brevet rank of First Class Assistant Department Magistrate[80] and for using his influence with the Department Director of the Board of War, To-lung-wu, to expedite this matter.[81] In addition, Kao P'u told Hsiung-lien, "You go on to Soochow and, if in the future the enterprise makes a profit, I will give you 4,000 taels."[82] Hsiung-lien, who had been intending to return to the capital for several months, finally acquiesced. In addition, Kao P'u also ordered his indentured servant Li Fu to go with them. Accordingly, on the eleventh day of the tenth month of 1777, Chang, Hsiung-lien, Li, and Feng left Yarkand for Soochow carrying about 2,800 catties of jade in sixteen carts.

Kao P'u's administration of matters in Yarkand up until his acquaintance with Chang Luan was undistinguished. It seems that he appointed two *begs* during this period and demanded bribes from both of them.[83] He probably continued the sale of government jade in the same way as his predecessor Ma Hsing-a had done. At least part of the money Kao P'u made on these illegal dealings he sent back to the capital through friends and fellow officials in Sinkiang who were returning to Peking. For example, he entrusted a clerk with 1,500 taels of silver.[84] The clerk arrived in Peking in the winter of 1777 with four packages of silver which he gave to Ku-pen, one of Kao P'u's indentured servants, to deliver to Kao P'u's wife who had remained in Peking. Of this amount, about 800 taels were used to buy 200 mou of land in Cho department just southwest of Peking, while the remainder was spent on redeeming pawned articles, paying for rice debts at the end of the year, and various household expenses at Kao P'u's residence in Peking. Also in 1777 Kao P'u sent back 500 taels through a senior bodyguard in order to purchase the brevet rank for Hsiung-lien for 360 taels and to contribute 140 taels to attain a higher rank of posthumous honor for one of Kao P'u's ancestors.[85]

Several times during early 1778, after his acquaintance with Chang Luan, friends of Kao P'u returned to the capital with silver and gold. Two who transported Kao P'u's money and goods to Peking were a friend named Ch'i-li-t'u and a senior bodyguard named Ch'o-k'o-t'o.[86] Another senior bodyguard, Na-su-t'u, was a good friend of Kao P'u who also brought back various items to Peking. When he arrived at Kao's residence in Peking, he had dinner with Ku-pen and Kao P'u's nephew, Shuang-ch'ing, who was a student in a government school.[87] On that occasion Ku-pen noticed that the list of items Na-su-t'u had brought did not correspond to that which Kao P'u had sent them in a letter and inquired why this was so. Na-su-t'u replied that Ch'ang Yung would come with the other items he had not brought.

Kao P'u's other financial activities at this time seem to have involved substantial business transactions both in Yarkand and in Peking. Early in 1778, for instance, Kao P'u borrowed 1,300 taels from a friend of his named Sung Kuo-ts'ung, a Department Director in the Board of War.[88] The year before Kao P'u, while in Yarkand, had bought some land just east of Peking for 2,600 taels, and so now he had a friend named Wang Ch'i go back to the capital to receive this land.[89] Later Kao P'u's indentured servant, Ch'ang-sheng, rented out this land for his master and received the yearly rents for him.[90]

On their journey to China proper, Chang, Hsiung-lien, Li, and Feng took the southern route from Yarkand, passing along the southern rim of the Tarim Basin, crossing the border into Kansu, and passing through Tunhuang before arriving in the town of Ansi, where the northern and southern routes around the Tarim Basin meet. From Ansi they proceeded on through the Jade Gate and shortly afterwards they came to the Chia-ku Customs Bureau. Previously Ch'ien-lung had heard that large pieces of jade were slipping through this major customs office on the route from Sinkiang and had ordered the officials there to take their duties more seriously. When Li Fu and the others arrived at the bureau they were asked who they were and what they were carrying. Li replied, "I am Kao P'u's indentured servant and I am going to the capital with my companions. We are carrying only some light luggage and it is really nothing (*mei-yu shen-ma tung-hsi*)."[91] Those in charge of the bureau then allowed him and the others to pass through without further ado. At other customs bureaus on the way Chang Luan was familiar with the men who worked there, so for a small bribe he was able to reach an understanding with them.[92]

On the twenty-fourth day of the twelfth month they arrived in the town of Su-chou, Kansu, where they spent two weeks resting and hiring pack mules to carry the jade.[93] When they left Su-chou they proceeded to Liang-chou (modern Wuwei), then to

Chungwei district in present day Ninghsia province, and from there
they crossed the river into Shensi's Ching-pien district. They passed
through Wu-pao district and across the river into Shansi to Fenyang, the home area of Feng Chih-an, on the nineteenth day of
the second month. From here Hsiung-lien split off from the others
and proceeded directly to the capital. From Fenyang the others
went south to Kaifeng in Honan and passed through Fengyang and
Chuchou in modern Anhwei. In the third month they landed at
Pukou and proceeded by boat across the Yangtze to Nanking. On
the way they passed through the Lung-chiang Customs Bureau,
where the Nei-wu-fu *pao-i* Mu-t'eng-o was superintendent, without
paying any taxes.[94] In Nanking they moored just outside the city.

When Li Fu had started out from Yarkand, Kao P'u had told
him to visit his uncle, Kao Chin, the Governor-General of Kiangsu,
Anhwei, and Kiangsi, and to request a travel pass in order to insure
protection from search by customs officials on the last part of their
journey. Thus, upon arrival in Nanking, Li Fu went to the governor-
general's office and sent in the gifts Kao P'u had entrusted to him
for delivery to Kao-chin—a dark jade bowl, a black sheepskin coat,
four bolts of Moslem cloth, one stone Buddha head, and a courtesy
letter.[95] Kao Chin invited Li Fu in to see him and inquired why he
had come. Li answered that his master had sent him to Soochow
to buy several jade articles and some silk. He mentioned that Kao
P'u had told him to request a travel pass. Kao Chin handed over
four boxes of jade articles and two bolts of Nanking silk and told
him to give them to Kao P'u. He also presented Li with a travel
pass with his official seal on it which said,

> The Imperial Commissioner for Yarkand, the high official
> Kao, sends the present indentured servant, Li•Fu, and others
> to the south to Soochow to arrange for the transport of tribu-
> tary gifts to the capital. He has been presented with this travel
> pass in order to avoid inspections along the route.[96]

Kao Chin told Li not to cause trouble along the way and that if
he carried any other goods he should pay taxes according to the

regulations when he reached a customs bureau.[97] Kao said that he was very busy just then and had no free time to reply to Kao P'u's letter, but would do so when he had an opportunity.[98]

From Kao Chin's offices Li, Feng, and Chang proceeded to those of the Nanking Imperial Manufactory Superintendent, Chi-hou, another *pao-i* who was a distant relative of Kao P'u, to send him Kao's greetings. When Li came in, Chi-hou inquired what brought him there. Li replied as he had to Kao Chin—that he was going to Soochow to purchase tribute articles for presentation at court. He presented Chi-hou with a black goatskin and some Moslem cloth in addition to the letter.[99]

When Li, Feng, and Chang left, they proceeded to Soochow, passing down the Yangtze through Chinkiang, then proceeding through I-hsing and T'ai-hu. On the twenty-fifth of the third month, just before entering Soochow, they passed through the Hu-shu Customs Bureau, which was under the supervision of the Soochow Imperial Manufactory Superintendent, Shu-wen, a *pao-i* who was Chi-hou's father. Here Li and Chang flourished their travel pass and stated that they had no taxable goods. They were allowed through without either a strict inspection or the imposition of taxes.[100]

Feng, Li, and Chang arrived in Soochow two days later and stayed in Chang Luan's shop near the Ch'ang-men in Ch'uan-chu Lane.[101] When they had the 90 pieces of jade weighed in Soochow they learned that the scales were somewhat different there, so that, instead of approximately 2,800 catties of jade, which they expected, they discovered that they had some 3,200 catties.[102] Li and Chang secretly agreed that the unexpected surplus of over 400 catties would go to Li as his share, and Li set up a method of double bookkeeping to hide this fact from Kao P'u.[103] Of the 90 pieces, Chang Luan sold 62 of them for 119,067 taels, of which 75,704 taels went to Kao P'u, 30,281 taels to Chang, and 13,082 taels to Li Fu.[104] Of the remaining pieces, 2 were given to Chang Luan and 2 were handed over to craftsmen for carving. Li Fu used part of his share to buy for 2,190 taels the other 24 pieces of ordinary jade (weighing a total of 547 catties) which had not found a ready market.

He seems to have spent the rest of his income from this venture on the purchase of 12 jade articles from two merchants, and loans to Hsiung-lien in the eighth month totaling 4,000 taels. Among his smaller miscellaneous disbursements, Li Fu, an indentured servant himself, incurred expenditures for the acquisition of two indentured servants of his own—one named Fang Pa-erh on a conditional sales (*tien*) contract for 20 taels, the other named Li San-yuan on an outright sale (*mai*) contract for 24 taels in Soochow.[105] Kao P'u received part payment in drafts for 11,790 taels paid by Chang Luan to the Chung-sheng, Wen-yin, and other stores in the capital and also in postdated checks signed by Chang Luan and payable in the second month of 1779 when Chang was planning to return to Peking.

Chang Luan seems to have used his income from the venture for various business purposes. He gave 4,000 taels to Hsiung-lien and used small amounts for purchases of gold (938 taels), for payments to jade craftsmen, and for renting boats, etc. (281 taels).[106] In Soochow he and his brother owned a house worth 4,000 taels and wooden and copper utensils worth 583 taels.[107] He also loaned out 2,321 taels and forwarded a shipment of tea worth 500 taels to the Three Righteous Principles Shop in Su-chou. In addition, he entrusted 500 taels' worth of porcelain to the merchants Chai An-kuo and Li I-t'ing to transport to Kansu for sale and gave a gold Buddha head to another merchant to carry to Kwangtung for sale there. Chang Luan kept considerable supplies of jade and other riches in his house. He had, for instance, over 1,000 catties of rough and polished jade and held over 3,000 taels of silver for Li Fu.[108] During this period Chang was also in communication with Chia Yu-k'u of the Kuei-hua Three Righteous Principles Shop about business matters in Urumchi.[109]

Feng Chih-an left Soochow in the fifth month to attend his father's funeral and received 300 taels from Chang Luan as his salary.[110] He took with him a letter from Chang Luan to a certain Wei Hsiang-chi telling him to "collect the money due from the indentured servant named Yuan (of the Su-chou Tao-t'ai Ch'en Chih-ch'üan)."[111] He arrived home in Shansi in the next month and spent 200 taels on funeral expenses. Later, in the seventh month, he received a letter from Chang Luan promising him 3,000 taels for his contribution to the jade venture, but he never received it. Two months later Chang Luan wrote him again requesting that he transport some goods to Yarkand, but he was unable to do so because the anniversary of his father's death fell on the seventeenth day of the tenth month.[112]

While Chang, Li, Hsiung-lien, and Feng were en route to Soochow, Kao P'u was planning the expansion of his successful jade operations. The native Moslem *begs*, named A-pu-tu-shu-k'u-erh-ho-cho and Kuo-p'u-erh, aided and encouraged him in this scheme.[113] Kao P'u's indentured servant Shen T'ai also urged him to expand his dealings in jade. Accordingly, in the second month of 1778, Kao P'u sought permission from Peking to open the jade deposits at Mi-erh-tai mountain to government supervised jade mining for one year.[114] Previously officials had sealed up this mountain, strictly prohibited the gathering of jade there, and established an inspection office (*k'a-tso*) to enforce this policy. Kao P'u based his petition to Ch'ien-lung on the pretext that opening the mountain to official exploitation for one year would help prevent illicit exploitation of the site by the local Moslems.[115] Even before he received a reply from Peking, however, Kao had begun to mine jade from the mountain. He may have started immediately in the second month to carry out his plan, but it seems more likely that he waited until after the death of O-tui, the *ak'im beg* who owed money to Chang Luan, on the twenty-first of the third month.[116] At this point Kao P'u grew so eager to expand mining operations that he drafted over 3,000 Moslem laborers into this project without pay.[117]

The jade the Moslems collected went mainly for Kao P'u's personal use, although he had to make considerable concessions to the local Moslem leaders and other Chinese officials to keep them quiet. The secretary, Ta-san-t'ai, and the *ishhan beg*, or assistant governor, A-pu-tu-shu-k'u-erh-ho-cho, even sent out another 200 miners of their own to find jade.[118] Kao P'u himself sent silver ingots worth 2,500 taels, which had been found by the Moslem laborers, to the *ak'im beg*, Se-t'i-pa-erh-ti, to try to gain his acquiescence in the expanded jade mining.[119] In addition to these purposes, at least some of the jade was sent to court as tribute, but this was only a very small part of the total. The largest number of finished jade items that he had sent to Peking was nine, and all of them were of ordinary, rather than exceptional, quality. The fine pieces Kao P'u obviously kept for his own use or sale for profit.[120]

Not only did Kao P'u himself profit from these commercial dealings; his indentured servants as well enjoyed prosperity. Shen T'ai, for example, carried on considerable commercial dealings in gold, silver, silks, and jade with the indentured servant Yuan Ping-t'ang of the Su-chou Tao-t'ai Ch'en Chih-ch'uan.[121]

The death of O-tui, which marked the beginning of greater abuses by Kao P'u, also initiated a significant change in the personnel in the Yarkand region. After O-tui's death Kao P'u memorialized, requesting permission to appoint O-tui's son, O-ssu-man, to his father's post of *ak'im beg* of Yarkand.[122] Ch'ien-lung feared that the appointment of O-ssu-man would lead to the development of hereditary succession and to a possible trend towards regional commanders similar to the type which had plagued the T'ang Dynasty. Instead of O-ssu-man, Ch'ien-lung decided to appoint Se-t'i-pa-erh-ti as O-tui's successor and to send O-ssu-man to assume a post in Kashgar.

A more important change in personnel came after the second month of 1778, when Ch'o-k'o-t'o, the Imperial Agent in Wu-shih, another town in the Tarim Basin, fulfilled his tour of duty. In appointing a successor, Ch'ien-lung's choice fell upon Yung-kuei, an elderly official who had risen to President of the Board of Rites and Board of Civil Appointments.[123] This unusual choice may have been the result of two considerations. On the one hand, the appointment was an intentional rebuke to Yung-kuei because of his "selling favors" (*shih-en*) as President of the Board of Civil Appointments to another official, Li Su-fang.[124] On the other hand, Yung-kuei was qualified for the post because he possessed a familiarity with the Sinkiang region acquired during the military campaigns there in the 1750s.

During the early months of 1778, as Kao P'u was beginning to exploit the jade deposits in Mi-erh-tai mountain, Chao Chün-jui mentioned his desire to return home and asked for government certificates for some jade he had bought.[125] Kao P'u took advantage of this opportunity to urge Chao to transport some of his jade to Su-chou for sale. Chao was reluctant, but, realizing that Kao P'u was adamant, he finally acquiesced.[126] In order to help Chao with the shipping, Kao P'u ordered his indentured servant Ch'ang Yung to accompany him and gave him over 200 certificates, which he was to display at the inspection bureaus (*k'a-lun*) along the way.

On the nineteenth day of the fourth month, Ch'ang Yung left Yarkand with two companions. He may have taken some jade with him, but it seems more likely that Chao, who stayed behind to conclude some business in Yarkand and Akosu, transported most of the 4,000 catties of jade (3,000 belonging to Kao P'u, 1,000 belonging to his indentured servants).[127] In the fourth month, he ran into his old acquaintance Fu Te, a merchant from Kuyuan department in Kansu who did business in Su-chou.[128] They arranged a business deal which they concluded the next month in Akosu when Fu Te, in partnership with the merchants Li Pu-an, Hsu Tzu-chien (a former employee of Chao Chün-jui), and others, put up a total of 14,000 taels to buy 1,000 catties of jade from Chao.[129] Fu and his partners then prepared to ship the jade to Soochow for sale.

Ch'ang Yung set out directly for Su-chou in Kansu, where he was to wait for Chao to arrive, then sell the jade and take the silver earned on to Kao P'u's house in the capital.[130] On the way he passed through Kuche, where he met T'ien Shih-chieh, the indentured servant of Ma Hsing-a, the former Imperial Agent in Yarkand.[131] Ma had received an appointment as Commandant of the Forces in Khotan, another town in the Tarim Basin, and had sent T'ien on to the capital with five boxes of clothing as engagement gifts for a young lady in Peking. Ch'ang and T'ien traveled together to Su-chou and lived together while they were there.

Later, Ch'ang Yung was taken ill and stayed for a while in Chao's house in Liang-t'ien-po in Weinan county in Shansi before

returning again to Su-chou.[132] Chao finally arrived in Su-chou sometime after Ch'ang, but found the price of jade too low to sell. In
view of the low prices for jade in Su-chou, he thought it would be
best for Ch'ang to proceed with the jade to Soochow and to try to
sell it there, while he himself stayed behind to settle some accounts
in Su-chou.[133]

On the twenty-second day of the eighth month, Ch'ang's
party left Su-chou on his way to the lower Yangtze. Ten days later
they arrived in Liang-chou and the next day proceeded to Ta-ho-i,
still in the Kansu corridor. At the postal station in the last location,
the personal servant of the local official who managed the postal
system inquired into Ch'ang Yung's background. Upon discovering that Ch'ang was dealing in illicit jade, he impounded one cart
and refused to let it proceed. Ch'ang sent a man to Liang-chou to
borrow 1,000 taels from a merchant who operated a variety store.
When the man returned with the sum, Ch'ang gave 970 taels to the
servant, who then allowed them to go on their way.[134]

While Ch'ang Yung and Chao Chün-jui were en route to Soochow, the newly appointed *ak'im beg* of Yarkand, Se-t'i-pa-erh-ti,
and the newly appointed Imperial Commissioner of Wu-shih, Yung-
kuei, had assumed their duties and were learning of Kao P'u's
activities. Se-t'i-pa-erh-ti, a Moslem, was upset by Kao P'u's op-
pression of his fellow believers through his demands for gold and
jewels from them and through forced labor at Mi-erh-tai mountain.[135]
Realizing that Kao P'u was his superior and had closer contact
with the court, Se-t'i-pa-erh-ti was careful to collect clear evidence
by which he could establish Kao P'u's guilt in illicitly selling jade
before denouncing him to his superiors. When Kao P'u offered to
send out some extra laborers for his benefit, Se-t'i-pa-erh-ti readily
agreed, and later he received fifty silver ingots from Kao-P'u, hand-
ing them over to his translator, Sa-mu-sa-k'o, to preserve as evidence against Kao.[136] At the same time, he reported what he had
learned only to Yung-kuei, because the other officials in the area
seemed to be actively participating in or passively tolerating Kao's
activities.

After receiving the denunciation of Kao P'u from Se-t'i-pa-erh-ti, Yung-kuei went from Wu-shih to Yarkand to investigate the situation personally. He verified the allegations against Kao P'u, deprived him of his feathered button, interrogated the other officials involved, and reported his findings to the emperor.[137] Pending the completion of the investigation, Kao P'u was removed from his post.[138] Some time in the ninth month of 1778, Ch'ienlung received Yung-kuei's report and ordered the governor-generals, governors, and customs superintendents to search out and arrest Chao Chün-jui and Ch'ang Yung as well as Chang Luan, Hsiunglien, Li fu, and Feng Chih-an and impound their jade.

In retrospect Ch'ien-lung noted that his refusal to appoint O-ssu-man as *ak'im beg* was more significant than he realized at the time. He remarked afterwards that, if he had followed Kao P'u's suggestion and made O-ssu-man the *ak'im beg*,

> he would have been very reluctant to report Kao P'u's misdeeds because, knowing that his father had been on good terms with Kao P'u, he would have lost face by reporting his misdeeds. Besides, he was young and inexperienced and would necessarily have followed Kao P'u's wishes, supporting him and conniving with him.[139]

While these events were transpiring in Sinkiang and in the capital, Li Fu, after spending several months in Soochow, agreed with Jen Hsiao-tsai and Hsiung-lien to proceed by boat from Soochow to Peking.[140] Jen, the relative and business partner of Chang Luan, had recently come to Soochow with a shipment of black sheepskins and asked Chang to help him sell them. After Chang had aided him in disposing of the sheepskins for 700 taels, he requested Jen to take some mirrors and lamps to the capital for him.[141] In addition, another business partner of Jen, Wei Ch'üan-i, gave him three jade articles to carry to Peking for sale.

Hsiung-lien had borrowed 550 taels from Chang Luan and left the original group of four in Fenyang, Shansi, to proceed to Peking to visit his aged mother.[142] Later, in the sixth month, he left Peking and went first to Chinkiang to attend to the family tombs and later to Soochow, where he arrived on the twelfth day of the eighth month.[143] Soon afterwards Li Fu and Chang Luan told him that they had sold all the jade and handed over to him a total of 3,450 taels. In the next three weeks Hsiung-lien spent over 1,000 taels of this money on purchases of clothes and other personal items and took the remainder with him when he left for Peking.[144] According to the agreement between the three men, Hsiung-lien departed from Soochow first on the seventh day of the ninth month, then Li Fu and Jen Hsiao-tsai left by boat on the tenth day, and Hsiung-lien joined them in Chinkiang.[145]

Li and Jen chartered two boats, loaded them with purchases and receipts resulting from the sale of jade in Soochow, and attached an official banner of a Senior Vice President in the Board of War to the mast.[146] The cargo included 84 jade articles, 24,080 taels of impure silver, 249 ounces of gold, 2 gold bracelets, over 40 boxes of silks and miscellaneous goods, four drafts for 11,790 taels to the Chung-sheng and Wen-yin stores in Peking, one post-dated check for 35,571 taels, and account books noting receipts of 128,859 taels for sales in jade.[147] In addition, Hsiung-lien's indentured servant, Kuo Hsing, and the two indentured servants Li Fu had recently bought accompanied them.[148]

After leaving Soochow, Li and Jen first came to the Hu-shu Customs Bureau under the management of the Nei-wu-fu *pao-i* Shu-wen. Li Fu took out the travel pass Kao Chin had given him and showed it to Shu-wen's indentured servant, who then went in to confer with his master. Later he reappeared and conveyed to Li a message from Shu-wen, saying, "The goods which you are carrying for your own use have to be taxed. Write out a list of your master's things and I (Shu-wen) will pay the tax for you."[149] Li then filled out a list of the silks and other items he was carrying and sent it in to Shu-wen who paid a tax of 79 taels for him. Li then proceeded on through the customs.

When Ch'ien-lung learned on the sixth day of the tenth month that Shu-wen had allowed Li and Jen through without even questioning them and inspecting their cargo, he first expressed his disillusionment, because Shu-wen had previously conscientiously performed his duties at the imperial manufactories and the Hu-shu Customs Bureau.[150] Later, recalling that the natives of Soochow were devoted gossips about anything new and unusual and concluding that they certainly must have spoken of the large shipments of jade from Sinkiang which Li Fu and the others had managed, Ch'ien-lung became incensed. During the half year Li spent in Soochow making his sales of jade, word of this must certainly have reached Shu-wen, a customs and manufactory superintendent who often dealt in jade articles and had contacts with jade artisans, and he should have arrested Li and Jen as soon as they appeared at the customs bureau.[151] If Shu-wen did not have the courage to arrest them, Ch'ien-lung thought that at least he should have memorialized to him about their activities. If he feared that the advisers (*mu-yu*) who drafted his memorials would divulge this information to the public, then he should have mentioned it to the emperor when the latter asked him about matters in Soochow during a court audience in Peking in the sixth month.[152] Ch'ien-lung came to the conclusion that Shu-wen was probably trying to cover up for Li Fu and ordered him to make a "voluntary contribution" to the Secret Accounts Bureau and had him removed from his post, although in fact he was allowed to continue to manage matters there in an unofficial capacity.[153]

From the Hu-shu Customs Bureau Li and Hsiung proceeded north along the Grand Canal. On the seventeenth day of the ninth month, they came to the Yangchow customs office under the supervision of Sun K'uo, the taotai of Ch'ang-chen.[154] At this time Sun was away in another department investigating the property of an official who had been impeached. He had left behind two secretaries (*shu-pan*) and two indentured servants to inspect the traffic and levy taxes. Upon arrival, Li Fu took out Kao P'u's calling card and showed it to the secretaries and indentured servants. At the same time he explained that the boxes in his two boats were all tribute goods from Soochow which Kao P'u was sending to Peking, and that he had no taxable goods. Sun's subordinates went aboard the boats and saw that Li was carrying jade artifacts, clothing, and silver, but interpreted these articles as falling within the category of tax-free tribute goods. Li and Hsiung thus went on their way without paying any taxes.

A month later when Sa-tsai, the Acting Governor-General of Kiangsi, Kiangsu, and Anhwei, reported that Li Fu and Hsiung-lien had slipped through the Yangchow customs bureau, Ch'ien-lung removed Sun K'o from his post, fined him 10,000 taels, and ordered his secretaries and indentured servants to wear the cangue for three months in front of the customs offices.[155]

Li, Hsiung-lien, and Jen proceeded up the Grand Canal, arriving at the Huai Customs Bureau on the twenty-sixth day of the ninth month. There the Superintendent, Yin-chu, acting on a tip from his indentured servant, captured Li, Hsiung-lien, and Jen and attached their property.[156] He made a complete inventory of all the goods they were carrying and sent them along to the Board of Punishments, the Ch'ung-wen Gate, and the Nei-wu-fu for examination and expropriation.[157] The postdated checks and drafts were to be cashed and the receipts paid to the Nei-wu-fu.[158] The rest of the goods were sold at the Ch'ung-wen Gate with the proceeds going also to the Imperial Household Department.

The Nei-wu-fu did not receive all the property seized, however, for Yin-chu did not report everything he found. One item he concealed was the travel pass Kao Chin had given to Li Fu. When Ch'ien-lung learned a few weeks later of the existence of the travel pass from the testimony of Li Fu and others, he ordered Yin-chu to make a "voluntary contribution" of 20,000 taels to the Nei-wu-fu's workshops as a fine for trying to hide Kao Chin's aid to Li Fu.[159] Sa-tsai, who knew of Yin-chu's concealment of the travel pass but did not mention this, was also told to contribute funds to the Secret Accounts Archives.[160]

The two accomplices of Li, Hsiung-lien and Jen, were seized soon afterwards. Chang Luan, who had remained behind in the area of the Yellow Oriole Ward Bridge in Soochow to pay off his debts, was captured on the thirtieth day of the ninth month by Yang K'uei, the Governor of Kiangsu.[161] Feng Chih-an was arrested at his home in Fen-chou by the department magistrate about three weeks later.[162]

Meanwhile Ch'ang Yung was still in Kansu. On the twelfth day of the ninth month, he stayed in the house of the teamster Ma Shou-pin in Mi-tzu-t'an in Tsingyuan county.[163] Since Ch'ang was afraid that officials might discover the jade when they later crossed the Yellow River, he took about 4,000 catties of jade and left them at Ma's house covered over with firewood and straw and told Ma Shou-pin and his companion, Ma Wan-lung, to look after them until Chao Chün-jui arrived. Ch'ang Yung then went ahead with the remainder of the jade, while Ma Wan-chin, a teamster, followed behind. Near the Shensi border in the town of Wa-t'ing, however, Ma Wan-chin overtook Ch'ang, who told him to return to Mi-tzu-t'an and order Ma Shou-pin to take the hidden jade and devise a means to ship it across the river without being discovered. Ma Wan-chin returned and told Ma Shou-pin of these instructions; then he went on to Nao-ch'üan where he met Chao Chün-jui and informed him of these developments.[164] Ma Shou-pin took over 3,000 catties of jade from those hidden in his house and transported them one postal step, to Ta-lao-ch'ih, where he hid them in the shop of Ma Pao. Officials investigating Li Fu's and Chao Chün-jui's jade dealings for Kao P'u discovered this store of jade shortly afterwards.[165] Ch'ang Yung was arrested on the twenty-fifth of the ninth month in Changwu district just inside Shensi province, and Chao Chün-jui was apprehended about the same time at K'ai-ch'eng in the same province.[166]

Aftermath

Rewards and punishments followed swiftly after the exposure of Kao P'u's illicit commercial dealings and the capture of him and his accomplices. When Yung-kuei interrogated Kao P'u about each aspect of his dealings, Kao P'u simply lowered his head and refused to defend his actions.[167] Ch'ien-lung, having read Yung-kuei's account of Kao P'u's activities and of his interrogation, declared that Kao P'u's peculation superseded even that of his father and, true to his word, he ruled out any leniency for Kao P'u based on his grandfather's or aunt's position.[168] He told Yung-kuei to administer the proper punishment—execution—to him there in Yarkand.[169]

Kao P'u's major accomplices, the Moslem *ishhan beg* A-pu-tu-shu-k'u-erh-ho-cho, and the minor official Ta-san-t'ai, were also executed.[170] Chang Luan, Chao Chün-jui, Li Fu, Ch'ang Yung, Shen T'ai, and Shu-pao were all sent to the capital for questioning by the Board of Punishments; their fate is unknown. Ch'o-k'o-t'o was punished by apparent dismissal from his post, although in fact he was allowed to remain on the job.[171] He suffered only this administrative sanction because his guilt lay not in malfeasance but in nonfeasance.

These punishments were balanced to a certain degree by rewards which went to the *ak'im beg* Se-t'i-pa-erh-ti and Yung-kuei. The former received the honorary title of Prince for his denunciation of Kao P'u, while the latter received an appointment as the powerful and prestigious President of the Board of Civil Appointments.[172]

The wealth Kao P'u had accumulated in Yarkand during his term of office, which amounted to 16,000 taels of silver, 500 ounces of gold, and countless silver ingots, was expropriated.[173] The jade remaining in Sinkiang was sent to the capital, rather than sold on the spot, in order to prevent further abuses.[174] As for the future of the jade mines, Ch'ien-lung considered a suggestion to open them to trade at prices fixed by the state. He rejected this proposal, which was based on the experience of the ginseng trade in nearby Manchuria, because it would be difficult to implement for jade mined in distant Sinkiang.[175] Instead, he decided to close the mines to all exploitation by the state. Only a few soldiers on duty at the site and Moslem laborers in the area would be allowed to gather a little jade for themselves. In addition, he established another agent in the Yarkand area to bolster the administration there and offered rewards in the future for imperial agents who reported the misdeeds of *begs* and for *begs* who did the same for the corrupt practices of agents.[176]

The officials, indentured servants, and merchants directly involved in Kao P'u's activities in Sinkiang were not the only ones affected by the settlement of the case. The Board of Civil Appointments recommended dismissal or dismissal and demotion for all the responsible provincial officials whose territory Kao P'u's indentured servants had traversed.[177] Ch'ien-lung thought that such harsh punishment would be unfair, since negligence of this type was very common. He ordered the board not to dismiss the officials deserving this punishment, but merely to make a note in their file and allow them to remain at their posts. As for those deserving both dismissal and demotion, they too were to stay in their positions, but the board was to deliberate on their demotion. In general, Ch'ien-lung adopted a tolerant attitude towards those officials who failed to report the exactions from the postal station by Kao P'u's indentured servants. Perhaps he surmised that these officials had kept quiet because they had feared reprisals against themselves by Kao P'u, who, as Senior Vice President of the Board of War, had been in charge of the postal system.[178]

The officials in charge of the customs bureaus who failed to detect and stop the shipments of jade, however, received harsh treatment. These were often Nei-wu-fu *pao-i* occupying positions as customs superintendents. The sanctions in these cases did not consist merely of the regular administrative measures, but of the new and unusual practice of contributing large sums of money to the Secret Accounts Bureau of the Nei-wu-fu. The sum total contributed "voluntarily" by officials involved in this case is unknown, but the total contributions mentioned in the extant records was 270,000 taels. The contributors[179] were twelve officials, at least four of them Nei-wu-fu *pao-i*, whom Ch'ien-lung criticized for their failure to detect or arrest Kao P'u's merchant partners or indentured servants as they transported illegal jade across the breadth of China. See Table 1.

Pressure or outright demands for these "voluntary" contributions stemmed from Ch'ien-lung's anger upon learning how Chang Luan, Li Fu, Ch'ang Yung, and Chao Chün-jui had traveled about the empire with impunity. High provincial officials and Nei-wu-fu *pao-i* serving in the customs bureaus were not anxious to hand over large sums to the Secret Accounts Bureau, so when they first learned of Ch'ien-lung's anger they offered excuses for their conduct or apologized for their carelessness. Often it was

Table 1

CONTRIBUTORS TO THE SECRET ACCOUNTS BUREAU
IN KAO P'U'S CASE

Name	Position	Contribution (in taels)
Yang-K'uei Shu-wen	Governor of Kiangsu	30,000[a]
(Nei-wu-fu *pao-i*)	Superintendent of Hu-shu Customs	40,000[b]
Pi Yuan	Governor of Shensi	30,000[c]
Sa-tsai	Acting Governor-General of Kiangsi, Kiangsu, and Anhwei	20,000[d]
Kao Chin (Nei-wu-fu *pao-i*)	Governor-General of Kiangsi, Kiangsu, and Anhwei	5,000[e]
Yin-chu (Nei-wu-fu *pao-i*)	Superintendent of Imperial Manufactories at Nanking	20,000[f]
Le-erh-chin	Governor-General of Shensi and Kansu	40,000[g]
Hsi-ning (Nei-wu-fu *pao-i*)	Ch'ang-lu Salt Censor	15,000[h]
Pa Yen-san	Governor-General of Shansi	40,000[i]
Wang T'an-wang	Governor of Chekiang	20,000[j]
Sun K'uo	Taotai of Ch'ang-chen	10,000[k]
TOTAL		over 270,000 taels

a. *SLHK*, 21:748,750b (December 1930).
b. *SLHK*, 21:748 (December 1930); 24:876b (January 1931).
c. *SLHK*, 22:792 (January 1931); 23:822b (January 1931).
d. *SLHK*, 23:817b, 818b (January 1931).
e. *SLHK*, 23:833 (January 1931).
f. *SLHK*, 23:817b, 820 (January 1931).
g. *SLHK*, 23:821 (January 1931); 24:868 (January 1931).
h. *SLHK*, 25:908 (February 1931).
i. *SLHK*, 24:873b (January 1931).
j. *SLHK*, 27:981b (February 1931).
k. *SLHK*, 22:785b-86 (January 1931).

only after Ch'ien-lung had made a number of stinging criticisms of their conduct that the officials felt it necessary to forward several thousand taels to his privy purse.

For example, when Shu-wen, the Superintendent of the Hu-shu Customs, told Ch'ien-lung that he did not know of Li Fu's passage through the customs in the third month because he had been in Soochow at the time, Ch'ien-lung replied, "You still have the nerve to say you didn't know! This is utter and incorrigible stupidity!"[180] At the same time, Shu-wen tried to excuse himself for not knowing that Li Fu had later passed through his bureau in the ninth month. Ch'ien-lung told him, "How can you say you didn't know when you paid the taxes for him? You must be stark raving mad to say this. I can tell you that the good fortune I have bestowed upon you has now come to an end."[181] Soon afterwards Shu-wen offered a contribution of 20,000 taels to the Secret Accounts Bureau to redeem himself, but Ch'ien-lung demanded that he pay more. Eventually he contributed 40,000 taels.[182]

Another example of a Nei-wu-fu *pao-i* who aroused Ch'ien-lung's ire was Yin-chu, the Superintendent of the Imperial Manufactories at Nanking. Ch'ien-lung was disturbed by the cooperative attitude he displayed towards Li Fu and was further annoyed by his efforts to cover up his faults by expressing repentance and a desire to do better in the future. Ch'ien-lung replied to these self-serving comments, "You are good at talking about how to administer your post with the proper concern for the public welfare, but that's all. I see that you *pao-i* will never change your base manners. What can I do? What can I do?"[183] Within two weeks, Yin-chu had committed himself to a contribution of 20,000 taels.

An example of a Nei-wu-fu *pao-i* reprimanded for his poor administration in connection with Li Fu's travels from Soochow up the Grand Canal, but apparently not fined, was I-ling-a, the Lianghuai Salt Censor. Ch'ien-lung asked him:

Although you are not in charge of the Yangchow Customs Bureau, still how can it possibly be that these large boats went through in broad daylight without your knowing it?

Your guilt is only slightly less than that of Shu-wen. What
good is it to appoint useless and venal officials like you to
government posts?[184]

The punishments meted out involved mostly Chinese or
Manchus. This was not only because Kao P'u and many of his aides
were either Chinese or Manchu, but also because Ch'ien-lung did
not want to stir up the Moslem community in Sinkiang by punishing their leaders. This accorded with the aim of Ch'ing policy in
Sinkiang, which was to rule over the Moslem populace by preventing the development of issues that would unify them against their
Manchu-Chinese overlords. Ch'ien-lung made these considerations
clear in an edict to Pi Yuan, the Governor of Shensi, in the eleventh
month of 1778, when he said:

> There is no need to interrogate the Moslems such as A-pu-tu-
> la, who were mentioned as vendors . . . of illegal jade in Chao
> Chün-jui's testimony. These ignorant Moslems have been se-
> cretly selling illegal jade for a long time. . . You tell Yung-
> kuei that if he discovers cases of Moslems selling illicit jade,
> he should not bother to interrogate them unless he receives
> a special rescript ordering him to do so. In this way he will
> not be able to stir up trouble unnecessarily.[185]

In fact, considerations of effective administration and a real-
ization of the inherent limitations in the bureaucratic system led
Ch'ien-lung to admonish officials not to press their investigations
too far in several respects. Once the high provincial officials began
to trace Kao P'u's traffic in jade they discovered much about the
shipping of jade by Chinese traders, the sale of jade in retail shops,
and the ultimate buyers of jade. In their desire to make amends
for their previous laxity, these officials were ready to apprehend
and interrogate any traders, retailers, or consumers who seemed to
be connected even most tenuously with Kao P'u's activities. Ch'ien-
lung, far from welcoming a rigorous and thorough disclosure of
misconduct on the part of large sectors of the bureaucracy or the
merchant community, admonished officials not to probe too deeply.

Thus, he instructed them that the criterion for official scrutiny of the various aspects of jade sales should be the extremity of the misbehavior. "My method of dealing with these matters is to eradicate the extreme abuses," he said, "and not to bother with cases that are *de minimis*."[186]

As for the Chinese merchants who transported jade from the western regions to China proper, he noted that he previously had not bothered to investigate their misdeeds and implied that this policy should not be changed.[187] As for the jade shops in Soochow, he ordered officials not to search them because a widespread investigation would undoubtedly lead to misconduct by the clerks and runners of the officials carrying out this task.[188] In addition, since the ultimate buyers of much of this jade were the wealthy and prestigious salt merchants, governors, and governor-generals, he discouraged any attempt to inquire into this aspect of the jade trade as "grossly improper."[189]

Ch'ien-lung's express desire not "to carry an investigation beyond its proper limits and unnecessarily implicate uninvolved persons" (*chu-lien*) was not limited to the scrutiny of Kao P'u's case, but seems to have been a common assumption of bureaucratic management in this period. The Chia-ch'ing Emperor (reigned 1796-1820) employed this same expression, for example, in telling investigating officials that bringing Ho-shen himself to justice would be sufficient and that they should not bother about his many accomplices who, he said, should be given the chance to reform themselves without undergoing judicial sanctions.[190] This attitude probably was a reflection of the emperor's narrow view of his own self-interest, which perceived the discovery and punishment of wide-scale peculation in the government as injurious to bureaucratic morale, conducive to abuses by those carrying out the investigations, and tending to tarnish the image of the state in the eyes of the people.

Ch'ien-lung's self-interest was by no means limited, however, to his ruminations on bureaucratic management. Indeed, the one who benefited most from Kao P'u's misdeeds and their investigation was the Ch'ien-lung Emperor himself. As noted above, the fines paid by officials involved in the case totaled over 200,000 taels. All these went into the Secret Accounts Bureau and became part of Ch'ien-lung's personal treasury, which was handled by the Nei-wu-fu. In addition, the expropriation of Kao P'u's property provided further income for the Nei-wu-fu's vaults. All Kao P'u's money went directly to the Nei-wu-fu, and his jade and personal belongings were forwarded to the Ch'ung-wen Gate for sale, with the proceeds sent to the Nei-wu-fu.[191] The latter procedure was also followed with all the goods Li Fu was carrying in his two boats. The drafts and postdated checks, totaling over 46,000 taels, were chased and the receipts transferred to the Nei-wu-fu.[192] Some of Kao P'u's property, such as his real estate (given to the Board of Revenue) and his indentured servants (handed over to his banner), was not taken over by the Nei-wu-fu.[193] It seems, however, that the Nei-wu-fu, as the representative of Ch'ien-lung's private interests, benefited more than any other government bureau. The total income to the Nei-wu-fu from Kao P'u's corruption and its ramifications was probably several hundreds of thousands of taels.

The benefit to Ch'ien-lung, however, was not merely monetary. In inspecting the carved jade artifacts expropriated from Chang Luan's house, he noted that the craftsmanship was better than that of any of the jade carvers in Peking. Officials informed him that the artisans were two brothers, P'ing-ch'i and P'ing-pa, from Soochow, who possessed a secret method of carving jade.[194] Ch'ien-lung ordered Shu-wen to find the brothers and send one of them to the capital with all the necessary tools and implements to carve for him. Shu-wen fulfilled this task and reported back that P'ing-pa, upon learning of Ch'ien-lung's wishes, had purportedly replied, "For a humble craftsman like myself to be summoned to the capital to serve there is a great honor. I am really very willing to go."[195]

Kao P'u's case provoked no fundamental reordering of the bureaucratic structure. Aside from the institutional changes mentioned above which took place in Sinkiang, the only other structural innovation resulting from this case was a reorganization of the postal systems in all provinces. Ch'ien-lung first suggested that

postal management be transferred from the grain and salt intendants to the resident and circuit intendants (*shou-hsun-tao*) and the
provincial judicial officers, in order to overcome the abuses evident
from the details which had emerged from the investigation into Kao
P'u's affairs. Finally, however, he accepted a suggestion from the
Board of War that it would be best to allow the grain and salt intendants to continue to handle postal matters in those places where
they patrolled a given area. In those places where they did not, the
board proposed to split the authority for the administration of the
postal system between the several circuit intendants (*hsun-tao*).
These officials were to examine the horses at the postal stations
to assure that they were suitable for use and were to send monthly
registers to the board as verification.[196]

Ch'ien-lung was probably not taken completely by surprise
at the discovery that Kao P'u was engaged in some form of corruption, but he does seem to have been outraged at the scale of his
activities. He claimed at one point that Kao P'u's case was the
biggest scandal in over a decade.[197] Kao P'u's case was unusual for
its size and ramifications at the time, but it was dwarfed by other
scandals, such as that of Ho-shen, which broke in the decades that
followed. Kao P'u's case, however, does illustrate the conditions
of governmental and social decline of the late eighteenth century
which rendered China so vulnerable to the West only a few decades
later.

Chapter VI

CONCLUSIONS

The Imperial Household Department, or Nei-wu-fu, was a distinctive, perhaps unique, institution. Its organizational form reflected a variety of influences, and its functions affected significantly the society and economy of the whole empire. Socially, the department was an outgrowth of the developing Manchu state of the seventeenth century. Institutionally, however, the department resulted from the influence of Chinese political organization, particularly the knowledge and understanding of the experience of previous Chinese dynasties in creating institutions to deal with the emperor's personal affairs. The origins and development of the Nei-wu-fu are closely linked with substantive themes and forces in Chinese and Manchu history as well as in the Ch'ing period itself. But the institution did not play a merely passive role in Ch'ing history; rather it exerted considerable influence, particularly in the eighteenth century, on the tenor of Ch'ing government and society. Accordingly, the Nei-wu-fu can be seen from two perspectives, one from the background of Chinese and Manchu history, and the other from the more immediate surroundings of Ch'ing society and government of the seventeenth and eighteenth centuries.

Looking at the origins of the Nei-wu-fu in the context of Chinese history, we can see that the major problem that confronted the founders of Manchu rule was how to avoid the eunuch abuses that had plagued previous dynasties. The causes of eunuch mismanagement of government in earlier periods were not uniform. They arose both from specific institutional weaknesses, such as unstable succession procedures in the T'ang, and from more general trends in governmental evolution, such as the increasing power of the emperor in Han and Ming times. And some of these same institutional defects (an uncertain succession arrangement) and trends (increasing autocracy) were present in Ch'ing times.

173

The principal difference between the Ch'ing and earlier dynasties was not that the political institutions of the dynasty as a whole or the trend of Ch'ing government were essentially different from previous periods. The fundamental distinction lay, rather, in the institutional form the management of the emperor's personal affairs assumed. The final compromise worked out after the death of the Shun-chih Emperor in 1661 was essentially a double-tiered organization with the Nei-wu-fu bondservants, or *pao-i* on top and the eunuchs on the bottom. This arrangement differed from the institutions created by Chinese dynasties, but was reminiscent of the predominantly non-eunuch administration of palace affairs under the Chin Dynasty of the Jurchen, the distant ancestors of the Manchus. The subordination of the eunuchs to the bondservants, however, did not mean that the eunuchs were managed only by *pao-i*. A hierarchy of eunuch authorities supervised directly the work of the lowest levels of the eunuch administration. The highest levels of the eunuch administration had contact with the emperor, but they and all their subordinates were under the general supervision of the Nei-wu-fu managers and, at times, the close scrutiny of a specific Nei-wu-fu sub-department.

The Nei-wu-fu employed a combined policy of general control by *pao-i* and of specific control by a eunuch hierarchy, which had three advantages over a uniform policy of using only bondservants to oversee eunuch activities. It both permitted the Nei-wu-fu to employ fewer *pao-i* to oversee eunuch activities and left the eunuchs some vestige of self-control and self-esteem, which probably improved their morale. Finally, it helped to minimize contact between the bondservants and the eunuchs and thus to prevent the growth of friendships between them, which would have hindered effective control over the eunuchs.

This is not to say, however, that lapses never occurred. One example of such a lapse involved a eunuch who divulged confidential information on governmental appointments to various civilian officials. This was a particularly sensitive case, since it involved the transmission of documents from high officials in the provinces to the emperor and thus brought to mind eunuch control of document transmission in the Ming period. Even this instance, however, was discovered by the Nei-wu-fu and reported to the emperor before it had developed into a major incursion into governmental decision-making. Furthermore, the case resulted in further restrictions on the eunuchs' role in the transmission of documents, which would prevent a similar occurrence in the future. In comparison with previous Chinese dynasties, therefore, the early and mid-Ch'ing periods were relatively free from eunuch abuses. It appears that the Nei-wu-fu successfully fulfilled the primary task Chinese history had bequeathed to it.

Examination of the Imperial Household Department from its historical background indicates that the various different influences that played a part in its formation make generalizing perilous. Perhaps the financial functions of the Nei-wu-fu best reflect its unusual background. In certain aspects, such as the imperial estates and the ginseng trade, the Imperial Household Department's role in the economy was a result of its Manchu heritage and the conquest of China. The close relationship between the Imperial Household Department and certain merchants was typical of other conquest dynasties, notably the Mongols. In other aspects, such as the manufactories and the customs bureaus, however, the appointment of Nei-wi-fu *pao-i* can be seen as a continuation of Ming practices, but with the substitution of bondservants for eunuchs. Accordingly, a characterization of the Nei-wu-fu as a mere expression of native Manchu practices seems too simplified. The employment of bondservants to manage the ruler's personal affairs was indeed a Manchu innovation. The establishment of the Imperial Household Department and the use of bondservants, however, did not signal the disappearance of the traditional Chinese eunuchs, but only their subordination to the bondservants. In the same manner, the department, although organized in accordance with the Manchu banner system, was a Chinese bureaucratic institution as well. If the Nei-wu-fu did indeed represent primarily native Manchu tendencies, it was a nativism adapted to Chinese historical and institutional traditions.

Nor does the term "Sinicization" seem to describe precisely

the department's development. The Manchu conquerors did not adopt Chinese culture in an historical vacuum, but under concrete historical circumstances. China for them meant primarily Ming China. In the Chinese state of that time they saw defects, such as eunuch usurpation of power, which they sought to avoid rather than emulate. This conscious rejection of Chinese experience in certain respects may itself have been the result of advice from Chinese scholars or of an examination of Chinese history. It seems very likely, however, that it was also linked very directly to the Manchus' own customs and experience. Whether these developments can all be subsumed under the general rubric of "Sinicization," therefore, seems doubtful. If they do indeed represent a process of Sinicization, this was not a mere blind imitation of the most immediate Chinese precedents, but a deliberate and judicious process of selective borrowing, perhaps the highest form of Sinicization.

Viewed from the more immediate context of seventeenth and eighteenth century China, the Imperial Household Department appears as an influential force in both government and society and, in many ways, a reflection of them. Institutionally, many of the Nei-wu-fu's departments resembled organs of the public bureaucracy. The Department had functional equivalents of the Boards of Revenue, Public Works, Ceremony, War, and Punishments and a censorial organ as well. The Nei-wu-fu also possessed its own school to train prospective officials and exams to select them. Accordingly, recruitment into the Nei-wu-fu bureaucracy showed certain similarities to that in the public bureaucracy. Promotion within the department, however, seems to have been considerably different from that in the government; elevation into the Nei-wu-fu *pao-i* elite often depended on personal relationships, particularly those between a *pao-i* nurse or concubine and a future emperor. As in the society at large, maintaining a position in the elite over several generations was not easy. While members of the elite tried to perpetuate their positions by purchasing degrees for their sons, their decline, like their rise, was often the result of another succession to the throne.

Of the sub-departments of the Nei-wu-fu, the largest was the Privy Purse, and the financial functions of the Nei-wu-fu were the most important part of its operations. This emphasis on financial matters distinguishes the Nei-wu-fu in part from the public bureaucracy. Furthermore, the department's economic role was not primarily in agriculture. The Nei-wu-fu lands, while not insignificant, did not constitute a large percentage of the empire's land, nor did they provide substantial income to the department. The Nei-wu-fu's economic role was rather in trade and industry. The copper, ginseng, silk, and salt trade were the major areas from which the Nei-wu-fu profited. Members of the Nei-wu-fu also manned the most important domestic and foreign customs posts. In industry, the Nei-wu-fu bondservants managed the largest textile enterprises in the empire.

The most significant aspect of the Nei-wu-fu's role in the economy was perhaps the institutionalization of the master-bondservant relationship as the means of exploiting the empire's most profitable economic activities. In this respect the Nei-wu-fu was an accurate reflection of Chinese society in the seventeenth and eighteenth centuries, although it differed from many other institutions in Chinese history. The Nei-wu-fu's management of the salt monopoly, the customs bureaus, and the manufactories, and its participation in other commercial activities, was in many ways simply the institutionalization at the highest levels of the master servant relationship common in Ch'ing society.

The use of indentured servants in Ch'ing China served to strengthen the authoritarian nature of the government and society. Truly authoritarian government depends not so much on a public bureaucracy which has an identity and sense of purpose that may conflict with the autocrat's, but on private institutions more pliant to the leader's will and ready to implement his policies. In the Ch'ing period all levels of government from the emperor to the district magistrate possessed both formal public institutions and informal private institutions. The formal public institutions were those recognized as the governmental bureaucracy. The informal private institutions were those personal relationships of dependence which linked bondservants to the emperor, indentured servants to officials, and even indentured servants to other indentured servants. The Nei-wu-fu, as the highest organ in the informal private hierarchy, offered the emperor a convenient and effective means of assuring that the exploitation of the empire's largest commercial enterprises was in loyal hands.

The Nei-wu-fu, as an informal private institution, strengthened the trend towards increasing autocracy in several ways. One example is the demands of the Secret Accounts Bureau for "voluntary contributions" to the Nei-wu-fu treasuries in the eighteenth century. These payments were prompted by suggestions from Ho-shen or the emperor to an official, often a *pao-i* customs or manufactory superintendent, that they might help him atone for his mismanagement or corruption. They were essentially a private exaction by the emperor on the officials who occupied the most lucrative and powerful posts in the provinces. This system of payments through the Secret Accounts Bureau, then, was a partial institutionalization of the system of squeeze which characterized the operations of the Nei-wu-fu *pao-i* generally.

It is no accident that the Secret Accounts Bureau arose in the last half of the eighteenth century. The evolution of the Nei-wu-fu's financial functions in general indicates that its role in the economy increased considerably during this century. Thus, the department, which had only a limited role early in the dynasty, began to assert a considerable influence over the society and economy in the eighteenth century. Of course, the *pao-i* were closely linked to the major themes of Manchu history before the conquest, but they did not at that time play the active role they did later. In the early period, the functions of the *pao-i* both before the conquest and afterwards were largely determined by prior precedent or by the nature of their institutional structure. In the eighteenth century, however, the department assumed a greater, more active role and contributed generously to the peculiar malaise and decline that characterized the last years of Ch'ien-lung's reign.

One key to the rising influence of the Nei-wu-fu was the peace and prosperity China enjoyed in the eighteenth century. A century of pax sinica starting from the late seventeenth century meant that the society and economy were not disrupted by major external concerns. The Ch'ing emperors were happy to see trade flourish and the economy develop, not only for the sake of the country, but also for the opportunity it afforded them to increase their private wealth. Thus, when the customs bureaus began to show a surplus in the late seventeenth century, the K'ang-hsi Emperor sent out Nei-wu-fu *pao-i* to remit these funds to the Privy Purse. Later Ch'ing emperors employed the Nei-wu-fu *pao-i* to manage or participate in the largest financial enterprises in the empire; the Nei-wu-fu also took part in commercial activities itself through large loans to salt merchants, the management of pawn shops, and the sale of silks from the imperial manufactories. In all these activities the bondservants acted as agents of the emperor and thus contributed to the growing power of the emperor over the economy and government, to the trend towards increasing autocracy.

The *pao-i* were indeed the emperor's agents, but they were not mere robots. Their appointment to financial posts and the involvement of the Nei-wu-fu in the economy had implications beyond simply increasing autocracy. In large part the influence of the *pao-i* on the economy and society was a result of their peculiar situation. Their bondservant status, like the degraded status of the eunuchs, made them dependent on their master for status and dignity, and thus willing instruments of the autocrat. Furthermore, bondservant status was based on the assumption that economic incentives were not effective or were too expensive to induce the desired conduct in the bondservant. Thus, resort was made to noneconomic measures in order to evoke a response that could not be elicited by mere economic self-interest. The consequence of inducing conduct in this manner was that the Nei-wu-fu *pao-i* never acquired the normative principles or psychological association with the goals of their master or with the values of proper government which other officials possessed. Accordingly, the bondservants and indentured servants were more predisposed by their previous experience and current insecurity to maximize their opportunities for enriching themselves through peculation and to take their master's conduct as a model for their own. Since the *pao-i* in large part did not internalize the desires of their master or the principles of Confucian government, they were restrained from peculation only by fear of punishment or of demotion. When they served in the provinces, far removed from their superior banner officials, from the emperor, and from high Nei-wu-fu officials, however, they were free of the most common and effective restraints on their misbehavior. That they engaged in large-scale corruption under these circumstances is no wonder. Indeed, the Ch'ien-lung Emperor was so familiar with the misdeeds of the *pao-i* officials appointed to the salt monopolies and the customs bureaus that he despaired of their ever abandoning their base bondservant habits.

Other factors further aggravated the natural tendency for bondservants to exploit their positions in the provinces. One of these was the nature of the funds handled by the Nei-wu-fu *pao-i*. The amounts of money that passed through the hands of the *pao-i* salt censors and customs and manufactory superintendents were large and varied from year to year. This situation provided ample opportunity to misrepresent the amount of funds collected in any year and to misappropriate a significant portion of them. Furthermore, it was a general practice among Ch'ing officialdom as a whole to take at least small amounts of public funds for their personal use. Still another element was the instability of *pao-i* official tenure. The *pao-i* were personal appointees and lacked the standing and legitimacy regular officials gained from their *chin-shih* degrees as well as their solidarity with the governmental bureaucracy as a whole. These factors meant that, in an age when the emperor and other members of the official elite were themselves taking advantage of every chance that presented itself for enlarging their fortunes, there was little to prevent the informal institutions from being converted into gouging operations by the emperor or his officials and much to foster in the bondservants and indentured servants the ethic of corruption they observed in their masters.

This can be most clearly seen in the network of squeeze and exaction of which the *pao-i* were an indispensable part. At the highest level, the emperor enriched himself by sending out bondservants to remit funds to his personal treasury. They, of course, took some of these funds for themselves, but he tried to regain these losses in part by demanding voluntary contributions and in part by confiscations. Below the emperor the Nei-wu-fu managers, most notably Ho-shen, exploited their propinquity to the emperor to demand bribes from the Nei-wu-fu *pao-i* at the salt monopolies, customs bureaus, and manufactories. The privileged bondservants who occupied these lucrative posts in the provinces, in turn, exploited the merchants or local officials under their supervision, mulcting them for all they could get. Often these *pao-i* and other officials employed their own indentured servants as their agents of exaction, much as the emperor used his *pao-i*. At times even the indentured servants of the *pao-i* had their own indentured servants whom they likewise employed as their tools of extortion. The most powerful positions in the Ch'ing economy and government, then, were enmeshed in a network of exploitative relationships that extended throughout the society.

Certainly, the Nei-wu-fu was the institutional antithesis of the eunuch-controlled palace organization of the Ming period. Yet ironically the corruption and mismanagement of the imperial bondservants in the eighteenth century might well be compared with the eunuch excesses of the sixteenth and seventeenth centuries. The Nei-wu-fu *pao-i* did not control the decision-making process at the throne, nor did they enjoy the military power of the Ming eunuchs. Nevertheless, the economic power of the *pao-i* resembled in significant ways the eunuch supervision of the imperial manufactories and the customs bureaus in the Ming era. In both cases the source of power came from a direct grant from the emperor personally, which by-passed the regular bureaucracy. The Nei-wu-fu bondservants, like the Ming eunuchs, were private agents of the emperor who misused the authority granted to them and contributed substantially to the major social, economic, and foreign problems that confronted the dynasty. In the Ch'ing period it was the bondage of the *pao-i* to the emperor which assured that in most cases they, as faithful servants, would carry out his desires, but which also ingrained in them attitudes that were inappropriate to an efficient and public-spirited bureaucracy. The Imperial Household Department, by providing a bureaucratic form for them, institutionalized and intensified these attitudes and the behavior that was their natural consequence.

List of Abbreviations

CYYC		*Chung-yang yen-chiu-yuan li-shih yu-yen yen-chiu-suo chi-k'an*
CSL:		*Ta-Ch'ing li-ch'ao shih-lu*
	CL	Ch'ien-lung
	KH	K'ang-hsi
	SC	Shun-chih
	TT	T'ai-tsu
HTSL		*Ch'in-ting Ta-Ch'ing hui-tien shih-li*
SLHK		*Shih-liao hsun-k'an*
TCHT		*Ta-Ch'ing hui-tien*

NOTES

I. The Background to the Imperial Household Department

1. Perspicacious scholars such as Ku Yen-wu, Huang Tsung-hsi, and Chao I bitterly criticized the eunuchs, but all admitted that they were indispensable. See Ku Yen-wu, *Jih-chih-lu chi-shih* (Shanghai, 1935), IV, 33; Huang Tsung-hsi, *Ming-i tai-fang lu* (Taipei, 1959), p. 109; Chao I, *Nien-erh-shih cha-chi* (Peking, 1963), I, 97. The only scholar we have discovered who advocated abolishing the eunuchs entirely was T'ang Chen, a late Ming—early Ch'ing philosopher. See T'ang Chen, *Ch'ien-shu* (Peking, 1955), pp. 167–169

2. T. Guilland, "Les Eunuques dans l'Empire Byzantin," *Etudes Byzantines*, I:205, 218 (1943).

3. Aisin-Gioro Pu Yi, *From Emperor to Citizen: The Autobiography of Aisin-Gioro Pu Yi*, tr. W. J. F. Jenner (Peking, 1964), pp. 61-62; Ai-hsin-chüe-lo P'u-i, *Wo ti ch'ien-pan-sheng* (Hong Kong, 1964), I, 69.

4. Mitamura Taisuke, *Kangan* (Tokyo, 1963), p. 7.

5. Katō Shigeru, "Kandai ni okeru kokka zaisei to teishitsu zaisei to no kubetsu oyobi ni teishitsu zaisei ippan," in *Shina keizaishi kōshō* (Tokyo, 1952), p. 106.

6. Wang Yu-ch'uan, "An Outline of the Central Government of the Former Han Dynasty," *Harvard Journal of Asiatic Studies* 12 (1949), 170-172.

7. Chao I, *Cha-chi*, I, 96.

8. Ibid., pp. 95-96.

9. Ibid., p. 96.

10. Ibid., p. 383.

11. Ch'en Yin-k'o, *T'ang-tai cheng-chih-shih shu-lun kao* (Chungking, 1943), p. 44.

12. Ibid., p. 50.

13. Chao I, *Cha-chi*, I, 383-384.

14. Ch'en Yin-k'o, *T'ang-tai*, pp. 79-82, 86.

15. Ibid., p. 82.

16. T'o-t'o, *Sung-shih* 1739 ed. (Taipei, 1956), 466:1.

17. Ibid., 466:1b.

18. Ibid., 466:5.

19. Ibid., 466:1b.

20. Saeki Tomi, "Sōdai no kōjōshi ni tsuite," *Tōhō gakuhō* (Kyoto), 9:164, 166, 170, 173, 174 (October 1938).

21. Saeki Tomi, "Sōdai no sobajōjū no kenkyū," *Tōhō gakuhō* (Kyoto), 14.2:89, 101 (February 1944).

22. Saeki, "Sōdai no kōjōshi," p. 194.

23. Saeki, "Sōdai no sobajōjū," p. 102.

24. T'o-t'o, *Chin-shih*, 1739 ed. (Taipei, 1956), 131:1b-2a.

25. Ibid., 131:1a-b.

26. Ibid., 8:19.

27. Ibid., 114:3a, 114:4b.

28. Ibid., 101:7b.

29. Ku Yen-wu, *Jih-chih lu*, IV, 317.

30. Ibid.

31. Charles Hucker, "Governmental Organization of the Ming Dynasty," *Harvard Journal of Asiatic Studies* 21:28 (1958).

32. Ting I, *Ming-tai t'e-wu cheng-chih* (Peking, 1950), pp.292-293.

33. Ibid., p. 306.

34. Ibid., p. 46.

35. Ibid., p. 93. For an analogous development, see James E. Dunlap, "The Office of the Grand Chamberlain in the Later Roman and Byzantine Empires," in James E. Dunlap and Arthur E. R. Boak, *Two Studies in Later Roman and Byzantine Administration* (New York, 1924), pp. 254, 256.

36. Ting I, *T'e-wu*, pp. 111-112.

37. Ibid., pp. 35-36.

38. Ibid., p. 33.

39. Ibid., p. 102.

40. Ibid., pp. 176-177.

41. Ibid., p. 248.

42. Ibid., p. 256.

43. Ibid., p. 23.

44. Shimizu Taiji, "Jiku kangan no kenkyū," *Shigaku zasshi* 43 (January 1932), 127-128.

45. Ting I, *T'e-wu*, p. 170.

46. Chao I, *Ou-pei ch'üan-chi* (Chia-ch'ing ed.) 18:21b-24b.

47. *Ming-shih-lu* (1940), Wu-tsung, 66.15b.

48. Wang Shih-chen, "Ch'ih-pei ou-t'an," in *Pi-chi hsiao-shuo ta-kuan* (Taipei, 1962), V, 2:1b.

49. Wang Ch'eng-en's loyalty has been immortalized in an unusual expression in the Peking dialect. When a person encounters a very difficult or hopeless situation, it is said that his only recourse is to "call Wang Ch'eng-en." Chin Shou-shen, *Pei-ching-hua yü-hui* (Peking, 1965), p. 103.

50. The term "Manchu" became the official designation for these people only in 1635. The most accurate term for the Manchus before this time seems to be "Jurchen." For the history of these terms, see Meng Sen, *Ch'ing-ch'ao ch'ien-chi* (Shanghai, 1930), pp. 1-5, 9-25.

51. Mo Tung-yin, "Ming-ch'u Nü-chen ti she-hui hsing-t'ai," in *Man-chou-shih lun-ts'ung* (Peking, 1958), p. 35.

52. For the most exhaustive study of Ming relations with the Jurchen, see Meng Sen, *Ming-yuan Ch'ing-shih t'ung-chi* (Peking, 1934).

53. Ejima Toshio, "Mindai Joshin chōkō bōeki no kaikan," *Shien* 77:1-2 (December 1958).

54. This translation is taken from Lien-sheng Yang, "Historical Notes on the Chinese World Order," in J. K. Fairbank, ed., *The Chinese World Order* (Cambridge, Mass., 1968), pp. 20-33.

55. Ejima Toshio, "Mindai Joshin no uma," *Shien* 63:93-115 (November 1954).

56. Ejima, "Mindai bōeki," pp. 13, 15.

57. Ibid., pp. 17-22.

58. Muramatsu Yūji "Nujihashaku no Joshinkoku to sono buzokuteki chitsujo to no kōshō," *Hitotsubashi ronsō* 17.3-4:48-49 (April 1947).

59. Wada Sei, "Some Problems Concerning the Rise of T'ai-tsu, the Founder of the Manchu Dynasty," *Memoirs of the Research Department of the Toyo Bunko*, 16:72-73 (1957).

60. Ejima, "Mindai bōeki," pp. 18-23.

61. A. Hummel, ed., *Eminent Chinese of the Ch'ing Period* (Washington, D.C. 1943-1944), p. 596.

62. The historian was Inaba Iwakichi. See Imanishi Shunjū, "Bauzen taru ninjin shi," *Tōyōshi kenkyū* 6.1:52 (August 1936).

63. Kawakubo Teirō, "Shindai jinshin saishu seido ni tsuite no ichi kōsatsu" in *Suzuki Jun kyōjū kanreki kinen tōyōshi ronsō* (Tokyo, 1964), pp. 166-168; Toda Shigeki, ed., *Seikyō Naimufu Junchi nenkan tōsatsu* (Mukden, 1943), pp. 94-95.

64. Wang Chung-han, "Huang-t'ai-chi shih-tai Man-tsu hsiang feng-chien-chih ti kuo-tu," *Ch'ing-shih tsa-k'ao* (Peking, 1957), pp. 52, 92.

65. Mikami Tsugio, "Kinchō zenki ni okeru Kanjin tōchi seisaku," *Toa kenkyūjo hō*, 21:2-3, 11-12, 17-20, 23-24 (April 1943).

66. For the varying interpretations on this question, see Wada Sei, "Minchō ni okeru Joshin shakai no hensen," *Shigaku zasshi*, 48.9:91-92 (September 1937); Hatada Takashi, "Kenshū san'ei no toku ni tsuite," in *Ikeuchi Hakase kanreki kinen tōyōshi ronsō* (Tokyo, 1940), pp. 670-672; and Kawachi Yoshihiro, "Kenshū Joshin shakai kōzō no ichi kōsatsu," in Tamura Jitsuzō, ed. *Mindai Man Mōshi kenkyū* (Kyoto, 1963), pp. 297-339. For an interesting Marxist interpretation of the evolution of Jurchen-Manchu society, see Cheng T'ien-t'ing, "Ch'ing ju-kuan-ch'ien man-chou-tsu ti she-hui hsing-chih," *Li-shih yen-chiu* 6:87-96 (December 1962).

67. Kawauchi Yoshihiro, "Atsudarizoku ni okeru dobi no kyokyūgen mondai," *Chōsen gakuhō* 21-22:590-627 (October 1961).

68. Hatada Takashi, "Mindai Joshinjin no tekki ni tsuite," *Tōhō gakuhō* (Tokyo) 11.1:260-267 (March 1940).

69. Ch'en Wen-shih, "Ch'ing-jen ju-kuan-ch'ien ti shou-kung-yeh," *Chung-yang yen-chiu-yuan li-shih yü-yen yen-chiu-suo chi-k'an* (hereafter cited as *CYYC*) 34:299 (December 1962).

70. Ibid., 315-318.

71. Inaba Iwakichi, *Shinchō zenshi*, 2 vols. (Tokyo, 1914), I, 258-261, 298-299.

72. Wang Chung-han, "Man-tsu tsai Nu-erh-ha-ch'i shih-tai ti she-hui ching-chi hsing-t'ai," in *Ch'ing-shih tsa-k'ao* (Peking, 1957), p. 29; Osabuchi Hajime, "Shinchō zenki shakai zakō," *Tōyō no shakai* (Tokyo, 1948), p. 300.

73. Wang Chung-han, "Man-tsu tsai," p. 25.

74. Toda Shigeki, "Shinsho ni okeru nikan irgen no hassei to sono igi," *Tōyōshi kenkyū* 5.4:27-43 (August–September 1941) and Kitamura Hironao, "Shinsho ni okeru seiji to shakai (1)–nyūkanzen ni okeru hakki to kanjin mondai," *Tōyōshi kenkyū* 10.4:60-69 (November 1949).

75. These estimates and the figures below are based on a count of the *pao-i* families from the upper three banners included in O-erh-t'ai, ed., *Pa-ch'i Man-chou shih-tsu t'ung-p'u* (1744).

76. The genealogical records give four answers to the question of when *pao-i* joined the Jurchen: unknown; *kuo-ch'u* (during the early years of the state); the T'ien-tsung period (1627-1636); and the K'ang-hsi period (1662-1722). We have taken the term *kuo-ch'u* to mean pre-1627 for two reasons. In the first place, we have not found any internal evidence in the entries implying that this term refers to the period after 1627. In the second place, we have found definitive evidence in some entries indicating that this term refers to the pre-1627 period. The slaves Sui Hsun and Ning-ku-ch'i, for instance, joined the Jurchen in the *kuo-ch'u* period and were especially honored by Nurhachi, who lived only till 1626. See O-erh-t'ai, *Pa-ch'i t'ung-p'u*, 1:29b and 33:5b.

77. Sudō Yoshiyuki, "Shinchō no nyūkanzen ni okeru kichi no hatten katei," *Tōhō gakuhō* (Tokyo) 12.2:38 (July 1941).

78. Ibid. The size of an estate is given as 13 male adults, but Nei-wu-fu documents from the mid-1660s seem to indicate an average size of 9 male adults per estate. See Toda, *Seikyō tōsatsu*, pp. 90-93.

79. Sudō, "Shinchō no nyūkan zen," p. 39.

80. Amakai Kenzaburō, *Naimufu kanshō* (Dairen, 1914), p. 85.

81. Sudō, "Shinchō no nyūkanzen," p. 39.

82. Amakai, pp. 11-12, 18.

83. Ibid., pp. 18-19.

84. Osabuchi Hajime, "Shin Taisojidai keisei kō," *Haneda Hakase shōju ju kinen tōyōshi ronsō* (Kyoto, 1950), p. 328.

85. Perhaps the first scholar to note the similarities between the Chin and Ch'ing social-military organizations was Toriyama Yoshikazu, "Moanbōkoku to Kin no kokusei," in *Chōsen Shina bunka no kenkyū* (Seoul, 1929), p. 535.

86. Osabuchi Hajime, "Shinsho haigara kō," *Inaba Hakase kanreki kinen Mansenshi ronsō* (Seoul, 1938), pp. 217-268.

87. Osabuchi Hajime, "Shinsho no hachi kozan kakushin ni tsuite," *Yamashita sensei kanreki kinen tōyōshi ronbunshū* (Tokyo, 1938), pp. 16-87.

88. Meng Sen, "Pa-ch'i chih-tu k'ao-shih," *Ming-Ch'ing-shih lun-chu chi-k'an* (Shanghai, 1959), pp. 233-234.

89. Ch'en Wen-shih, "Ch'ing T'ai-tsung shih-tai ti chung-yao cheng-chih ts'o-shih," *CYYC* 40:308 (October 1968).

90. Cheng T'ien-t'ing, "Ch'ing-tai pao-i chih-tu yü huan-kuan," *Ch'ing-shih t'an-wei* (Chungking, 1946), p. 60.

91. Amakai (p. 19) gives 1631 as the date for the original establishment of the Nei-wu-fu, but gives no source. Chang Te-ch'ang presents ambiguous evidence that suggests the year 1628 as the year of origin for the organization. Chang Te-ch'ang, "The Economic Role of the Imperial Household (Nei-wu-fu) in the Ch'ing Dynasty," *Journal of Asian Studies* 31.2: 245 (February 1972).

92. Ts'ao Tsung-ju, "Tsung-kuan nei-wu-fu k'ao-lueh," *Wen-hsien lun-ts'ung* (1936), pp. 85-86.

93. Cheng T'ien-t'ing, "Ch'ing-tai pao-i," p. 65.

94. Ibid., pp. 65-66.

95. Ibid., p. 66. This harsh measure was mitigated, however, by a clause allowing parents with more than four children to entrust one son to the proper officials in preparation for service as a palace eunuch.

96. *Ta-Ch'ing li-ch'ao shih-lu* (Taipei, 1964), Shun-chih, 76:16b-17. Hereafter cited *CSL* by reign: *TT* (T'ai-tsu), *SC* (Shun-chih), *KH* (K'ang-hsi), and *CL* (Ch'ien-lung).

97. *CSL:SC*, 76.17. Different sources give different names to the bureaus: see Cheng T'ien-t'ing, "Ch'ing-tai pao-i," pp. 73-76.

98. *CSL:SC*, 76:17b.

99. *CSL:SC*, 77:2-3b.

100. *CSL:SC*, 92:12.

101. Cheng T'ien-t'ing, "Ch'ing-tai pao-i," pp. 68-69.

102. Ibid., pp. 69-71.

103. Chang Te-ch'ang, p. 248.

104. Ibid., p. 71.

II. A General View of the Imperial Household Department

1. *Tsung-kuan Nei-wu-fu hsien-hsing tse-li* (1852 ed.), t'ang shang, 1:18b. For other references to the Nei-wu-fu censors, see *CSL:CL*, 72:20, 139:18, 147:22, 331:19. The Yung-cheng Emperor established these censors in 1726. Hsiao Shih, *Yung-hsien lu* (Shanghai, 1959), p. 290.

2. See the diagram attached to Ts'ao Tsung-ju.

3. These figures and those below, which are taken from the chapters on Nei-wu-fu organization in *Ch'in-ting Ta-Ch'ing hui-tien shih-li*, 1899 ed. (Taipei, 1967), 1170-1173 (hereafter cited as *HTSL*), include permanent "posts" (*ch'üeh*) and not temporary or joint appointments. Nor do they include appointments to positions such as customs superintendents, salt censors, and other posts which were not officially part of the Nei-wu-fu organization. Appointment of Nei-wu-fu personnel to these positions was an informal, although regular, custom rather than a formally recognized procedure.

4. The information provided here and below is drawn from *HTSL*, 1170-1173.

5. See diagram, p. 31.

6. Chu Hsieh, *Ming-Ch'ing liang-tai kung-yuan chien-chih yen-ko t'u-k'ao* (Shanghai, 1947), p. 90. See also *Ch'ien-lung ching-ch'eng ch'üan-t'u* (Peking, 1941).

7. Yü Min-chung, *Kuo-ch'ao kung-shih*, Ch'ien-lung ed. (Taipei, 1965), 11:19.

8. Compare the diagrams of the Ming and Ch'ing forbidden cities in Chu Hsieh, *Ming-Ch'ing*, p. 52.

9. Ts'ao Tsung-ju, p. 88.

10. *HTSL*, 1170:1-2b. The Nei-wu-fu ministers (*tsung-kuan nei-wu-fu ta-ch'en*) appear to be the same officials as the Nei-wu-fu managers (*nei-wu-fu tsung-kuan*).

11. This list of duties, like those for other officials below, is taken from the work of Ts'ao Tsung-ju, who utilized Nei-wu-fu documents unavailable to us. See Ts'ao Tsung-ju, pp. 89-90.

12. Ibid.

13. *HTSL*, 1170:2.

14. Ibid., 1170:2b-6.

15.   Ts'ao Tsung-ju, pp. 91-92.

16.   See below, pp. 127–129.

17.   *HTSL*, 1170:10-11b.

18.   Ts'ao Tsung-ju, p. 96.

19.   Haneda Tōru, *Man Wa Jiten* (Kyoto, 1937), p. 6.

20.   *HTSL*, 1171:1-3b.

21.   Jerry Norman, *A Manchu-English Dictionary* (Taipei, 1967), p. 347. I
      appreciate Silas Wu's pointing out the Manchu term to me.

22.   For an explanation of this term, see Nieh Ch'ung-ch'i, "Man-kuan Han-
      shih," *Yen-ching hsueh-pao* 32:113 (June 1947).

23.   Ts'ao Tsung-ju, p. 103.

24.   *Pao-i* could, if they wished, take the regular government examinations
      and accept positions in the state bureaucracy. *HTSL*, 1218:12b. For
      information on the Nei-wu-fu schools, see *HTSL*, 1200.

25.   *HTSL*, 394:19b.

26.   See below, p. 49.

27.   *HTSL*, 1200:11.

28.   *HTSL*, 1200:13b.

29.   *CSL:CL*, 557:3b-4.

30.   *HTSL*, 1200:2b.

31.   *CSL:CL*, 605:1b, 611:14b.

32.   *CSL:CL*, 1009:6-7.

33.   *HTSL*, 1173:14.

34. For these aspects of the department, see the material drawn from Nei-wu-fu archives in Wu Hsiang-hsiang, *Tzu-chin-ch'eng mi-t'an* (Taipei, 1953), pp. 79-94.

35. See, for instance, Ch'i Ju-shan, "Ch'ien-Ch'ing ti Nei-wu-fu ya-men," in *Ch'i Ju-shan ch'üan-chi*, 9 vols. (Taipei, n.d.), III, 71-78. I am indebted to Peter Li for this reference.

36. *HTSL*, 1216:9b.

37. *HTSL*, 1216:11b.

38. *HTSL*, 1216:12.

39. *HTSL*, 1216:2.

40. *HTSL*, 1216:12b.

41. *HTSL*, 1216:14.

42. Yü Min-chung, 4:20.

43. For the pronunciation of this name, see Ts'ao Tsung-ju, p. 5.

44. The standard reference work on Ch'ing administration, H. S. Brunnert and V. V. Hagelstrom, *Present Day Political Organization of China*, tr. A. Beltchenko and E. E. Moran (Shanghai, 1912), p. 104, explains this term as one which refers to officials below the rank of a secretary, Rank 6a. Here, however, the term probably refers to department (*ssu*) directors.

45. *HTSL*, 1216:1b.

46. *CSL:CL*, 106:2b-3.

47. *HTSL*, 1216:15.

48. Unfortunately, we have no hard figures but only indirect hints that the number of eunuchs was increasing. See, for instance, Yü Ming-chung, 4:14b-15, 4:19b, and *HTSL*, 1216:2b.

49. *HTSL*, 1216:2b-3.

50. *HTSL*, 1216:1.

51. *HTSL*, 1216:1.

52. Yü Min-chung, 2:7.

53. *HTSL*, 1216:8b.

54. *HTSL*, 1216:1.

55. *HTSL*, 1216:14b.

56. Yü Min-chung, 4:19b.

57. *HTSL*, 1216:14b.

58. Yü Min-chung, 4:16b.

59. Ibid., 2:3b.

60. Ibid., 2:3b; 3:9.

61. *HTSL*, 1216:8.

62. *HTSL*, 1216:8.

63. Yü Min-chung, 2:1b.

64. Yü Min-chung, 3:12.

65. Ibid., 4:15.

66. Ibid., 4:21b-22.

67. *HTSL*, 1216:15.

68. The edicts in Yü Min-chung, *Kuo-ch'ao kung-shih*, are mostly addressed to *Erh-teng tsung-kuan*, i.e., "you assistant chief eunuchs."

69. Yü Min-chung, 2:2b.

70. See the revealing letters to him by K'ang-hsi in Jonathan Spence, *Emperor of China* (New York, 1974), pp. 155-166.

71. Yü Min-chung, 3:8b-9.

72. Ibid., 4:21b.

73. Ibid., 4:17b.

74. Ibid., 3:7b-8, 4:7, 4:19b, 4:20, 4:22b-23.

75. Ts'ao Tsung-ju, p. 98; and *KCKS*, 2:4.

76. Yü Min-chung, 4:11b, 21b.

77. *HTSL*, 1212:4b; Brunnert and Hagelstrom, p. 16; and Ts'ao Tsung-ju, p. 105. See also *CSL:CL*, 20:22b, 347:13b, 376:22.

78. *HTSL*, 1216:12b-13.

79. Yü Min-chung, 3:6.

80. Ibid., 3:6b.

81. *HTSL*, 1216:6b.

82. Yü Min-chung, 2:7.

83. Yü Min-chung, 2:6b-7. Spence, *Emperor of China*, p. 123, gives the figure of 300 for "women around the palace."

84. Ch'ing-k'uei, *Kuo-ch'ao kung-shih hsu-pien* 1816 ed. (Peking, 1933), 2:12b.

85. *HTSL*, 1200:16b.

86. This analysis is taken from Peter Blau, *Bureaucracy in Modern Society* (New York, 1963), pp. 32-90.

87. See Blau's discussion of supervisors, ibid., pp. 70-72.

88. Yü Min-chung, 3:3b.

89.   Yü Min-chung, 3:4.

III. The Social Organization of
the Imperial Household Department's Bondservants

1.   Brunnert and Hagelstrom, p. 10.

2.   E. G. Pulleyblank, "The Origins and Nature of Chattel Slavery in China,"
      Journal of the Economic and Social History of the Orient, 1.2:211
      (April 1958).

3.   Niida Noboru, *Shina mibunhō shi* (Tokyo, 1943), p. 860.

4.   Ibid., pp. 905-915.

5.   Ibid., pp. 914-936.

6.   George T. Staunton, *Ta Tsing Leu Lee* (London, 1810), p. 293.

7.   Jonathan Spence, *Ts'ao Yin and the K'ang-hsi Emperor* (New Haven, 1967),
      and Chang Te-ch'ang.

8.   Ch'ien Mu, *Chung-kuo li-tai cheng-chih te-shih* (Hongkong, 1956),
      pp. 102-105.

9.   Suzuki Tadashi, "Mindai katei kō," *Shikan* 37:23-40 (June 1952).

10. Fujii Hiroshi, "Shinan shōnin no kenkyū," *Tōyō gakuhō* 36.3:82-85
      (December 1953).

11. The term *chia-jen*, literally "house person," meaning an indentured
      servant, seems to date from a usage that was current in the lower
      Yangtze in late Ming times (Niida, p. 892). This Chinese term is thus,
      by coincidence, very similar to the Manchu term for bondservant,
      pao-i. In Ch'ing times the Manchu term referred only to the bond-
      servants of the emperor and banner leaders, while the Chinese term
      acquired a broader meaning, referring not only to indentured servants
      but also to younger and older brothers, sons, and nephews, i.e., male
      relatives of the master who resided in his household. (Hsueh Yun-sheng,
      Tu-li ts'un-i [1905], 41:35). The Chinese term seems to have been used
      most often, however, to describe indentured servants rather than simply

relatives. The legal literature refers only to *chia-ien* of officials, probably not because influential commoners, such as wealthy merchants, did not have relatives living with them, but because only officials were allowed to own slaves according to Ch'ing law (Niida, p. 892). In addition, all the *chia-jen* for whom our sources give names have different surnames from their masters. In view of the fact that the Chinese family was patrilocal and connections with the wife's relatives were often tenuous, it seems logical that these *chia-jen* with surnames different from their masters were not relatives but indentured servants. For an example of the use of different terms to describe the same person, see the memorialist's use of the terms *chia-jen, ch'i-jen nu-p'u,* and *chia-nu* in *SLHK*, 13:452-454 (October 1930).

12. Nakayama Hachiro, "Minmatsu Joshin to hakki teki tōsei ni kansuru sobyō, *Rekishigaku kenkyū* 5.2:146 (December 1935).

13. Wang Chung-han, "Huang t'ai-chi," pp. 52, 60; and Mo Tung-yin, "Pa ch'i chih-tu," *Man-chou-shih lun-ts'ung*, p. 102.

14. *CSL:TT*, 9:12b-13.

15. Mo Tung-yin, "Pa-chi chih-tu," *Lun-ts'ung*, p. 102.

16. Ibid., pp. 146-147.

17. Cheng T'ien-t'ing, "Pao-i chih-tu," p. 60.

18. *Yü-chih lu* (n.p., n.d.), 1727, 9:76-80.

19. See below, pp. 144–146.

20. *HTSL*, 133:19b.

21. See below, pp. 135, 158.

22. Sasaki Masaya, "Shindai kanryō no kashoku ni tsuite," *Shigaku zasshi* 63.2:39-43 (February 1954).

23. Ch'ing Shih-tsung, *Chu-p'i yü-chih* (1887 ed.), 5:110b.

24. *Shang-yü pa-ch'i* (1732), 1725, 1:46.

25. *Shih-liao hsun-k'an* (hereafter *SLHK*) 40:452-454 (July 1931).

26. *Shang-yü t'iao-li*, 1757, 213b.

27. Hsueh Yun-sheng, 41:36b.

28. *HTSL*, 133:17b.

29. *SLHK*, 4:118b (July 1930) and *CSL:CL*, 594:15.

30. O-erh-t'ai, ed., *Pa-ch'i t'ung-chih ch'u-chi* 1739 ed. (Taipei, 1957), passim.

31. Spence, *Ts'ao Yin*, p. 22.

32. This interpretation was suggested by P. T. Ho.

33. O-erh-t'ai, *Pa-ch'i ch'u-chi*, 3:passim, 4:passim, 5:passim.

34. Hsueh Yun-sheng, 41:35.

35. *CSL:KH*, 83:8b. It is assumed in all the laws that the bondservants belong to officials, because in theory commoners without official positions were not permitted to own them. This, of course, did not correspond to reality. See Niida, p. 892.

36. See below, p. 72.

37. *CSL:KH*, 47:9b, 48:12b.

38. O-erh-t'ai, *Pa-ch'i ch'u-chi*, 1:12b, 17:4b.

39. Ibid., 1:17b-18b.

40. Ibid., 17:5b; and *Shang-yü nei-ko*, 1725, 8:2b.

41. Ibid., 8:3.

42. *Shang-yü pa-ch'i*, 1724, 34:11; *Yü-chih lu*, 2:97-100.

43. O-erh-t'ai, *Pa-ch'i ch'u-chi*, 1:26.

44. Jerry Norman, *Manchu-English Dictionary* (Taipei, 1967), p. 246. I appreciate Silas Wu's referring me to this work.

45. *Shang-yü nei-ko*, 1725, 8:8b. Manchu princes, just as they had *pao-i*, also had *hsin-che-k'u*. See *CSL:KH*, 250:76. This fact was kindly brought to my attention by Silas Wu.

46. *Shang-yü nei-ko*, 1725, 8:8b.

47. Ibid., 8:5b.

48. *CSL:CL*, 73:12.

49. *CSL:KH*, 43:6b-7, 44:15b; and *HTSL*, 99:7.

50. *CSL:KH*, 83:8b-9b; and *HTSL*, 106:8b-9.

51. *HTSL*, 105:6b.

52. *CSL:KH*, 42:16b-17; Hsueh Yun-sheng, 36:18b.

53. Hsueh Yun-sheng, *Tu-li*, 36:10.

54. See, for example, Li Fu and Shen T'ai, below, pp. 153, 156.

55. Saeki Tomi, "Shindai Shinkyō ni okeru gyokuseki mondai," *Shirin* 53.5:43 (March 1970).

56. See *CSL:CL*, 605:1b, 1114:2b.

57. See, for example, *CSL:CL*, 1190:2b.

58. *CSL:CL*, 343:7b-8 and pp. 136–137.

59. *CSL:CL*, 120:41.

60. *CSL:CL*, 102:15.

61. *CSL:CL*, 339:6b, 341:31b.

62. *CSL:CL*, 327:23.

63. *CSL:CL*, 1059:12b-13b. These merchants were probably connected to the Nei-wu-fu lumber trade. See *CSL:CL*, 408:21, 412:8b.

64. *CSL:CL*, 1208:9-10b.

65. *CSL:CL*, 441:18, 576:30b.

66. This discussion is from Amakai, pp. 32–42, 96–108.

67. See also *CSL:CL*, 40:32b.

68. *CSL:CL*, 1316:12.

69. *CSL:CL*, 1316:12.

70. Amakai, p. 106.

71. Spence, *Ts'ao Yin* (p. 14) gives four. Another from the mid-eighteenth century was Li Chih-ying.

72. *Shang-yü pa-ch'i*, 1725, 3:39b.

73. *CSL:KH*, 32:9b-10.

74. Hsu Ta-ling, *Ch'ing-tai chüan-na chih-tu* (Peking, 1950), p. 24.

75. *Man-Han wen-wu kuan-sheng ming-tz'u lu* (1798).

76. These were secretary, *chu-shih*, 150 men; clerk, *pi-t'ieh-shih*, 549; warden of the Board of Punishments, *hsing-pu ssu-yü*, 107; police-master and jail-warden in the capital, *ping-ma-ssu li-mu*, 101; second-class sub-prefect, *t'ung-p'an*, 134; district magistrate, *chih-hsien*, 102; salt receiver, *yen-k'o ta-shih*, 124; lower prefectual official, *fu-ching*, 210; assistant district magistrate, *hsien-cheng*, 1,258; district registrar, *hsien-chu-pu*, 227; departmental police-master and jail warden, *chou-li-mu*, 279.

77. Hsu Ta-ling, *Chüan-na*, p. 169.

78. *HTSL*, 1218:11.

79. O-erh-t'ai, *Pa-ch'i ch'u-chi*, 145:14.

80. Spence, *Ts'ao-Yin*, pp. 23-24.

81. Hsiao Shih, *Yung-hsien lu*, p. 266.

82. *CSL:CL*, 120:41-42, 167:5.

83. *CSL:CL*, 1498:11b-12.

84. Aisin-Gioro, *From Emperor*, pp. 71-72.

85. Cheng T'ien-t'ing, "Man-Ch'ing huang-shih chih shih-tsu yü hsueh-hsi," *T'an-wei*, p. 17.

86. *HTSL*, 1218:7.

87. *CSL:CL*, 1083:4-5.

88. Spence, *Emperor of China*, p. 123.

89. *CSL:CL*, 172:12b.

90. Yü Min-chung, 2:2b.

91. Ibid., 4:6.

92. Ibid., 2:3.

93. Ibid., 2:5b.

94. *HTSL*, 1218:7b.

95. T'ang Pang-chih, *Ch'ing huang-shih ssu-p'u* (1923), 2:14.

96. Chang Ts'ai-t'ien, *Ch'ing lieh-ch'ao hou-fei chuan-kao* (1929), 1:97.

97. T'ang Pang-chih, 2:27-28.

98. Hummel, pp. 412-413.

99. Chang Ts'ai-t'ien, 2:23.

100. Hummel, pp. 159-160.

101.   Chang Ts'ai-t'ien, 2:19b.

102.   Hummel, p. 969.

103.   Chang Ts'ai-t'ien, 2:34.

104.   Hummel, p. 968.

105.   O-erh-t'ai, *T'ung-p'u*, 7:1; 10:8b-9; 17:8; 20:14b.

106.   T'ieh-pao, *Pa-ch'i t'ung-chih*, 318:9b-319:56b.

107.   Ch'ing Shih-tsung, *Chu-p'i*, 4:89b.

108.   Ibid., 4:89.

109.   Ibid., 4:91b.

110.   Ibid., 4:97.

111.   Ibid., 17:20.

112.   Ibid., 17:20b.

113.   Ibid., 17:24.

114.   Ibid., 17:29.

115.   Ibid., 17:33.

116.   Ibid., 17:34b.

117.   *CSL:CL*, 165:26.

118.   *CSL:CL*, 184:3b.

119.   *CSL:CL*, 186:14.

120.   *CSL:CL*, 204:18b, 220:11, 238:7, 240:3b, 241:11, 244:13, 251:4, 255:14b.

121.   *CSL:CL*, 271:4b.

122. *CSL:CL*, 311:11b.

123. *SLHK*, 21:748b (December 1930). See also *CSL:CL*, 469:10, 676:3b, 686:19b-25, 816:4b.

IV. The Financial Functions of the Imperial Household Department

1. The only work on the Nei-wu-fu's financial role is the recent article by Chang Te-ch'ang, p. 43.

2. The locations of these vaults are taken from *Shun-tien-fu chih* (1885 ed.), 10:4-7. See also the diagram, p. 31.

3. For the location of this and other storehouses and Nei-wu-fu offices outside the palace, see the index and maps in *Ch'ien-lung ching-cheng ch'üan-t'u*.

4. The treasury in the Summer Palace is referred to in *SLHK*, 15:538 (October 1930). For these and other grain storehouses, see *Ta Ch'ing hui-tien* (1764), 87:11b-12 (hereinafter cited as *TCHT*), and *HTSL*, 1190:passim.

5. *HTSL*, 1190:2b-3.

6. *HTSL*, 1175:1.

7. *HTSL*, 1200:11.

8. *HTSL*, 1200:1.

9. *HTSL*, 1175:1b.

10. *HTSL*, 1175:3, 4b.

11. *HTSL*, 1175:4b.

12. *HTSL*, 1170:4b.

13. *HTSL*, 1170:6.

14. See, for example, *CSL:CL*, 475:5, 911:9b, 912:31, 1291:43b, 1377 28b-29b, 1378:2b-3b.

15. Amakai, pp. 9-10.

16. Ibid., p. 5.

17. Ibid., pp. 11-12.

18. Muramatsu Yūji, "Shin no maimufu shōen," *Hitotsubashi daigaku kenkyū nenpō* 12:107 (1968).

19. Ibid., pp. 18-19.

20. *TCHT* (1764), 87:11, and (1818), 2-4.

21. Muramatsu Yūji, "Shin no naimufu shōen," p. 12.

22. Amakai, pp. 109-110, 114-117.

23. Ibid., pp. 137-141.

24. Ibid.

25. Ibid., pp. 146-147.

26. Ibid., pp. 144-145.

27. Ch'ing shih-tsung, *Chu-p'i*, 5:3b-4.

28. Ibid., 5:3b.

29. Ibid., 5:3b.

30. *HTSL*, 1197:10b-11.

31. *HTSL*, 1196:4b.

32. *HTSL*, 1198:1.

33. *HTSL*, 1198:2b.

34. *HTSL*, 1196:6b.

35. *HTSL*, 1196:11b.

36. *TCHT* (1764), 87:passim, and (1818), 74:passim.

37. Nankai University History Department, ed., *Ch'ing shih-lu ching-chi tzu-liao chi-yao* (Peking, 1959), pp. 635-636; and *HTSL*, 1196:15b.

38. Imamura Tomo, *Ninjin shi*, 7 vols. (Seoul, 1936), III, 6.

39. *HTSL*, 232:1.

40. Toda, *Seikyō tōsatsu*, pp. 94-95.

41. *HTSL*, 232:4b.

42. *HTSL*, 232:4b.

43. *HTSL*, 233:1.

44. *HTSL*, 233:4b.

45. *HTSL*, 233:1.

46. Ku-kung po-wu-yuan Ming-Ch'ing tang-an pu, ed., *Kuan-yü Chiang-ning chih-tsao Ts'ao-chia tang-an shih-liao* (Peking, 1975), p. 66.

47. Ibid., pp. 148, 155.

48. *HTSL*, 232:7b.

49. *HTSL*, 232:8, 9, 10b.

50. *HTSL*, 1213:3b. The term *jen-mai*, literally "recognize and buy," seems to imply that they were allowed to purchase this ginseng on credit.

51. *HTSL*, 1213:3b.

52. *HTSL*, 233:4b and *CSL:CL* 1444:5b-8; 1446:4, 11b-13b; 1448:4-8. For information on the ginseng trade in the nineteenth century, see Chang Te-ch'ang, "The Economic Role," pp. 261-263.

53. See Murakami Shozō, "Genchō ni okeru senfushi to atsudatsu," *Tōhō gakuhō* 13.1:143-151 (May 1942).

54. For a full account of the Fan clan, see Ping-ti Ho, *The Ladder of Success in Imperial China* (New York, 1962), pp. 283-286.

55. Saeki Tomi, "Shinchō no kōki to Sansei shōnin," *Shakai bunka shigaku* 1:17 (March 1966).

56. Ibid., p. 32.

57. Ping-ti Ho, p. 284.

58. Yamawaki Teijirō, *Kinsei Nitchū bōekishi no kenkyū* (Tokyo, 1961), pp. 41-42. Yamawaki draws the conclusion from this incident that Fan Yü-pin was a broker for the Nei-wu-fu's Department of the Privy Purse.

59. Yamawaki, *Kinsei Nitchū* (p. 42), suggests that the Fan lineage mentioned here included the famous Fan Wen-ch'eng of the seventeenth century and the high officials Fan Shih-ch'ung and Fan Shih-i of the eighteenth century.

60. *CSL:CL*, 5:18, 68:7, 77:8.

61. For the history of the copper trade, see also Spence, *Ts'ao Yin*, pp. 106-108 and Yamawaki, *Kindai Nitchū*, pp. 19-20, 31-34.

62. CSL:CL, 214:186.

63. *Ch'ing-ch'ao wen-hsien t'ung-k'ao* (Shanghai, 1936), p. 4976; Ku-kung po-wu-yuan, *Ts'ao-chia tang-an shih-liao*, pp. 15-17. The Nei-wu-fu manufactories may also have been involved in this trade with Japan. Ku-kung po-wu-yuan, *Ts'ao-chia tang-an shih-liao*, p. 14.

64. *HTSL*, 214:19b.

65. *Ch'ing t'ung-k'ao*, p. 4978.

66. Before the copper trade assumed its final form in the early Ch'ien-lung period, local officials in Kiangsu and Chekiang recruited local merchants and loaned them funds to buy Japanese copper, but they proved incapable of fulfilling the quotas. Yamawaki, *Kinsei Nitchū*, pp. 31-34, 40-41.

67. *HTSL*, 214:19b.

68. Yamawaki, *Kinsei Nitchū*, pp. 40-57.

69. Yamawaki Teijirō, "Shindai enshō to Nagasaki bōeki no dokusen," *Shigaku zasshi* 67.8:67 (August 1958).

70. Yamawaki, *Kinsei Nitchū*, p. 40.

71. Ibid., p. 15.

72. Ibid., p. 16.

73. Ibid., p. 19 and Yamawaki Teijirō, *Nagasaki no Tōjin bōeki* (Tokyo, 1965), pp. 193-196.

74. Yamawaki, *Kinsei Nitchū*, p. 38.

75. Ibid., p. 181; and *CSL:CL*, 334:12b.

76. Yamawaki, "Shindai enshō."

77. Yamawaki, *Nagasaki no Tōjin*, p. 179; and *CSL:CL*, 39:7b.

78. *SLHK*, 6:198b (July 1930); and *CSL:CL*, 597:9.

79. *CSL:CL*, 550:10b-13.

80. Yamawaki, *Kinsei Nitchū*, p. 44.

81. *CSL:CL*, 708:15b; 1175:1-2b.

82. *CSL:CL*, 1175:1-2b.

83. *CSL:CL*, 1172:15-16 mentions the transfer of his interest in the copper trade to a nephew, Fan Ch'ai, but this seems to have been only a temporary measure. See Yamawaki, *Kinsei Nitchū*, p. 46.

84. *CSL:CL*, 1184:2-3b.

85. Yamawaki, *Kinsei Nitchū*, p. 43.

86. Ibid., p. 44.

87. For further information on the customs bureaus, see also Chang Te-ch'ang, pp. 256-259.

88. Hosea Ballou Morse, *The International Relations of the Chinese Empire*, 3 vols. (London, 1910), I, 52.

89. *SLHK*, 10:354 (September 1930).

90. Liang T'ing-nan, 8:4b.

91. Ibid., 41:2.

92. Ibid., 10:9.

93. Ibid., 14:30b.

94. *Wen-hsien ts'ung-pien* 11:8b (May 1931).

95. Liang T'ing-nan, 11:8. For procedures on shipping these funds to the Nei-wu-fu, see *CSL:CL*, 712:1b.

96. *Hu-pu tse-li* (1776 ed.), 52.4. There were no quotas for the bureaus at Ch'ung-wen Gate, Shan-hai-kuan, Kalgan, and Sha-hu-k'ou.

97. Liang T'ing-nan, 14:28-30.

98. Nei-wu-fu clerks and others were also appointed to many of the customs bureaus. See Hsiao Shih, p. 105 and *CSL:CL*, 595:5, 599:55, 672:8, 1059:20b-21b.

99. Liang T'ing-nan, 7:20b.

100. Ibid., 7:30-31b.

101. The information here and below comes from the biographies indexed in Tu Lien-che and Fang Chao-ying, ed., *Index to Thirty-Three Collections of Ch'ing Dynasty Biographies*, Harvard-Yenching Institute Sinological Index Series, Vol. IX (Peking, 1932) and from the lists of officials in the gazetteers in the following notes and in the discussions of the salt monopoly and the Imperial Manufactories below.

102. *Hu-pu tse-li*, 52:5-6.

103. *Che-chiang t'ung-chih* (1736 ed.), 121:15; and *Chiu-chiang-fu chih* (1874 ed.), 25:17.

104. Hsiao Shih, pp. 82-83.

105. Hsiao Shih, p. 125.

106. *CSL:CL*, 9:38b.

107. *CSL:CL*, 323:40b-42.

108. *CSL:CL*, 670:4b. An-ning had appropriated 70,000 taels.

109. Li Huan, ed., *Kuo-ch'ao ch'i-hsien lei-cheng ch'u-pien* (1890), 165:44. Yang gave 19,000 of these to salt merchants to earn interest.

110. Liang T'ing-nan, 8:5-6b, 8:16, 7:3b, 8:21b, 14:31b.

111. Spence, *Ts'ao Yin*, p. 105.

112. John K. Fairbank, *Trade and Diplomacy on the China Coast* (Cambridge, 1964), p. 51.

113. Ch'ing Shih-tsung, *Chu-p'i*, 3:76a.

114. See below, pp. 117-120.

115. For shipping procedures, see *CSL:CL*, 400:20, 692:5.

116. See the extensive treatment of this salt administration and the Nei-wu-fu *pao-i* salt censors in Spence, *Ts'ao Yin*, pp. 166-212.

117. *Liang-huai yen-fa chih* (1806 ed.), 34:17-19.

118. Ibid., 34:16-21.

119. Ibid., 34:18-21.

120. *Liang-che yen-fa chih* (1801 ed.), 22:36-38.

121. *Chi-fu t'ung-chih* (1884 ed.), 30:43b-52b.

122. Spence, *Ts'ao Yin*, pp. 192-193.

123. Spence, *Ts'ao Yin*, pp. 192-193.

124. Ch'ing Shih-tsung, *Chu-p'i*, 6:88. See also Spence, *Ts'ao Yin*, p. 212.

125. Nankai, *Ch'ing tzu-liao*, p. 635. See also *CSL:CL*, 159:1b.

126. *CSL:CL*, 343:7b and Kao Heng, *Huai-pei tso-cheng* (n.d.), 3:60-67.

127. *CSL:CL*, 218:2-3, 343:7b.

128. *CSL:CL*, 427:15.

129. *Liang-huai yen-fa chih* (1806 ed.), 20:18.

130. Ibid., 20:18.

131. *Hu-pu tse-li*, 48:22b.

132. *CSL:CL*, 1396:10.

133. Only governors, governor generals, salt censors, customs superintendents, and imperial manufactory superintendents were permitted to send gifts to the emperor in the eighteenth century. See *CSL:CL*, 66:5b, 119:12, 1025:30. These presents were received by the Chancery of Palace Memorials. See *CSL:CL*, 1112:16b.

134. See below, p. 138.

135. Spence, *Ts'ao Yin*, p. 103; *Wen-hsien ts'ung-pien* 29:5b-6 (August 1935).

136. Spence, *Ts'ao Yin*, p. 103.

137. *Wen-hsien tsung-pien* 26:82b (March 1937).

138. Ibid., 10:11 (April 1931).

139. Spence, *Ts'ao Yin*, p. 190.

140. Ch'ing Shih-tsung, 5:76b.

141. *Liang-huai yen-fa chih* (1806 ed.), 17:3.

142. Ibid., 17:3b.

143. *Ch'ang-lu yen-fa chih* (1726 ed.), 2:26.

144. *Liang-huai yen-fa chih* (1806 ed.), 17:1b.

145. Ibid., 17:4; and Ping-ti Ho, "The Salt Merchants of Yang-chou: A Study of Commercial Capitalism in Eighteenth Century China," *Harvard Journal of Asiatic Studies* 17:160-161 (June 1954).

146. *Liang-huai yen-fa chih* (1806 ed.), 17:4b-6.

147. *CSL:CL*, 1438:10b.

148. Ku-kung po-wu-yuan, *Ts'ao-chia tang-an shih-liao*, p. 36.

149. *HTSL*, 1213:20.

150. *HTSL*, 1213:1.

151. See, for example, *CSL:CL*, 253:21.

152. *Liang-huai yen-fa chih* (1806 ed.), 17:2, 11b.

153. For details on the transport of cloth to Peking in the 1700s, see *CSL:CL*, 265:22, 777:9, 1142:21.

154. *Su-chou-fu chih* (1881 ed.), 22:41b.

155. *HTSL*, 1190:13.

156. See Spence, *Ts'ao Yin*, pp. 87-123.

157. P'eng Tse-i, "Ch'ing-tai ch'ien-ch'i chiang-nan chih-tsao ti yen-chiu," *Li-shih yen-chiu* 4:93 (August 1963).

158. *Liang-huai yen-fa chih* (1748 ed.), 8:46-47.

159. Ibid., 8:47b.

160. *Su-chou-fu chih*, 22:43b-44.

161. *HTSL*, 1190:20b.

162. *CSL:CL*, 550:10b-13. This trade may have started as early as 1726.
      Ku-kung po-wu-yuan, *Ts'ao-chia tang-an shih-liao*, p. 174.

163. *CSL:CL*, 557:23b.

164. *CSL:CL*, 1040:14b-15.

165. *CSL:CL*, 594:4.

166. *CSL:CL*, 600:25, 648:1b.

167. *CSL:CL*, 1112:1b.

168. *Wen-hsien ts'ung-pien*, 10:9b (May 1931).

169. *HTSL*, 1190:14b.

170. See, for example, *CSL:SC*, 23:17. Also see Hsueh Yun-sheng, 4.

171. *HTSL*, 1219:10b, 15.

172. The Nei-wu-fu rightfully received pawn shops that were expropriated,
      but Ch'ien-lung seems to have disapproved of active measures by the
      Nei-wu-fu to acquire pawn shops. *CSL:CL*, 194:13b.

173. *HTSL*, 1213:2.

174. *HTSL*, 1219:15.

175. See also the account of this by Chang Te-ch'ang, p. 267.

176. Hummel, p. 288.

177. See below, pp. 117–120 for details on the Secret Accounts Bureau.

178. Li Huan, 96:37-40.

179. Ibid., 96:40.

180. *SLHK*, 8:282 (August 1930).

181. Ibid., 279b.

182. Ibid., 7:240-242 (August 1930).

183. Ibid., 237b.

184. Ibid., 242-243b.

185. *Wen-hsien ts'ung-pien*, 25:1b (April 1925). The earliest reference we have found to the term *tzu-hsing i-tsui* (see below) and associated with contributions to the Secret Accounts Bureau dates to 1768 and involves the Nei-wu-fu *pao-i* Yu Pa-shih. *CSL:CL*, 816:4b.

186. *Wen-hsien ts'ung-pien*, 25:1 (April 1925) and Chang Te-ch'ang, p. 263.

187. *Wen-hsien ts'ung-pien*, 25:passim, and 26 (May 1935):passim.

188. Ibid., 25:9.

189. Ibid., 25:1-4, 5b-8b and 26:1-4, 5b-8b.

190. Ibid., 25:1b, 25:4b, 26:3, 25:4b, 25:9b, 25:4b, 25:9, 25:5, 25:3b, 25:2b.

191. Ibid., 26:1-4.

192. Ibid., 26:1-9b.

193. Ibid., 25:5b.

194. Ibid., 25:5b.

195. Nakamura Yūichi, "Tōdai naizōkō no henyō," *Machikaneyama ronsō* 4:140-141 (March 1971).

196. *HTSL*, 503:2.

197. *HTSL*, 503:8b-9.

198. *CSL:CL*, 442:2, 1108:5.

199. Haijong Chun, "Sino-Korean Tributary Relations in the Ch'ing Period," in *The Chinese World Order*, ed. by J. K. Fairbank (Cambridge, Mass., 1968), pp. 90-111. This study does not seem to deduct travel expenses within China from the value of the gifts received by the Chinese side. Thus it refers to gross, rather than net, income. Of course, transport costs for the Koreans within China certainly were not substantial, and the Nei-wu-fu undoubtedly still made a net profit on the tributary missions from that country. The low transport costs may make the Korean missions unrepresentative of the system as a whole but, if the discrepancy in the value of the gifts in the Korean case is representative, it seems unlikely that transport costs within China for many missions would be large enough to cause the Nei-wu-fu a net loss on any particular tributary mission or on the system as a whole.

200. Ibid., pp. 102, 105-106.

201. Ch'ing Shih-tsung, *Chu-p'i*, 5:107.

202. Matteo Ripa, *Memoirs of Father Ripa*, tr. Fortunato Prandi, in *Ancient Moral Tales* (New York, 1845), p. 138.

203. Ch'ing Shih-tsung, *Chu-p'i*, 5:107-108.

204. *CSL:CL*, 422:4.

205. *HTSL*, 514:8b. Randle Edwards was kind enough to bring this reference to my attention.

206. *CSL:CL*, 1428:9b-11.

207. *HTSL*, 514:4b.

208. *HTSL*, 514:5.

209. *CSL:CL*, 167:8.

210. *HTSL*, 514:7b.

211. See, for example, *CSL:CL*, 505:7, 535:11, 874:23b.

212. *HTSL*, 1214:5.

213. Cheng T'ien-t'ing, "Ch'ing-tai pao-i," p. 72.

214. Carroll B. Malone, *History of the Peking Summer Palaces under the Ch'ing Dynasty*, Illinois Studies in the Social Sciences 19.1-2:23, 62.

215. *SLHK*, 5:163 (July 1930).

216. *SLHK*, 26:932b-933 (February 1931).

217. *SLHK*, 25:893b (February 1931); 26:931 (February 1931).

218. *SLHK*, 14:479b and 481 (October 1930).

219. Wang Wei, *Yuan-ming-yuan* (Peking, 1957), p. 2.

220. Ibid., p. 10.

221. *CSL:KH*, 82:18.

222. *CSL:KH*, 59:25b.

223. Li Huan, 43:16.

224. *CSL:CL*, 456:16b, 754:27.

225. *CSL:CL*, 762:9b-10.

226. *CSL:CL*, 1202:1b.

227. *Shun-t'ien fu chih*, 12:2.

228. *HTSL*, 1218:7b.

229. *HTSL*, 1213:passim.

230. Li Huan, 52.25.

231. *CSL:CL*, 920:24.

232. *CSL:CL*, 578:4b.

233. *CSL:CL*, 748:14b, 751:1b.

234. *CSL:CL*, 811:7b-8.

235. Chang Te-ch'ang, p. 271.

236. Na-yen-ch'eng, *A-wen-ch'eng-kung nien-p'u* (1813), 25:38 and *CSL: CL*, 920:24.

237. *CSL:CL*, 920:24.

238. *CSL:CL*, 694:12.

239. *CSL:CL*, 773:7b.

240. *CSL:CL*, 811:7b-8.

241. *CSL:CL*, 1210:18.

242. *CSL:CL*, 1396:10.

243. Na-yen-ch'eng, 25:35b-37b.

V. Two Illustrative Cases

1. *CSL:CL*, 963:17.

2. *CSL:CL*, 963:23b.

3. *CSL:CL*, 963:35b. This terminology is taken from Silas Wu, *Communication and Imperial Control in China* (Cambridge, Mass., 1970), p. 49. The source used here mentions only the *tsou-shih* officials and eunuchs without reference to "inner" or "outer," but this distinction seems analytically helpful.

4. Silas Wu, pp. 43, 161.

5. *CSL:CL*, 1115:25b-26. In 1780 quotas were set reserving four posts for the Nei-wu-fu and two for the general bureaucracy.

6. *CSL:CL*, 963:34.

7. *CSL:CL*, 963:20.

8. *CSL:CL*, 963:19b.

9. *CSL:CL*, 963:40.

10. *CSL:CL*, 963:17b.

11. *CSL:CL*, 963:18.

12. *CSL:CL*, 963:33.

13. *CSL:CL*, 966:6.

14. For a short description of this Nei-wu-fu office, see Chao Lien, 1:37.

15. Liang T'ing-nan, 7:20b.

16. *CSL:CL*, 963:29.

17. *CSL:CL*, 964:26b; 965:4b.

18. *CSL:CL*, 964:12; 965:5.

19. *CSL:CL*, 964:12.

20. *CSL:CL*, 963:31b.

21. *CSL:CL*, 963:29b.

22. *CSL:CL*, 963:25.

23. *CSL:CL*, 963:32; 964:12; 966:55; 964:27b.

24. *CSL:CL*, 963:37.

25. *CSL:CL*, 963:36b.

26. See Chang Te-ch'ang, p. 265; Sasaki, pp. 39-43; Saeki, "Shindai Shinkyō," pp. 27-54. This last article is the most extensive, but it does not utilize any of the materials in *SLHK*.

27. This biography and that of Kao P'u, except where noted, are taken from *Ch'ing-shih lieh-chuan* (Taipei, 1962), 16:44b-46.

28. *CSL:CL*, 354:10b-11.

29. *CSL:CL*, 380:7.

30. *CSL:CL*, 437:17.

31. *CSL:CL*, 624:18b.

32. *CSL:CL*, 672:16b.

33. *CSL:CL*, 692:5.

34. *CSL:CL*, 741:13b-14.

35. *CSL:CL*, 741:14b.

36. *CSL:CL*, 444:14.

37. *CSL:CL*, 812:13.

38. *CSL:CL*, 813:20-21.

39. Although his grandfather, Kao Pin, had been released from *pao-i* status, Kao P'u was considered a "Nei-wu-fu man" by other Nei-wu-fu *pao-i*. See *SLHK*, 19:663, 668 (December 1930). One possible explanation for this seeming contradiction is that Kao P'u was returned to *pao-i* status because of his father's crimes.

40. *Ch'ing-shih lieh-chuan*, 16:45.

41. Ibid., 16:45b.

42. *CSL:CL*, 1018:9b, 1020:2. Later Ma's appointment in the capital was deferred, and he was ordered to serve as Commandant of the Forces in Khotan. See below, p. 157.

43. *CSL:CL*, 1068:3.

44. *CSL:CL*, 1067.5, 1067.14.

45. *CSL:CL*, 1050:15.

46. *Shin-chiang wai-fan chi-lueh* (1777 ed.), 1:25b.

47. Ibid., 1:26.

48. *SLHK*, 26:949 (February 1931).

49. *SLHK*, 26:949 (February 1931).

50. *CSL:CL*, 1071:1b-2.

51. *CSL:CL*, 1020:2; *SLHK*, 24:874b (January 1931).

52. *SLHK*, 19:669, 20:709 (December 1930).

53. *CSL:CL*, 1070:24.

54. *CSL:CL*, 1070:26.

55. *SLHK*, 25:908b (February 1931).

56. *SLHK*, 25:908b (January 1931).

57. *SLHK*, 24:875 (January 1931).

58. *SLHK*, 24:875 (January 1931).

59. *SLHK*, 25:908b (February 1931).

60. *SLHK*, 24:874 (January 1931).

61. *SLHK*, 25:904, 910b (February 1931); 20:715b (December 1930); 27:985b (February 1931).

62. *SLHK*, 27:985b (February 1931).

63. *SLHK*, 25:911 (February 1931).

64. *SLHK*, 25:910b, 904 (February 1931).

65. *SLHK*, 22:784 (January 1931).

66. *SLHK*, 22:784 (January 1931).

67. *SLHK*, 28:9 (March 1931).

68. *SLHK*, 28:9 (March 1931).

69. *SLHK*, 28:9 (March 1931); 22:784 (January 1931).

70. *SLHK*, 20:709 (December 1930).

71. *SLHK*, 24:877 (January 1931).

72. *SLHK*, 25:905b (February 1931).

73. *Chi-tzu*, the son of a relative.

74. *SLHK*, 25:906 (February 1931).

75. *SLHK*, 25:905 (February 1931); 23:823 (January 1931).

76. *SLHK*, 22:784b (January 1931).

77. *SLHK*, 19:671b–672 (December 1930).

78. *CSL:CL*, 1068:3b-4.

79. *SLHK*, 20:707b (December 1930).

80. *SLHK*, 19:669 (December 1930).

81. *SLHK*, 19:669 (December 1930).

82. *SLHK*, 20:709b (December 1930).

83. Saeki, "Shindai Shinkyō," p. 33.

84. *SLHK*, 19:660b (December 1930).

85. *SLHK*, 19:660b (December 1930).

86. *CSL:CL*, 1067:13b, 24.

87. *SLHK*, 19:661 (December 1930).

88. *SLHK*, 19:660 (December 1930); Saeki, "Shindai Shinkyō," p. 31.

89. I appreciate Joseph Cheng's help in interpreting this passage. *SLHK*, 19:661 (December 1930).

90. *SLHK*, 19:661 (December 1930).

91. *SLHK*, 22:791 (January 1931).

92. *SLHK*, 22:791b (January 1931).

93. *SLHK*, 23:823 (January 1931).

94. *SLHK*, 27:989 (February 1931).

95. *SLHK*, 20:708b-709 (December 1930).

96. *SLHK*, 26:947 (February 1931).

97. *SLHK*, 23:817 (January 1931).

98. *SLHK*, 20:709 (December 1930).

99. *SLHK*, 25:902b (February 1931).

100. *SLHK*, 21:754 (December 1930).

101. *SLHK*, 23:823b (January 1931).

102. *SLHK*, 20:707b-708b (December 1930).

103. *SLHK*, 20:707b, 709 (December 1930).

104. At *SLHK*, 19:670b.20:708 (December 1930) it says Chang's share was 31,600 taels, but that he received it in jade rather than silver.

105. *SLHK*, 20:708b (December 1930).

106. *SLHK*, 20:708 (December 1930).

107. *SLHK*, 26:948b (February 1931).

108. *SLHK*, 19:671 (December 1930); 20:708 (December 1930).

109. *SLHK*, 25:903b (February 1931).

110. *SLHK*, 23:823b (January 1931).

111. *SHLK*, 26:949b-50 (February 1931).

112. *SLHK*, 23:823b (January 1931).

113. *CSL:CL*. 1067:37.

114. *Ch'ing-shih lieh-chuan*, 16:46.

115. *CSL:CL*, 1067:9b-10.

116. *CSL:CL*, 1067:6b; 1055:1b-2.

117. *CSL:CL*, 1068:2b.

118. *CSL:CL*, 1068:23b-24.

119. *CSL:CL*, 1067:10b.

120. *CSL:CL*, 1067:13.

121. *CSL:CL*, 1075:21b, 1078:10, 1080:2b-3. Yuan Ping-t'ang was mentioned above, p. 154.

122. *CSL:CL*, 1068:3b-4.

123. *CSL:CL*, 1051:126, 1033:10.

124. *CSL:CL*, 1067:38b.

125. *SLHK*, 24:870b (January 1931).

126. *SLHK*, 24:871 (January 1931).

127. The evidence on these details is conflicting. See *SLHK*, 20:715 (December 1930); 21:757 (December 1930); 24:870b (January 1931).

128. *SLHK*, 28:17 (March 1931).

129. *SLHK*, 26:950b (February 1931).

130. *SLHK*, 20:715 (December 1930).

131. *SLHK*, 21:759 (December 1930); *CSL:CL*, 1023:15.

132. *SLHK*, 20:711, 715 (December 1930).

133. *SLHK*, 20:715b (December 1930).

134. *SLHK*, 24:872b (January 1931).

135. *CSL:CL*, 1068:2b.

136. *CSL:CL*, 1067:10.

137. *CSL:CL*, 1067:4b-5.

138. *CSL:CL*, 1067:6b.

139. *CSL:CL*, 1068:4b.

140. *SLHK*, 20:708b (December 1930).

141. *SLHK*, 20:709b-710 (December 1930).

142. *SLHK*, 20:709b (December 1930).

143. *SLHK*, 19:669 (December 1930).

144. *SLHK*, 20:709b (December 1930).

145. *SLHK*, 20:708b (December 1930).

146. *SLHK*, 20:707 (December 1930); 21:748 (December 1930).

147. *SLHK*, 20:707 (December 1930).

148. *SLHK*, 21:748b (December 1930); 20:707 (December 1930).

149. *SLHK*, 21:754b (December 1930); 23:817 (January 1931).

150.   *CSL:CL*, 1068.19b.

151.   *SLHK*, 24:875b (January 1931). Shu-wen was not the only *pao-i* involved in purchasing jade. Indeed, it seems to have been a common custom for the *pao-i* superintendents to collect expensive jade ornaments. I-ling-a, the Superintendent of the Huai Customs Bureau, for instance, bought on credit two jade pieces for a total of 10,500 taels through his indentured servant Min Tung-shen in the second month of 1778. *SLHK*, 27:980 (February 1931). Shu-wen himself bought jade worth 8,200 taels in the first month of 1778 alone. *SLHK*, 26: 954b (February 1931). See also purchases by merchants of jade and other articles for I-ling-a worth 600,000 taels. *CSL:CL*, 1208:9b.

152.   *CSL:CL*, 1068:19b-20.

153.   *SLHK*, 21:754 (December 1930).

154.   *SLHK*, 22:786b-787 (January 1931).

155.   *SLHK*, 22:787 (January 1931).

156.   *SLHK*, 21:748 (December 1930).

157.   *SLHK*, 22:785b (January 1931).

158.   *CSL:CL*, 1068:14b.

159.   *SLHK*, 23:817 (January 1931).

160.   *SLHK*, 23:817 (January 1931).

161.   *SLHK*, 20:708b (December 1930); 21:749b (December 1930).

162.   *SLHK*, 23:823 (January 1931).

163.   *SLHK*, 24:872b (January 1931); *CSL:CL*, 1070:20.

164.   *SLHK*, 21:755 (December 1930).

165.   *SLHK*, 22:788b (January 1931).

166.   *SLHK*, 21:745 (December 1930); *SLHK*, 20:715 (December 1930).

167.   *CSL:CL*, 1067:36b.

168.   *CSL:CL*, 1274:22.

169.   *CSL:CL*, 1067:6; 1067:38b. We do not know under what particular statute Kao P'u was put to death, but merchants who later illicitly dealt in jade from Sinkiang received the severest punishment prescribed for theft—strangulation. *CSL:CL*, 1070:5b.

170.   *CSL:CL*, 1070:30b, 1071:11.

171.   *CSL:CL*, 1081:19b.

172.   *CSL:CL*, 1070:30b-31, 1067:38b.

173.   *Ch'ing-shih lieh-chuan*, 16:46, *CSL:CL*, 1067:36b, 37b.

174.   *CSL:CL*, 1070:31b.

175.   *CSL:CL*, 1070:17-19b.

176.   *CSL:CL*, 1070:32b-33.

177.   *CSL:CL*, 1072:35.

178.   *SLHK*, 25:906b (February 1931).

179.   See Table 1, p. 166.

180.   *SLHK*, 21:754 (December 1930).

181.   *SLHK*, 21:754 (December 1930).

182.   *SLHK*, 22:783 (January 1931); 24:876b (January 1931).

183.   *SLHK*, 21:748b (December 1930).

184.   *SLHK*, 19:668b (December 1930).

185.   *SLHK*, 28:17 (March 1931). As a further measure to placate the Moslems, Ch'ien-lung ordered that taxes be commuted for the 3,000 Moslems whom Kao P'u had impressed into mining jade. *CSL:CL*, 1070:31.

186. *CSL:CL*, 1070:40b.

187. *CSL:CL*, 1070:41b.

188. *SLHK*, 23:827b (January 1931).

189. *SLHK*, 27:984b (February 1931).

190. *SLHK*, 8:282b (August 1930).

191. *SLHK*, 19:663b (December 1930).

192. *SLHK*, 20:708 (December 1930). Ch'ien-lung realized that the Nei-wu-fu was not receiving all of Kao P'u's fortune. The total income from the jade sales in Soochow was over 120,000 taels, while the amount recovered in drafts, postdated checks, and in cash was only about 70,000 taels. Ch'ien-lung probably suspected the *pao-i* superintendents and high provincial officials of pocketing the unaccounted-for 50,000 taels and may have demanded the payments to the Secret Accounts Bureau as a way of recouping it. *SLHK*, 23:827, 828 (January 1931).

193. *SLHK*, 19:663b (December 1930).

194. *SLHK*, 28:21b (March 1931).

195. *SLHK*, 28:21b (March 1931).

196. *CSL:CL*, 1070:25.

197. *SLHK*, 19:666b (December 1930).

BIBLIOGRAPHY

Ai-hsin-chue-lo P'u-i 愛新覺羅溥儀 . *Wo ti ch'ien-pan-sheng* 我的前半生 (Autobiography). Hongkong, 1964.

Aisin-Gioro Pu Yi. *From Emperor to Citizen: The Autobiography of Aisin-Gioro Pu Yi.* Tr. W. J. F. Jenner. Peking, Foreign Languages Press, 1964.

Amakai Kenzaburō 天海謙三郎 . *Naimufu kanshō* 內務府 官莊 (The Nei-wu-fu's landed estates). Dairen, 1914.

Blau, Peter. *Bureaucracy in Modern Society.* New York, Random House, 1963.

Brunnert, H. S., and V. V. Hagelstrom. *Present Day Political Organization of China.* Tr. A. Beltchenko and E. E. Moran. Shanghai, Kelly and Walsh, 1912.

Chang-lu yen-fa chih 長蘆塩法志 (Ch'ang-lu salt gazetteer). 1726.

Chang Te-ch'ang. "The Economic Role of the Imperial Household (Nei-wu-fu) in the Ch'ing Dynasty," *Journal of Asian Studies* 31.2:243-273 (February 1972).

Chang Ts'ai-t'ien 張采田 . *Ch'ing lieh-ch'ao hou-fei chuan-kao* 清列朝后妃傳稿 (Draft biographies of empresses and concubines of the Ch'ing period). N.p., 1929.

Chao I 趙翼 . *Ou-pei ch'üan-chi* 甌北全集 (Complete works). Chia-ch'ing ed.

——Nien-erh-shih cha-chi 廿二史劄記 (Notes on the twenty-two histories). Peking, 1963.

Chao Lien 昭槤 . *Hsiao-t'ing tsa-lu* 嘯亭雜錄 (Collected essays). Shanghai, 1909.

Che-chiang t'ung-chih 浙江通志 (Chekiang gazetteer). 1736.

Ch'en Wen-shih 陳文石 "Ch'ing-jen ju-kuan-ch'ien ti shou-kung-yeh 清人入關前的手工業 (Handicrafts of the Manchus before the conquest), *Chung-yang yen-chiu-yuan li-shih yü-yen yen-chiu-suo chi-k'an* 34:291-321 (December 1962).

———"Ch'ing T'ai-tsung shih-tai ti chung-yao cheng-chih ts'o-shih 清太宗時代的重要政治措施 (The important political policies of Abahai's reign), *Chung-yang yen-chiu-yuan li-shih yü-yen yen-chiu-suo chi-k'an* 40:295-372 (October 1968).

Ch'en Yin-k'o 陳寅恪 *T'ang-tai cheng-chih-shih shu-lun kao* 唐代政治史述論稿 (A draft political history of the T'ang dynasty). Chungking, 1943.

Cheng T'ien-t'ing 鄭天挺 . "Ch'ing-tai pao-i chih-tu yü huan-kuan" 清代包衣制度與宦官 (The pao-i system and eunuchs in the Ch'ing period), in his *Ch'ing-shih t'an-wei* 清史探微 (Essays on Ch'ing history). Chungking, 1946.

———"Ch'ing ju-kuan-ch'ien Man-chou-tsu ti she-hui hsing chih" 清入關前滿洲族的社會性質 (The social nature of the Manchu tribes before the conquest), *Li-shih yen-chiu* 6:87-96 (December 1962).

Chi-fu t'ung-chih 畿輔通志 (Chi-fu gazetteer). 1884.

Ch'i Ju-shan 齊如山 . "Ch'ien-Ch'ing ti Nei-wu-fu ya-men" 前清內務府衙門 (The Ch'ing Nei-wu-fu), in *Ch'i Ju-shan ch'üan-chi* 齊如山全集 (Complete works). 9 vols. Taipei, n.d.

Ch'ien-lung ching-ch'eng ch'üan-t'u 乾隆京城全圖 (A complete map of the capital in the Ch'ien-lung period). Peking, 1941.

Ch'ien Mu 錢穆 . *Chung-kuo li-tai cheng-chih te-shih* 中國歷代政治得失 (The political strengths and weaknesses of the various Chinese dynasties). Hongkong, 1956.

Chin Shou-shen 金受申 *Pei-ching-hua yü-hui* 北京話語汇
(Dictionary of unusual terms in the Peking dialect). Peking,
1965.

Ch'in-ting Ta-Ch'ing hui-tien shih-li 欽定大清會典事例
(Ch'ing administrative statutes). 1899 ed. Taipei, 1967.

Ch'ing-ch'ao wen-hsien t'ung-k'ao 清朝文獻通考 (Materials
on Ch'ing institutional history). Shanghai, 1936.

Ch'ing-k'uei 慶桂 . *Kuo-ch'ao kung-shih hsu-pien* 國朝宮史
續編 (A continuation of the history of the palace in the
Ch'ing period). 1816 ed. Peking, 1933.

Ch'ing-shih lieh-chuan 清史列傳 (Ch'ing biographies).
Taipei, 1962.

Ch'ing Shih-tsung 清世宗 *Chu-p'i yü-chih* 硃批諭旨
(Vermilion endorsements of the Yung-cheng Emperor). 1732.

Chiu-chiang-fu chih 九江府志 (Kiukiang gazetteer). 1874.

Chu Hsieh 朱偰 . *Ming-Ch'ing liang-tai kung-yuan chien-chih
yen-ko t'u-k'ao* 明清兩代宮苑建置沿革圖考
(History of the palace buildings in the Ming and Ch'ing
periods). Shanghai, 1947.

Chun, Haijong. "Sino-Korean Tributary Relations in the Ch'ing
Period," in John K. Fairbank, ed., *The Chinese World Order*.
Cambridge, Harvard University Press, 1968.

Dunlap, James E. "The Office of the Grand Chamberlain in the
Later Roman and Byzantine Empires," in James E. Dunlap
and Arthur E. R. Boak, eds., *Two Studies in Later Roman
and Byzantine Administration*. New York, Macmillan Co.,
1924.

Ejima Toshio 江嶋壽雄 . "Mindai Joshin no uma" 明代
女真の馬 (The horses of the Jurchen in the Ming dynasty)
Shien 63:93-115 (November 1954).

———"Mindai Joshin chōkō bōeki no gaikan" 明代女真朝貢貿易の概觀 (A general view of the Jurchen tributary trade in the Ming period), *Shien* 77:1-25 (December 1958).

Fairbank, John K. *Trade and Diplomacy on the China Coast*. Cambridge, Harvard University Press, 1964.

Fujii Hiroshi 藤井宏 . "Shinan shōnin no kenkyū 新安商人の研究 (Investigations on the Hui-chou merchants), *Tōyō gakuhō* 36.3:65-118 (December 1953).

Guilland, T. "Les Eunuques dans l'Empire Byzantin," *Etudes Byzantines* 1:196-238 (1943).

Haneda Tōru 羽田亨 . *Man Wa Jiten* 滿和辭典 (A Manchu-Japanese dictionary). Kyoto, 1937.

Hatada Takashi 旗田巍 . "Mindai Joshinjin no tekki ni tsuite" 明代女真人の鐵器について (The iron implements of the Jurchen in the Ming dynasty), *Tōhō gakuhō* (Tokyo) 11.1:260-267 (March 1940).

———"Kenshū san'ei no kokō ni tsuite" 建州三衛の戸口について (The population of the three Chien-chou garrisons), in *Ikeuchi Hakase kanreki kinen tōyōshi ronsō* 池内博士還暦記念東洋史論叢 (Essays in honor of Professor Ikeuchi). Tokyo, 1940.

Ho, Ping-ti. "The Salt Merchants of Yang-chou: A Study of Commercial Capitalism in Eighteenth Century China," *Harvard Journal of Asiatic Studies* 17:130-168 (June 1954).

———*The Ladder of Success in Imperial China*. New York, Columbia University Press, 1962.

Hsiao Shih 蕭奭 . *Yung-hsien lu* 永憲錄 (A Record of Yung-cheng's reign). Shanghai, 1959.

Hsu Ta-ling 許大齡 . *Ch'ing-tai chüan-na chih-tu* 清代捐納制度 (The Ch'ing system of selling official degrees and offices). Peking, 1950.

Hsueh Yun-sheng 薛允升 . *Tu-li ts'un-i* 讀例存疑 (Commentaries on the Ch'ing Code). N.p., 1905.

Hu-pu tse-li 戶部則例 (Administrative regulations of the Board of Revenue). 1776.

Huang Tsung-hsi 黃宗羲 . *Ming-i tai-fang lu* 明夷待訪錄 (Essays on government). Taipei, 1959.

Hucker, Charles. "Governmental Organization of the Ming Dynasty," *Harvard Journal of Asiatic Studies* 21:1-66 (1958).

Hummel, A., ed. *Eminent Chinese of the Ch'ing Period*. Washington, Government Printing Office, 1943-1944.

Imamura Tomo 今村鞆. *Ninjin shi* 人蔘史 (A history of ginseng). 7 vols. Seoul, 1936.

Imanishi Shunjū 今西春秋 . "Bauzen taru shi ninjin" 耄然たる人蔘史 (The importance of the history of ginseng), *Tōyōshi kenkyū* 6.1:52 (August 1936).

Inaba Iwakichi 稻葉岩吉 . *Shinchō zenshi* 清朝全史 (A complete history of the Ch'ing dynasty). 2 vols. Tokyo, 1914.

Kao Heng 高恒 . *Huai-pei tso-cheng* 淮北鹺政 (The salt administration of Huai-pei). pre-1755.

Katō Shigeru 加藤繁 "Kandai ni okeru kokka zaisei to teishitsu zaisei to no kubetsu oyobi ni teishitsu zaisei ippan" 漢代に於ける國家財政と帝室財政との區別及びに帝室財政一般 (The distinction between the public and privy purse during the Han period), *Shina keizaishi kōshō* 支那經濟史考證 (Essays on Chinese economic history). Tokyo, 1952.

Kawauchi Yoshihiro 河内良弘 . "Atsudarizoku ni okeru dobi no kyokyūgen mondai" 斡朶里族に於ける奴婢の供給源問題 (The problem of the supply of slaves for the Wo-to-li tribe), *Chōsen gakuhō* 21-22:590-627 (October 1961).

———"Kenshū Joshin shakai kōzō no ichi kōsatsu" 建州女真社會構造の一考察 (A study of the structure of the Chien-chou Jurchen), in Tamura Jitsuzō 田村実造 , ed., *Mindai Man Mōshi kenkyū* 明代滿蒙史研究 (Essays on Manchu and Mongol history). Kyoto, 1963.

Kawakubo Teirō 川久保悌郎. "Shindai ninjin saishu seido ni tsuite no ichi kōsatsu" 清代人參採取制度について の 一考察 (A study of the system of ginseng gathering in the Ch'ing dynasty), in *Suzuki Jun kyōjū kanreki kinen tōyōshi ronsō* 鈴木俊教授還曆記念東洋史論叢 (Essays in honor of Professor Suzuki). Tokyo, 1964.

Kitamura Hironao 北村敬直 . "Shinsho ni okeru seiji to shakai (1)—nyūkanzen ni okeru hakki to kanjin mondai"清初に於ける政治と社會㈠入關前に於ける八旗と漢人問題(Early Ch'ing government and society: the eight banners and the problem of Chinese captives), *Tōyōshi kenkyū* 10.4:60-69 (November 1949).

Ku-kung po-wu-yuan Ming-Ch'ing tang-an pu 故宮博物院明清檔案部 , ed. *Kuan-yü Chiang-ning chih-tsao Ts'ao-chia tang-an shih-liao* 關於江寧織造曹家檔案史料 (Materials from archives relating to the Ts'ao family and the Nanking imperial manufactory). Peking, 1975.

Ku Yen-wu 顧炎武 . *Jih-chih lu chi-shih* 日知錄集釋 (A record of knowledge accumulated daily). Shanghai, 1935.

Li Huan 李桓 , ed. *Kuo-ch'ao ch'i-hsien lei-cheng ch'u-pien* 國朝耆獻類徵初編 (Biographies of eminent men of the Ch'ing period). N.p., 1890.

Liang-che yen-fa chih 兩浙塩法志 (Liang-che salt gazetteer). 1801.

Liang-huai yen-fa chih 兩淮塩法志 (Liang-huai salt gazetteer). 1748 and 1806 eds.

Liang T'ing-nan 梁廷枏. *Yueh-hai-kuan chih* 粵海關志 (Canton customs gazetteer). post-1839.

Malone, Carroll B. *History of the Peking Summer Palaces under the Ch'ing Dynasty*. Illinois Studies in the Social Sciences 19. 1-2 (1934).

Man-Han wen-wu kuan-sheng ming-tz'u lu 滿漢文武官生名次錄 (A record of Manchu and Chinese sons of officials awaiting appointment). 1798.

Meng Sen 孟森. *Ch'ing-ch'ao ch'ien-chi* 清朝前紀 (Studies in early Ch'ing history). Shanghai, 1930.

———*Ming-yuan Ch'ing-hsi t'ung-chi* 明元清系通紀 (Selected passages and commentaries on the Jurchen in the Ming period). Peking, 1934.

———"Pa-ch'i chih-tu k'ao-shih" 八旗制度考實 (An analysis of the eight-banner system), *Ming-Ch'ing-shih lun-chu chi-k'an* 明清史論著集刊 (Essays on Ming and Ch'ing history). Shanghai, 1959.

Mikami Tsugio 三上次男. "Kinchō zenki ni okeru Kanjin tōchi seisaku" 金朝前期に於ける漢人統治政策 (The policies employed to control the Chinese in the early period of the Chin dynasty), *Tōa kenkyūjo hō* 21:1-71 (April 1943).

Ming-shih-lu 明實錄 (Veritable records of the Ming dynasty). N.p., Kiangsu Provincial Library, 1940.

Mitamura Taisuke 三田村泰助. *Kangan* 宦官 (Eunuchs). Tokyo, 1963.

Mo Tung-yin 莫東寅. "Ming-ch'u Nü-chen ti she-hui hsing-t'ai" 明初女真的社會形態 (The social structure of the

Jurchen in the early Ming), *Man-chou-shih lun-ts'ung* 滿州
史論叢 (Essays in Manchu history). Peking, 1958.

Morse, Hosea Ballou. *The International Relations of the Chinese
Empire*. 3 vols. London, Longmans, Green, 1910.

Murakami, Shozō 村上正三 . "Genchō ni okeru senfushi
to atsudatsu" 元朝に於ける泉府司と斡脱 (The
ch'üan-fu-ssu and the *ortaq* in the Yuan dynasty), *Tōhō gakuhō*
13.1:143-151 (May 1942).

Muramatsu Yūji 村松祐次 . "Nujihashaku no Joshinkoku to
sono buzokuteki chitsujo tosono kōshō" 女兒哈赤の女真國
とその部族的秩序とその交渉(Nurhachi's Jurchen state: its
tribal order and contacts with other Jurchen), *Hitotsubashi
ronsō* 17:3-4, 12-50 (April 1947).

———"Shin no Naimufu shōen" 清の内務府莊園 (The
estates of the Nei-wu-fu in the Ch'ing period), Hitotsubashi
daigaku kenkyū nenpō, Keizaigaku kenkyū 一橋大学
研究年報 (Hitotsubashi University research year-
book, Research in economics) 12:1-118 (1968).

Na-yen-ch'eng 那彥成 . *A-wen-ch'eng-kung nien-p'u* 阿文
成公年譜 (Biography of A-kuei). 1813.

Nakamura Yūichi 中村祐一 . "Tōdai naizōkō no henyō 唐代
内蔵庫の変容 (The changes in the privy purse in the
T'ang period), *Machikaneyama ronsō* 待兼山論叢
4:137-168 (March 1971).

Nakayama Hachiro 中山八郎 . "Minmatsu Joshin to hakki
teki tōsei ni kansuru sobyō" 明末女真と八旗的統制
に關する素描 (A description of the late Ming Jurchen
and the eight banner system), *Rekishigaku kenkyū* 5.2:115-
146 (December 1935).

Nankai University History Department, ed. *Ch'ing shih-lu ching-
chi tzu-liao chi-yao* 清實錄經濟資料集要 (A

collection of economic materials from the Ch'ing veritable records). Peking, 1959.

Nieh Ch'ung-ch'i 聶崇岐 . "Man-kuan Han-shih" 滿官漢釋 (Explanations of Manchu governmental terms), *Yenching hsueh-pao* 32:97–115 (June 1947).

Niida Noboru 仁井田陞 . *Shina mibunhō shi* 支那身分法史 (A history of status law in China). Tokyo, 1943.

Norman, Jerry. *A Manchu-English Dictionary*. Taipei, 1967.

O-erh-t'ai 鄂爾泰 , ed. *Pa-ch'i t'ung-chih ch'u-chi* 八旗通志初集 (Records of the eight banners). 1739 ed. Taipei, 1968.

———, ed. *Pa-ch'i Man-chou shih-tsu t'ung-p'u* 八旗滿州氏族通譜 (The genealogies of the eight banners). 1744.

Osabuchi Hajime 鴛淵一 . "Shinsho haigara kō 清初擺牙喇考 (A study of the pai-ya-la of the early Ch'ing), in *Inaba Hakase kanreki kinen Man Senshi ronsō* 稻葉博士還曆記念滿鮮史論叢 (Essays in honor of Professor Inaba). Seoul, 1938.

———"Shinsho no hachi kozan gakushin ni tsuite" 清初の八固山額真について (The Ku-shan-o-chen officials of the early Ch'ing), in *Yamashita sensei kanreki kinen tōyōshi ronbunshū* 山下先生還曆記念東洋史論文集 (Essays in honor of Professor Yamashita). Tokyo, 1938.

———"Shinchō zenki shakai zakkō" 清朝前紀社會雜考 (A study of Manchu society before the conquest), in Hiroshima daigaku tōyōshi kenkyūshitsu, ed., *Tōyō no shakai* 東洋の社會 (East Asian societies). Tokyo, 1948.

———"Shin Taisojidai keisei kō" 清太祖時代刑政考 (The judicial administration in Nurhachi's reign), in *Haneda Hakase shōjū kinen tōyōshi ronsō* 羽田博士頌壽記念東洋史論叢 (Essays in honor of Professor Haneda). Kyoto, Tōyōshi kenkyūkai, 1950.

P'eng Tse-i 彭澤益. "Ch'ing-tai ch'ien-ch'i chiang-nan chih-tsao ti yen-chiu" 清代前期江南織造的研究 (Investigations on the imperial manufactories in Kiangnan in the early Ch'ing), *Li-shih yen-chiu* 4:91-116 (August 1963).

Pulleyblank, E. G. "The Origins and Nature of Chattel Slavery in China," *Journal of the Economic and Social History of the Orient* 1.2:185-220 (April 1958).

Ripa, Matteo. *Memoirs of Father Ripa*, tr. Fortunato Prandi. *Ancient Moral Tales*. New York, Wiley and Putnam, 1845.

Saeki Tomi 佐伯富. "Sōdai no kōjōshi ni tsuite" 宋代の皇城司について (On the imperial city department in the Sung period), *Tōhō gakuhō* (Kyoto) 9:164-203 (October 1938).

———"Sōdai no sobajōjū no kenkyū" 宋代の走馬承受の研究 (A Study of the itinerant inspectors of the Sung period), *Tōhō gakuhō* (Kyoto) 14.2:75-109 (February 1944).

———"Shinchō no kōki to Sansei shōnin" 清朝の興記と山西商人 (The rise of the Ch'ing dynasty and the Shansi merchants), *Shakai bunka shigaku* 1:11-41 (March 1966).

———"Shindai Shinkyō ni okeru gyokuseki mondai" 清代新疆における玉石問題 (An illicit jade operation in Sinkiang in the Ch'ing period), *Shirin* 53.5:27-54 (March 1970).

Sasaki Masaya 佐々木正哉 "Shindai kanryō no kashoku ni tsuite" 清代官僚の貨殖について (Ch'ing officials as merchants), *Shigaku zasshi* 2:22-57 (February 1954).

Shang-yü nei-ko 上諭内閣 (Edicts of the Yung-cheng Emperor to the cabinet). N.d.

Shang-yü pa-ch'i 上諭八旗 (Edicts of the Yung-cheng Emperor to the eight banners). 1732.

Shang-yü t'iao-li 上諭條例 (Judicial cases of the Ch'ien-lung reign). Chia-Ch'ing ed.

Shih-liao hsun-k'an 史料旬刊 (Periodical of historical materials). Peking, 1930-1931.

Shimizu Taiji 清水泰次 "Jiku kangan no kenkyū" 自宮宦官の研究 (A Study of self-castrated eunuchs), *Shigaku zasshi* 43:83-128 (January 1932).

Shin-chiang wai-fan chi-lueh 新疆外藩記略 (Sinkiang gazetteer). 1777.

Shun-t'ien-fu chih 順天府志 . (Shun-t'ien gazetteer). 1885.

Spence, Jonathan. *Ts'ao Yin and the K'ang-hsi Emperor, Bond-servant and Master*. New Haven, Yale University Press, 1966.

———*Emperor of China*. New York, Alfred A. Knopf, 1974.

Staunton, George T. *Ta Tsing Leu Lee*. London, Cadwell & Davies, 1810.

Su-chou-fu chih 蘇州府志 (Su-chou gazetteer). 1881.

Sudō Yoshiyuki 周藤吉之 . "Shinchō no nyūkanzen ni okeru kichi no hatten katei" 清朝の入關前に於ける族地の發展過程 (The process of development of the Ch'ing banner lands before the conquest), *Tōhō gakuhō* (Tokyo) 12.2:1-64 (July 1941).

Suzuki Tadashi 鈴木正 "Mindai katei kō" 明代家丁考 (A study of bondservants in the Ming period), *Shikan* 37:23-40 (June 1952).

Ta-Ch'ing hui-tien 大清會典 (Collected statutes of the Ch'ing dynasty). 1764. 1818 ed.

Ta-Ch'ing li-ch'ao shih-lu 大清歷朝實錄 (Veritable records of the Ch'ing dynasty). Taipei, 1964.

T'an Wen 譚文 . *Pei-ching chang-ku* 北京掌故 (Stories of Peking's history). Hong Kong, 1974.

T'ang Chen 唐甄 *Ch'ien-shu* 潛書 (Essays). Peking, 1955.

T'ang Pang-chih 唐邦治 . *Ch'ing huang-shih ssu-p'u* 清皇室四譜 (A genealogical study of the Ch'ing imperial house). N.p. 1932.

T'ieh-pao 鐵保 *Pa-ch'i t'ung-chih* 八旗通志 (Gazetteer of the eight banners). 1799.

Ting I 丁易 *Ming-tai t'e-wu cheng-chih* 明代特務政治 (Ming secret service government). Peking, 1950.

T'o-t'o 脫脫 *Chin-shih* 金史 (History of the Chin dynasty). 1739 ed. Taipei, 1956.

———*Sung-shih* 宋史 (History of the Sung dynasty). 1739 ed. Taipei, 1956.

Toda Shigeki 戶田茂喜 . "Shinsho ni okeru nikan irgen no hassei to sono igi" 清初に於けるニカン・イルゲン發生とその意義 (The origin and meaning of the nikan-irgen status in the early Ch'ing), *Tōyōshi Kenkyū*, 5.4: 27-43 (August–September 1941).

———, ed. *Seikyō Naimufu Junchi nenkan tōsatsu* 盛京内務府順治年間檔冊 (Original documents from the Shen-yang Nei-wu-fu in the Shun-chih period). Mukden, 1943.

Toriyama Yoshikazu 鳥山喜一 . "Moanbōkoku to Kin no kokusei" 猛安謀克と金の國勢 (*Meng-an mou-k'o* and the strength of the Chin dynasty), in *Chōsen Shina bunka no kenkyū* 朝鮮支那文化の研究 (Studies on Korean and Chinese Culture). Seoul, 1929.

Ts'ao Tsung-ju 曹宗儒 . "Tsung-kuan nei-wu-fu k'ao-lueh" 總管內務府考略(A study of the Nei-wu-fu). *Wen-hsien lun-ts'ung* 文献論叢 (Collected essays). N.p. 1936.

Tsung-kuan Nei-wu-fu hsien-hsing tse-li 總管內務府現行則例 . 1852.

Tu Lien-che and Fang Chao-ying, eds. *Index to Thirty-Three Collections of Ch'ing Dynasty Biographies.* Harvard-Yenching

Institute Sinological Index Series, Vol. IX. Peking, Harvard-Yenching Institute, 1932.

Wada Sei 和田清 . "Minchō ni okeru Joshin shakai no hensen" 明朝に於ける女真社會の變遷(Changes in Jurchen society in the Ming dynasty), *Shigaku zasshi* 48.9:91-92 (September 1937).

———"Some Problems Concerning the Rise of T'ai-tsu, the Founder of the Manchu Dynasty," *Memoirs of the Research Department of the Toyo Bunko*, 16:35-74 (1957).

Wang Chung-han 王鍾翰 "Man-tsu tsai Nu-erh-ha-ch'i shih-tai ti she-hui ching-chi hsing-t'ai" 滿族在努爾哈齊時代的社會經濟形態. (The form of economy and society of the Manchu tribes in Nurhachi's time), in his *Ch'ing-shih tsa-k'ao* 清史雜考 (Essays on Ch'ing history). Peking, 1957.

———"Huang-t'ai-chi shih-tai Man-tsu hsiang feng-chien-chih ti kuo-tu" 皇太極時代滿族向封建制的過渡 (The transition of the Manchu tribes to feudalism in Abahai's time), in his *Ch'ing-shih tsa-k'ao*. Peking, 1957.

Wang Shih-chen 王士禎 "Ch'ih-pei ou-t'an" 池北偶談 (Essays), in *Pi-chi hsiao-shuo ta-kuan* 筆記小説大觀 (Collection of essays and short stories). Taipei, 1962.

Wang Wei 王威 *Yuan-ming-yuan* 圓明園 (The summer palace). Peking, 1957.

Wang Yu-ch'uan. "An Outline of the Central Government of the Former Han Dynasty," *Harvard Journal of Asiatic Studies* 12:134–187 (1949).

Wen-hsien ts'ung-pien 文獻叢編 (Collected historical materials). Peking, 1936.

Wu Hsiang-hsiang 吳相湘 *Tzu-chin-ch'eng mi-t'an* 紫禁城秘譚 (Secrets of the Forbidden City). Taipei, 1953.

Wu, Silas. *Communication and Imperial Control in China.* Cambridge, Harvard University Press, 1970.

Yamawaki Teijirō 山脇悌二郎 . "Shindai enshō to Nagasaki bōeki no dokusen" 清代塩商と長崎貿易の獨占 (The monopoly of the copper trade with Japan by the salt merchants in the Ch'ing period), *Shigaku zasshi* 67.8:63–80 (August 1958).

———*Kinsei Nitchū bōekishi no kenkyū* 近世日中貿易史の研究 (Studies in modern Japanese-Chinese trade). Tokyo, 1961.

———*Nagasaki no Tōjin bōeki* 長崎の唐人貿易 (The China trade at Nagasaki). Tokyo, 1965.

Yang Lien-sheng. "Historical Notes on the Chinese World Order," in John K. Fairbank, ed., *The Chinese World Order.* Cambridge, Harvard University Press, 1968.

Yü-chih-lu 諭旨録 (Edicts and rescripts of the Yung-cheng Emperor). N.p., n.d.

Yü Min-chung 于敏中 *Kuo-ch'ao kung-shih* 國朝宮史 (A history of the palace in the Ch'ing period). Ch'ien-lung ed. Taipei, 1965.

GLOSSARY

A-erh-to 阿爾多
A-k'o-su 阿克蘇
A-pu-nai 阿布鼐
A-pu tu-shu-k'u-erh-ho-cho
阿布都舒庫爾和卓
a-tun shih-wei 阿敦侍衛
a-tun ya-men 阿敦衙門
ak'im beg 阿奇木伯克
An-hsi 安西
An-su 安肅
An-ting-men 安定門

bayara 擺牙喇
beile 貝勒

cha-erh-ku-ch'i 札爾固齊
Ch'a-ha-erh 察哈爾
Ch'a-k'u 茶庫
Chai An-kuo 柴安國
ch'ai-k'u 柴庫
Chang Ch'eng-yeh 張承業
chang-chü 賬局
Chang-i-ssu 掌儀司
Chang Luan 張鑾
Chang Pao 彰寶
Chang T'ai-p'ing 張太平
Chang T'ing-yü 張廷玉
Chang Yung-kuei 張永貴
Ch'ang-chen 常鎮

Ch'ang-fang kuan-hsueh
長房官學
ch'ang-men 閶門
Ch'ang-po-shan 長白山
Ch'ang-sheng 長生
ch'ang-sui 長隨
Ch'ang-wu 長武
Ch'ang-Yung 常永
Chao Chin-kuei 趙進貴
Chao Chün-jui 趙鈞瑞
Chao Liang-tung 趙良棟
chao-p'ei 招配
Chao Shih-pao 趙世保
che 摺
Che-hai 浙海
Ch'e-k'u 車庫
Chen-chiang 鎮江
Ch'en Chih-ch'üan 陳之銓
Ch'en Te-ch'ang 陳德昌
Cheng Chih-chin 鄭製錦
Cheng-jui 徵瑞
Cheng-ting 正定
Cheng-yang-men 正陽門
chi-cheng-fang 吉徵房
Chi-ch'ing 吉慶
Chi-hou 基厚
chi-mi 羈縻
chi-tzu 繼子
Ch'i-ch'eng-o 期成額

241

ch'i-hsia chia-jen 旗下家人
ch'i-hsia p'u-pei 旗下僕婢
ch'i-hsia t'ai-chien
旗下太監
ch'i-jen nu-p'u 旗人奴僕
Ch'i-li-t'u 奇理圖
chia-jen 家人
Chia-ku 嘉峪
chia-k'u 甲庫
chia-nu 家奴
Chia Yu-k'u 賈有庫
Chiang Chen-hung 江振鴻
Chiang Ch'un 江春
Chiang Kuang-ta 江廣達
Chiang P'u 蔣溥
Chiang Tz'u-ch'i 蔣賜棨
chieh-fei-yin 解費銀
chieh-sheng ch'e-chiao yin
節省車腳銀
Chieh-tu-shih 節度使
chien-chan 監戰
chien-sheng 監生
Ch'ien-ch'ing-kung tsung-kuan
乾清宮總管
Ch'ien-ch'ing-men 乾清門
chih-hsien 知縣
chih-hsien 職銜
chih-shih 執事
chih-tsao 織造
Chih-tsao-chü 織造局
Chin 金
Chin Chien 金簡

Chin-chou 錦州
Chin-chou chuang-t'ou ya-men
錦州莊頭衙門
Chin-ch'uan 金川
chin-i-wei 錦衣衛
Chin Pao 晉寶
chin-shih 進士
chin-shih-ch'u 近侍處
Chin-shih-chü 近侍局
ch'in-ch'ai 欽差
ching-fei yin 經費銀
Ching-hsing 井陘
Ching-ming-yuan 靜明園
Ching-pien 靖邊
Ching-shan kuan-hsueh
景山官學
Ching-yuan 靖遠
Ching-yun-men 景運門
ch'ing-chiang 清醬
Ch'ing-feng-ssu 慶豐司
Ch'ing-t'ai 清泰
Ch'ing-yuan 清苑
Chiu-ch'üan 酒泉
Cho-chou 涿州
Ch'o-k'o-t'o 綽克托
chou-li-mu 州吏目
chou-t'ung chih-hsien
州同職銜
chu-lien 株連
chu-shih 主事
Ch'u-chou 滁州
chü-jen 舉人

Ch'ü-wo 曲沃
Ch'uan-chu-hsiang 穿珠巷
Ch'üan Te 全德
chuang-ting 莊丁
chuang-t'ou 莊頭
ch'üeh 缺
Ch'un-ning 春寧
Chung-ho-tien 中和殿
Chung-sheng 中聲
chung-shu 中書
Chung-wei 中衛
Ch'ung-wen Gate 崇文門

En-yu-ssu 恩佑寺
erh-teng tsung-kuan
爾等總管

fa-yin 罰銀
Fan Ch'ing-chi 范清濟
Fan Ch'ing-chu 范清注
Fan Ch'ing-hung 范清洪
Fan Ch'ing-k'uang 范清曠
Fan Chung-ch'i 范重縈
Fan-i-ch'u 番役處
Fan Li 范李
Fan San-pa 范三拔
Fan Shih-ch'ung 范時崇
Fan Shih-i 范時繹
Fan Wen-ch'eng 范文程
Fan Yü-pin 范毓馪
Fan Yung-tou 范永斗
Fang Pa-erh 方八兒
Fen-chou 汾州

Fen-yang 汾陽
Feng-ch'en-yuan 奉宸苑
Feng Chih-an 馮致安
Feng-yang 鳳陽
Fo-lun 佛倫
fu-ching 府經
Fu-heng 傅恒
fu-huo pu-lu 俘獲捕虜
Fu-lung-an 福隆安
fu-shou-ling t'ai-chien
副首領太監
Fu-shun 撫順
Fu Te 傅德

Hai-pao 海保
Han-chün 漢軍
Ho-chin-erh 和晉兒
Ho-erh-ching-o 和爾經額
Ho-shen 和珅
Hou 侯
Hsi-Ning 西寧
hsiang-yüeh 鄉約
Hsiao-nan-chuang 小南莊
hsieh-t'ung pan-shih ta-ch'en
協同辦事大臣
hsieh-tzu-ch'u 寫字處
Hsien-an-kung kuan-hsüeh
咸安宮官學
hsien-cheng 縣丞
hsien-chu-pu 縣主簿
hsien-san 閒散
hsin-che-k'u 辛者庫

Hsin-chu 新柱

hsing-lu yü-shih 行路御史

hsing-pu ssu-yü 刑部司獄

Hsiung-lien 熊濂

hsu-shang 邺賞

Hsu Tzu-chien 徐子建

Hsuan-hui-shih 宣徽使

Hsun-shih Shan-tung ts'ao-wu 巡視山東漕務

hsun-tao 巡道

Hu-chün 護軍

Hu-shu 滸墅

Hu Te-lin 胡德琳

Huang-ch'eng-ssu 皇城司

Huang Kuang-te 黃光德

huang-tien 皇店

huang-ts'e 黃冊

Hui-chi-ssu 會計司

Hui-chou 徽州

Hui-fa 輝發

Hui-ling 惠齡

Hui-mien kuan-hsueh 回緬官學

hui-shen 會審

Hui-t'ung-kuan 會同館

Hui-tzu-hsueh 回子學

Hung-i-ko 弘義閣

Hung-jen Monastery 弘仁寺

Huo-ch'i-ying 火器營

Huo-lu 獲鹿

I-chou 易州

I-hsing 宜興

I-k'u 衣庫

I-la-ch'i 伊拉齊

I-ling-a 伊齡阿

i-tsui-yin 議罪銀

ishhan beg 伊什罕伯克

Jen Hsiao-tsai 任孝哉

jen-mai 認買

jen-tsui-yin 認罪銀

ju-i-kuan 如意館

ju-mu 乳母

k'a-lun 卡倫

k'a-tso 卡座

Kalgan 張家口

Kan-fu 趕福

Kan-yü hu-t'ung 乾魚衚衕

K'ang-shan-yuan 康山園

Kao 高

Kao Chin 高晉

Kao Heng 高恒

Kao Pin 高斌

Kao P'u 高樸

Kao Sheng 高陞

Kao Yun-chang 高雲彰

Kao Yun-hui 高雲惠

Kao Yun-lung 高雲龍

Kao Yun-ts'ung 高雲從

Kashgar 喀什噶爾

Keng Chung-ming 耿仲明

Khotan 和闐

Ko-ta-hun 噶達渾

K'o-erh-ch'in 科爾沁
Ku-pen 顧本
ku-shan-o-chen 固山額真
Ku Wen-hsing 顧問行
Ku-yuan 固原
k'u-chang 庫長
k'u-shou 庫守
k'u-shih 庫使
kuan-chuang 官莊
kuan-chuang-jen 管莊人
kuan-fang 官房
Kuan-fang tsu-fang
    官房租房
kuan-ling 管領
kuan-nei 關內
kuan-nu 官奴
Kuan-pao 觀保
kuan-shang 官商
kuan-shen 官蔘
Kuang-ch'u-ssu 廣儲司
Kuei-hua 歸化
kuei-li 規禮
kung-fei 公費
Kung-hsi-fang 宮戲房
kung-sheng 貢生
Kung-tien chien-tu ling-shih
    t'ai-chien 宮殿監督
        領事太監
kung-yung-shen 公用蔘
K'ung Yu-te 孔有德
Kuo Ching 郭敬
kuo-ch'u 國初

Kuo-fang 果房
Kuo Hsing 郭興
Kuo-p'u-erh 果普爾

Lai-pao 來保
Lang Shih-ning 郎世寧
lao-shih 老實
Li Ch'ao-tso 李朝佐
Li Chih-ying 李質頴
Li-fan-yuan 理藩院
Li Fu-kuo 李輔國
Li Hsu 李煦
Li I-t'ing 李以挺
Li Pu-an 李步安
Li San-yuan 李三元
Li Su-fang 李澍方
Li Wei-chün 李維鈞
Li Wen-chao 李文照
Li Yü 李玉
Liang-chou 涼州
Liang-hsiang 良鄉
Liang Liu 梁琉
Liang-t'ien-p'o 良天坡
liang-yen-tao 糧鹽道
Lin-ch'ing 臨清
Ling-ch'in shih-wu ta-yuan
    陵寢事務大員
Liu Ch'eng-kuei 劉承規
Liu Chin 劉瑾
Liu Ch'üan 劉全
lou-kuei 陋規
Lung-chiang 龍江

Ma Hsing-a 瑪興阿

Ma Pao 馬保

Ma Shou-pin 馬守賓

Ma Wan-chin 馬萬金

Ma Wan-lung 馬萬龍

mai 買

Man-tu-li 滿都禮

Mao-ch'in-tien 懋勤殿

mei-yu shen-ma tung-hsi 沒有甚麼東西

Meng-ku i-sheng 蒙古醫生

Meng-ku kuan-hsueh 蒙古官學

Mi-chi-ch'u 密記處

Mi-erh-tai 密爾岱

Mi-tzu-t'an 麋子灘

Min-ning 旻寧

Min Tung-shen 閔東濬

Ming-cheng 明正

mu-chang 牧長

mu-k'u 木庫

Mu-t'eng-o 穆騰額

mu-yu 幕友

muke 謀克

Na-su-t'u 納蘇圖

Na-yen-t'ai 那延泰

Nan-an-k'u 南鞍庫

Nan-shu-fang 南書房

Nao-ch'üan 腦泉

nei-ch'ang 內厰

nei-hsing-ch'ang 內行厰

Nei-hu-pu 內戶部

nei-kuan-ling 內管領

Nei-kuan-ling ch'u 內管領處

Nei-kung-pu 內工部

nei-t'ing 內廷

nei-t'ing shih-yao 內廷勢要

nei-wu-fu 內務府

Ni Ch'eng-k'uan 倪承寬

Ni-men chuang hu-t'u ma 你們裝糊塗嗎

Nien-kan-ch'u 粘竿處

Ning-ku-ch'i 寧古齊

Ning-shou-kung 寧壽宮

Ning-wu 寧武

Ning-yuan 寧遠

Ning Yuan-wo 寧元我

niru 牛祿

o-shang 額商

O-ssu-man 鄂斯瑪

O-tui 鄂對

pai-ch'i suo-mai 白契所買

pan-jen pan-wu 半人半物

pang-t'ieh 幫貼

pao-chieh 保結

Pao-ho-tien 保和殿

pao-i 包衣

pao-mu 保母

Pao-ti-ssu 寶諦寺

Pao-yueh-lou 寶月樓

Paoting 保定
pi-t'ieh-shih 筆帖式
p'i-chia 披甲
p'i-k'u 皮庫
ping-ma-ssu li-mu 兵馬司吏目
P'ing-ch'i 平七
P'ing-pa 平八
P'u-fu 普福
P'u-k'ou 浦口

Sa-mu-sa-k'o 薩木薩克
Sa-tsai 薩載
San-fa-ssu 三法司
San-i 三義
San-pao 三寶
Se-t'i-pa-erh-ti 色提巴爾第
Seng-tao-ssu 僧道司
Sha-hu-k'ou 殺虎口
shan-shih 山石
shang 賞
shang-lai 賞賚
Shang-shu-fang 尚書房
Shang-ssu-yuan 上駟院
Shen 沈
Shen-hsing-ssu 慎刑司
Shen Pao 申保
Shen T'ai 沈泰
sheng-jen 升任
sheng-yuan 生員
shih-en 市恩

Shih-lin 石麟
shih-mu 侍母
shih-p'u 世僕
Shih-san-t'ai 十三台
Shou-an-kung 壽安宮
shou-hsun-tao 守巡道
Shou-k'ang-kung 壽康宮
shou-ling t'ai-chien 首領太監
shu-hu 樹戶
shu-li 書吏
Shu-lin 書麟
shu-pan 書辦
Shu Pao 淑寶
shu-tsui-yin 贖罪銀
Shu-wen 舒文
Shuang-ch'ing 雙慶
ssu 司
ssu-k'u 司庫
Ssu-k'u-ch'üan-shu 四庫全書
ssu-kuan 司官
Ssu-li-chien 司禮監
Su-chou 肅州
Su-ho-te 舒赫德
su-la 蘇喇
Sui Hsun 隨遜
Sun 孫
Sun K'uo 孫括
Sung Kuo-ts'ung 宋國璁

ta-chih-ch'ien 大制錢

Ta-ho-i 大河驛
Ta-hsing 大興
Ta-lao-ch'ih 打勞池
Ta-san-t'ai 達三泰
Ta-sheng wu-la tsung-kuan
　　ya-men 打牲烏拉
　　　總管衙門
tai-ti t'ou-ch'ung 帶地投充
t'ai-chien 太監
T'ai-fei-yin 台費蔭
T'ai-hang 太行
T'ai-ho-tien 太和殿
T'ai-hu 太湖
t'an-k'u 炭庫
T'an-k'u 毯庫
tang-shen ping li-yu wen-chüan
　　當身並立有文券
t'ang-kuan 堂官
tao-fu 道府
tao-yuan 道員
T'ao Lung 陶隴
Te-k'ui 德魁
teng-hsien 登仙
T'i-jen-ko 體仁閣
tiao-yung 調用
t'ieh-k'u 鐵庫
tien 典
tien-mai 典賣
tien-shen 典身
t'ien-fang tsu-yin 田房租銀
T'ien Shih-chieh 田士傑
To-lung-wu 多隆武

t'ou-ch'ung 投充
t'ou-k'ao 投靠
tsai-hsiang 宰相
ts'an-ling 參領
Tsao-pan-ch'u 造辦處
Ts'ao Hsi 曹璽
Ts'ao Yin 曹寅
tso-ling 佐領
tso-sheng chia-jen 坐者家人

Tso-ssu 左司
tsou-che 奏摺
tsou-hsia 奏匣
Tsou-ma ch'eng-shou
　　走馬承受
Tsou-shih-ch'u 奏事處
Tsou-shih kuan-yuan
　　奏事官員
Tsou-shih t'ai-chien
　　奏事太監
Tsung-jen-fu 宗人府
tsung-kuan 總管
Tsung-kuan nei-ssu teng-hsiang
　　總管內司等項
tsung-kuan t'ai-chien
　　總管太監
Tsung-li kung-ch'eng ch'u
　　總管工程處
tsung-li yen-fa ta-ch'en
　　總理鹽法大臣
Tsung-pan hui-chiang shih-wu
　　ta-ch'en 總辦回疆事務大臣

tsung-shang 總商
Tsung Yun 宗筠
tu-t'ung 都統
Tu-yü-ssu 都虞司
T'u Lai 屠賴
Tuan-k'u 緞庫
t'un 屯
Tung-ch'ang 東昌
tung-ch'ang 東廠
T'ung-ch'i-k'u 銅器庫
T'ung I 佟義
t'ung-p'an 通判
tzu-hsing 自行
Tzu-ming-chung-ch'u 自鳴鐘處
Tz'u-k'u 磁庫

Wa-t'ing 瓦亭
wai-ch'ao 外朝
Wan Mien-ch'ien 萬縣前
Wang Ch'ang-kuei 王常貴
Wang Chen 王振
Wang Chi-en 王繼恩
Wang Ch'i 王七
Wang Chin 王進
Wang Erh 王二
Wang Hung 王洪
Wang Jui 王瑞
Wang Pao-yuan 王葆元
Wang P'u 王溥
Wei 衛
Wei Chia-shih 魏佳士

Wei-chia-wan 魏家灣
Wei Ch'üan-i 衛全義
Wei Hsiang-chi 魏象紀
Wei-nan 渭南
wei-so 衛所
wen-chieh 文結
Wen-hua-tien 文華殿
Wen-yin 聞銀
Wu Liang-fu 吳良輔
Wu-pei-yuan 武備院
Wu-shih 烏什
Wu-shih-i 武士宜
五十一
Wu T'an 吳壇
Wu-wei 武威
Wu-ying-tien 武英殿

Yang-hsin-tien 養心殿
Yang Wen-ch'ien 楊文乾
Yao Li-te 姚立德
Yao Ling-yen 姚令言
Ye-ho 葉赫
Yeh-erh-ch'iang 葉爾羌
yen-i-tao 鹽驛道
yen-k'o ta-shih 鹽課大使
Yen-liao-k'u 顏料庫
yin 蔭
yin 引
yin-ch'i suo-mai 印契所買
Yin-chu 寅著
Yin-hsiang 胤祥
yin-k'u 銀庫

Yin-liang chuang-t'ou-ch'u
銀糧莊頭處

yin-sheng 蔭生

Yin Yuan-shu 殷元舒

Ying-fang 鷹房

Ying-lien 英廉

Ying-t'ai-tien 瀛台殿

Ying-tsao-ssu 營造司

Yu-ssu 右司

Yü-ch'a-shan-fang
御茶膳房

Yü Ch'eng-lung 于成龍

Yü-ch'ien shih-wei
御前侍衛

Yü Chin-pao 余金寶

Yü-ch'uan-ch'u 御船處

Yü-ho-ch'iao 玉河橋

Yü Min-chung 于敏中

Yü-shu-ch'u 御書處

Yü-yao-fang 御藥房

Yü-yueh-k'u 御樂庫

Yü-yung-chien 御用監

yuan 願

Yuan-ming-yuan 圓明園

Yuan Ping-t'ang 遠炳堂

yuan-shih 緣事

yuan-wai-lang 員外郎

Yueh-hua Gate 月華門

Yun I 允禮

Yung-kuei 永貴

Yung-yen 顒炎

INDEX

A-erh-to, 126

A-pu-nai, 75

A-pu-tu-la, 168

A-pu-tu-shu-k'u-erh-ho-cho, 155; execution of, 164

a-tun shih-wei (supervisors of droves), 36

A-tun ya-men (Pastoral Office), 35

Abahai; household organization of, 16; government organization under, 19-20

Accounts Department (Hui-chi-ssu), 41, 44, 82

Agriculture: effect of Chinese captives in Manchuria on, 15; not of primary importance for Nei-wu-fu, 177

ak'im beg (Moslem local governor), 141, 156

Akosu, 146, 147, 157

An-ning, 102

An-su district, 144

An-ting-men (An-ting Gate), 123

Anhwei, 152

Annam, 121, 122; eunuch blunders in campaigns in, 8

Ansi, 151

Artillery and Musketry Division (Huo-ch'i-ying), 108

Audience, under the Ming, 10-11

Autocracy, Nei-wu-fu's part in increasing, 178-179

Banners: organized under Nurhachi, 19; eunuchs from , 41; *pao-i* organization of, 61; hereditary succession in, 61; and salt management, 104; Ch'ing heritage from, 175

bayara (select guard units), 19

beg (Moslem governor), 141-142, 164

beile (Manchu banner leaders), 18; organized by Nurhachi, 19; slave eunuchs of, 22; hereditary succession of, 61

Bondage, Chinese: pre-Ch'ing, 53-55; Ch'ing, 55-60; *see also* Bondservants; Slaves

Bondservants, imperial (*pao-i*): subordination of eunuchs to, 25; banner organization of, 60-64; tenure of, 61-62; causes of replacement, 62; social control of, 62-63; decline of martial heritage among, 64; social structure of, 64-69; aristocracy of, 67; of punished officials, 114; case of Kao Yun-tsung, 131-136; case of Kao P'u, 136-172; Ch'ing organization of eunuchs and, 174; institutionalization of, 177-178; misbehavior of, 181

Bondservants, Jurchen or Manchu: Chinese captives, 12, 14-18; role of on landed estates, 18, 55; under the banner system, 21; tasks of eunuchs taken over by, 25; in early organization of Nei-wu-fu, 27; compared to Chinese, 56-58

Buddhist and Taoist Priests, Office of (Seng-tao ssu), 30

HARVARD EAST ASIAN MONOGRAPHS